The Geometry of
Visual Phonology

DISSERTATIONS IN LINGUISTICS

A series edited by
Joan Bresnan, Sharon Inkelas, William J. Poser, and Peter Sells

The aim of this series is to make work of substantial empirical breadth and theoretical interest available to a wide audience.

The Geometry of
Visual Phonology

LINDA UYECHI

CSLI Publications
Center for the Study of Language and Information
Stanford, California

Library of Congress Cataloging-in-Publication Data

Uyechi, Linda, 1957–
    The geometry of visual phonology / Linda Uyechi.
        p.   cm.
    Revision of author's 1994 thesis.
    Includes bibliographical references and index.
    ISBN 1–57586–012–0. — ISBN 1–57586–013–9 (hardback)
    1. Sign language. 2. American Sign Language. 3. Grammar, Comparative
and general—Phonology. I. Title.
    HV2474.U88   1996
    419—dc20   96–33365
                                                            CIP

The images: ALL, APPOINTMENT, ASK, BICYCLE, BORROW, CHOOSE, CRITICIZE, DAY, DEAF, DREAM, FLOWER, GERMANY, GOOD, LIE, LIKE, LOAN, LONELY, NOW, OUR, SENTENCE, SORRY, UNDERSTAND, WANT and YES are reprinted with permission from *A Basic Course in American Sign Language*, Copyright © 1980, 1994, T.J. Publishers, Inc., Silver Spring, MD 20910, illustrated by Frank A. Paul.

The images: APPLE, CONFLICT, FIRE, HOSPITAL, INCOMPETENT, LOCALE, MEET-YOU, MILK, MISCHIEVOUS, MOTHER, NOW, OLD, PERCENT, PRINT, RESTAURANT, SHUTDOWN, and TWENTY-ONE are reprinted and adapted by permission of the publisher, Allyn & Bacon, from Humphries and Padden, *Learning American Sign Language*, Copyright © 1992 with illustrations by Rob Hills, Daniel W. Renner, and Peggy Swartzel-Lott.

The images: CHILDREN, DRY, STUDY, SUMMER, THING, UGLY, articulatory space, and various handshapes are reprinted by permission of the publisher from *The Signs of Language* by Edward Klima and Ursula Bellugi, Cambridge, Mass.: Harvard University Press, Copyright © 1979 by the President and Fellows of Harvard College.

The images: FIGHT, IT'S-NOTHING, LIAR, LOOK-AT$_{OVER-TIME}$, LOOK-AT$_{OVER-AND-OVER-AGAIN}$, and PRESIDENT are reprinted by permission of the publisher and authors, Charlotte Baker-Shenk and Dennis Cokely, of *American Sign Language: A Teacher's Resource Text on Grammar and Culture* (1980), Washington, DC: Clerc Books, an imprint of Gallaudet University Press, Copyright © 1980 by Gallaudet University, illustrated by Frank A. Paul.

"Fond orné. Nénuphar. (Fig. 112)," the drawing on the cover of the paperback edition of this book is by Maurice-Pillard Verneuil from his *Étude de la Plante: Son application aux industries d'art* (1903, Paris: Librairie centrale des beaux-arts). Courtesy Richard Manuck.

♾ The acid-free paper used in this book meets the minimum requirements of the American National Standard for Information Sciences—Permanence of Paper for Printed Library Materials, ANSI Z39.48-1984.

To the memory of
Kami Shinsato Inamine
and
Hatsuyo Inamine Higa

For Yasuko, Shizue, Otome, Toyoko, Haruko, Tokie, Elaine, Juliette, and Hideno

Contents

Preface

This is a slightly revised version of my doctoral dissertation, submitted to Stanford University in December 1994. The content of the thesis is unchanged, but its form has been altered to improve accuracy, readability, and consistency.

Explaining a three-dimensional system in a two-dimensional medium continues to pose a challenge. In this version of the thesis I have been greatly aided by the artistry of Iwao Peter Sano who created new graphics and taught me the skills to create some of my own. It is with his help that many ideas presented in the thesis have been rendered less opaque.

This thesis, in any form, would never have been completed without the invaluable guidance of my dissertation committee: Paul Kiparsky, William J. Poser, Diane K. Brentari, K.P. Mohanan, and Eve Clark. The ideas presented here would never have emerged from hiding without the coaxing of K.P. Mohanan – ideas that would not have been there in the first place if not for the linguists who inspire, nurture, and sustain my interest in linguistics: Joan Bresnan, Miriam Butt, Jennifer Fitzpatrick Cole, Henriette deSwart, Will Leben, Tara Mohanan, John Rickford, Peter Sells, and Whitney Tabor.

The work in this thesis would certainly not be meaningful without the groundwork laid by the sign language linguists whose footsteps I follow, and who at one time or another have been kind enough to challenge my ideas: Jean Ann, Diane Brentari, Robert Johnson, Scott Liddell, David Perlmutter, Wendy Sandler, Kelly Stack, and Harry van der Hulst. And the concepts would not be as clear without the challenges posed by my comrades in sign language linguistics (TNG): Onno Crasborn, Daisuke Hara, Chris Miller, Sybilla Nyhoff, Yutaka Osugi, Christine Poulin, Janine Toole, Els van der Kooij, and Inge Zwitserlood.

The work would not have been possible at all without those people who generously shared their languages with me: Mo Aiello, Tony Bloem,

Wim Emmerik, Cathy Haas, Lynn Jacobsen, Sandra (Bunny) Klopping, Brian Malzkuhn, Soya Mori – nor without the friends and family who share themselves with me: Rudy Busto, Jill Fujisaki, Debra Maxon, Malavika Mohanan, Jeannie Sibonga, Starla Miller, Minako Sano, Peter Sano, Stanford Taiko, Christine Taylor, Marlene Taylor, Michelle Taylor, Renee Taylor, Steve Taylor, and my folks. And, of course, work and life are possible but never as meaningful or fun without Steve. For all the excellent ideas and good feelings these people infuse me with, I can never repay or thank them enough – I can only accept sole responsibility for the content of this publication.

Palo Alto
July 1996

1

The Geometry of Visual Phonology

In this thesis I argue for a theoretical framework of *visual phonology*, the phonology of sign language, that is distinct from current theoretical frameworks of spoken language phonology. The division between sign language and spoken language phonology is motivated by an inherent asymmetry between sight and sound. Whereas a visual image can be seen in a moment, at a discrete point in time, an auditory signal requires an interval of time to hear. I demonstrate that this asymmetry is present in the phonological organization of language and argue, therefore, that language mode must be accounted for in phonological theory.

Hence, the theoretical frameworks of visual phonology and spoken language phonology are distinct, where by *theoretical framework* I mean a precise use of language to capture formal properties of a well-defined object of study. I take the domain of visual phonology to be the set of natural signed languages, and the domain of spoken language phonology to be the set of natural spoken languages. Using modality-free language to compare the phonological constructs of the frameworks, I conclude that they share modality-independent properties. Those properties form the basis for articulating a *theory* of universal phonology, where by *theory* I mean a set of laws that hold over all objects in the domain of the theory – the domain of universal phonology being the set of all natural languages.

I propose, then, that distinct theories of visual and spoken language phonologies must be formulated in modality-specific frameworks, and that the two are related by a theory of universal phonology, captured by the model of phonology in (1).

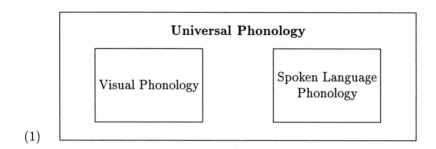

(1)

This proposal differs significantly from previous work on sign language phonology (Liddell and Johnson 1989, Sandler 1989, Wilbur 1990, Brentari 1990b, Perlmutter 1992).[1] The model of phonology adopted in those analyses is illustrated in (2). I refer to it as the transfer-and-test model because it is based on the premise that what we know about spoken language phonology is equivalent to our knowledge about universal phonology. As represented by the first and second boxes in (2), spoken language phonology maps onto universal phonology. In turn, because a universal theory of phonology should hold for all natural languages then, following a transfer-and-test approach to sign language phonology, it should also be applicable to and provide explanations for sign languages. This is represented by the second and third boxes in (2).

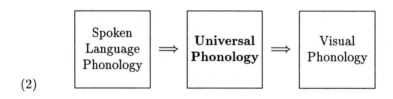

(2)

Clearly, modality-specific features such as *coronal*, *nasal*, and *labial* are not part of a transfer-and-test model, but constructs that reflect the organization of mode-specific features are. Hence, a research program to develop such a model is organized around questions such as: What is the segment in sign language? What is the structure of the syllable? How are segments organized into syllables? What role does sonority play

---

[1] Van der Hulst (1993) rejects the notion of using sign language as a testing bed for competing theories of spoken language phonology, and presents a more sign-oriented approach. Nevertheless, he adopts a feature-based representation, and depends on spoken language-based timing segments, specifically undifferentiated X-slots, to represent signs.

in syllable organization? The result is a single-framework-single-theory model of phonology.

Crucially, work that adopts the model in (2) downplays the modality difference between sign and spoken languages, focusing only on the similarities between them (Anderson 1993). This leads to complications when applying spoken language constructs to sign language data – an issue discussed at more length in Chapter 6. I therefore reject (2) and adopt the model in (1).

From this perspective, no independent theoretical framework for sign language has yet been proposed. Hence, the bulk of the thesis is devoted to laying the groundwork for a theoretical framework of visual phonology based on data from American Sign Language (ASL).[2] The main focus of the effort is to develop a set of constructs and propositions that provide contrastive representations of signs. To accomplish this I base the argument for each part of the framework on patterns of distribution and alternation and lexically distinctive properties of the data. I pay particular attention to presenting the data from ASL in images and descriptive terms that are clearly distinguished from the terms adopted into the theoretical framework.

The questions central to the thesis are basic to the enterprise of discovering the structure of phonological representations in this framework of *visual phonology*. What are the atomic and non-atomic constructs of the representation? What are the arguments to motivate each construct of the representation? What are the principles that govern the way the constructs are put together to form complex representations? What kind of mathematics is needed to formalize the structure of the representations and the principles that hold on the representations? The answer that emerges is the geometry of visual phonology.[3]

In the remainder of this chapter, I present one perspective on the inherent difference between the visual and auditory mode, and then preview the results of the thesis with a detailed description and representation of a sign. I conclude with an outline of the thesis.

---

[2] American Sign Language is the natural language of *Deaf* communities in the United States and other parts of North America (Humphries and Padden 1988).

[3] Note that this use of *geometry* is not to be confused with the notion of *feature* "geometry". I mean *geometry* in its formal sense, as a branch of mathematics. The *feature geometry* of spoken language phonology is, in fact, a misnomer. Phonological feature geometry is based on a mathematical object called a tree that is formally a rooted, directed, and connected graph without cycles, borrowing from the branch of mathematics called graph theory. In its original formulation (Mohanan 1983, Clements 1985), the sister nodes are unordered; the graph formally captures only dominance relations (constituency).

1.1 Sign and Speech

Sign language and spoken language represent two distinct modes of language. One is articulated with the hands and perceived with the eyes; the other is articulated with the vocal apparatus and perceived with the ears. Because both are languages, one possibility is that a single representation will account for both. Does mode matter? In previous generative models the effect of mode is downplayed, a transfer-and-test approach to sign analysis is adopted, and spoken language constructs are applied to the signs (Liddell and Johnson 1989, Sandler 1989, Perlmutter 1992, Brentari 1990b, Wilbur 1993, Stack 1988).

In this thesis I raise the question again: *Does mode matter?* The answer is a resounding *YES!* To defend this position I adopt a system internal strategy for sign analysis so that each construct and principle adopted into the model is based on arguments built on the properties of sign language data. The result is a framework for visual phonology that is distinct from the framework for spoken language phonology; each reflects the modality-specific characteristics of its domain. The differences between the frameworks provide support for a phonetic groundedness, or naturalness, of phonology. The similarities between them provide support for a theory of universal phonology.

But even before comparing the frameworks, it is enlightening to consider the inherent properties of vision and audition that might influence linguistic organization. Vision and audition are similar because they are both human senses, but they provide distinct windows on the world.[4]

Consider, for example, the following scenario. A backpacker comes across a magnificent upright redwood tree on Monday. Inspired by it, she stops to take its picture. She returns along the same path on Wednesday, only to find the same tree lying on the ground. Shocked that such a beautiful tree has fallen, she takes another picture of it. Did the tree make a sound when it fell?

Let us assume that our backpacker was so taken by the tree that she also left behind a camcorder to videotape it while she went on her two-day hike. The camera will record both the sound and image of the tree falling, so when our backpacker returns home she will have a range of documents of the event: (i) snapshots of the tree before and after it fell, (ii) a video image of the tree falling, and (iii) an audio recording of the noise the tree makes when it falls.

Our backpacker has captured two types of visual images, one discrete

---

[4]In terms of physics, the eyes and ears are tuned to different frequencies. Whereas the ears are tuned to a frequency range of about 20 to 20,000 Herz, the eyes are sensitive to a much broader range of frequencies.

and one continuous, but only one (continuous) audio "image" of the fallen tree. Notably, this asymmetry is due not to technical limitations, but rather to the same type of physical difference that differentiates the perception of signed and spoken language. Whereas the eye can perceive a state of affairs at a discrete point in time, as represented by a snapshot of the tree, the ear requires an interval of time to perceive an event, as indicated by the sole audio recording.

Another way to characterize this asymmetry is to imagine yourself in a room separate from the world and stopped in time. If you look around, you can gather visual information through your eyes; your ears perceive nothing. Now allow the room to exist in time, and listen. Clap your hands and you hear something. Stop clapping your hands and, as long as nothing else happens, it will be silent again. In other words, if nothing happens, you hear nothing. To hear something, something must happen.

Regardless of how we imagine it, there is an undeniable asymmetry between the perception of a visual image and of sound. As summarized in (3), a visual image can capture information in an instant or over an interval of time. In contrast, an audio image is only perceptible over an interval of time.

(3)

	Vision	Hearing
Discrete point in time	Discrete image (snapshot)	*
Interval of time	Continuous image (videotape)	Continuous sound (audio-tape)

So, on the basis of the observation that sign language is based on vision and spoken language on hearing, we would expect that similar asymmetries are likely to emerge in the analysis of the languages. At the least, we must be alert to the possibility that mode can matter.

In this thesis, I conclude that the language faculty exploits language mode, optimizing the organization of the information to fit the medium of communication. The most striking instance of this is the contrast in the representation of time. In spoken language, the atomic unit of time is an interval of time (the segment). In sign language phonology,

I argue that the atomic unit of time is a discrete point in time. A time interval is also important, but it is represented as a sequence of two points in time. Consequently, the phonological structure of signs requires two types of units: those that represent a static state, and those that capture a transition between two states. Language mode is, in short, of consequence to linguistic analysis.

1.2 Visual Phonology

Because the goal of the thesis is to develop a new theoretical framework, it is imperative to present arguments for the adoption of each construct and principle into the model of *visual phonology*. To that end, I abide by two rules of the thesis. The first part of rule one is to adhere to the careful separation between descriptive language and theoretical language. The second part of rule one is to argue for the constructs and principles adopted as part of the theory on the basis of data presented using descriptive terms. Rule two is to admit and explain any deviations from rule one.

By following those rules, my goal is to present a model that consists of a set of constructs suited to the properties of the data, along with a set of coherent and falsifiable propositions that make correct predictions about signs. Although the organization of the constructs may be familiar from spoken language phonology, most of the constructs argued for in this work are quite unlike those of traditional generative phonology. For the sake of previewing those novel constructs, I suspend the rules of the thesis for the remainder of this section in order to work through an example that introduces the general organization of the representation.

I start with a detailed description of the sign meaning *to dream*, and present the representation of the hand and signing space in the terms argued for in the body of the thesis. I then give a descriptive representation for the sign that illustrates the relation between space and time in visual phonology. By the end of the section, the reader should have grasped two things: (i) an overview of the model, and (ii) a feel for articulating the ASL sign DREAM.[5]

---

[5] Here, I adopt the convention from Baker-Shenk and Cokely (1980). Signs are referred to by a name that corresponds to the closest English equivalent set in small capitals, e.g., DREAM refers to the ASL sign that means *dream* in English. I include English meanings in italics only if the meaning is not apparent from the gloss, e.g., RED-SLICE *tomato*.

1.2.1 A Description of DREAM

To articulate the sign in (4), two things happen: (i) the hand moves away from the forehead, while (ii) the index finger alternately bends and extends.[6]

(4)   DREAM

The steps for articulating the sign are listed in (5). The reader should try them before proceeding with the rest of the section.

(5)   Step-by-step DREAM:

1. Choose the hand you write with. If you are right-handed, this will be your right hand; if you are left-handed, it will be your left.

2. Hold your hand as if pointing out the direction of the linguistics department to a stranger. Hold your index finger straight. Bend your middle, ring, and pinky fingers and fold your thumb around them (as in (6a)).

3. Place the tip of your index finger against the same side of your forehead as the hand that you are using, so that your fingertip is just above the outer edge of your eyebrow. The palm of your hand should be at about a 45° angle with respect to the front of the face.

4. Move your hand about an inch away from the forehead along a straight path along a slightly upward direction. Simultane-

---

[6](4) is a revised form of an image reprinted with permission from *A Basic Course in American Sign Language*, Copyright (c) 1980, 1994, T.J. Publishers, Inc., Silver Spring, MD 20910, illustrated by Frank A. Paul. Other images included with permission from that publication are ALL, APPOINTMENT, ASK, BICYCLE, BORROW, CHOOSE, CRITICIZE, DAY, DEAF, FLOWER, GERMANY, GOOD, LIE, LIKE, LOAN, LONELY, NOW, OUR, SENTENCE, SORRY, UNDERSTAND, WANT and YES.

ously bend the joints of the index finger so that the knuckle joint is straight while the others bend (as in (6b)).

5. Move your hand another inch in the same direction while extending the joints at the tip and middle of the index finger, so that it looks like it did in step 2.

6. Bend the joints once more, moving another inch along the same path.

7. Stop. Your hand should be a few inches from the forehead with the index finger bent. In all, you should have moved your hand through the four distinct positions illustrated in (4).

Practice articulating the sign until it flows smoothly. The repeated bending and extending of the index finger should be articulated in the same proportion as the movement away from the forehead. You might also try a variation of the sign: move the hand farther and farther away from the forehead while continuing to alternate between a bent and extended index finger, stopping only after the arm has reached its limit. That gesture can be roughly interpreted as *dream-for-a-long-time*.

With this example in mind (and on hand), consider that there are roughly two things about the gesture to represent: (i) the hand itself, and (ii) the space that it moves through. I discuss each of these parts of the sign in turn.

1.2.2 Hand

Two distinct postures of the hand, or *handshapes*, are needed to articulate DREAM. These are shown in (6). *Handshape* can be specified by two pieces of information: (i) the *selected finger(s)*, and (ii) the positions of their joints. For both handshapes in (6), the *selected finger* is the index finger. In (6a) all of the joints are straight, or *extended*. In (6b), the knuckle joint, or *base joint*, is straight; the other joints, called the *non-base joints*, are bent into a neutral position.

(6)   a. Hand Posture 1   b. Hand Posture 2

For the sake of completeness I include the representation for each hand posture in (7). The features and organization of the information are presented in Chapter 2. Of interest here is the minimal difference between the hand postures. In (7a) the non-base joints (-BASE) of the selected fingers are extended; in contrast, in (7b) the non-base joints of the selected fingers are in a neutral position.

(7)　　a.　Hand Posture 1

$$
\text{HS:} \begin{bmatrix} +Selected: & \begin{bmatrix} \text{I} \end{bmatrix} \\ & \quad \begin{bmatrix} +\text{BASE}: & \begin{bmatrix} +\text{EXT} \\ -\text{FLEX} \end{bmatrix} \end{bmatrix} \\ & \quad \begin{bmatrix} -\text{BASE}: & \begin{bmatrix} +\text{EXT} \\ -\text{FLEX} \end{bmatrix} \end{bmatrix} \\ -Selected: & \begin{bmatrix} \text{TMRP} \end{bmatrix} \\ & \quad \begin{bmatrix} +\text{BASE}: & \begin{bmatrix} -\text{EXT} \\ +\text{FLEX} \end{bmatrix} \end{bmatrix} \\ & \quad \begin{bmatrix} -\text{BASE}: & \begin{bmatrix} -\text{EXT} \\ +\text{FLEX} \end{bmatrix} \end{bmatrix} \\ Thumb: & \begin{bmatrix} +\text{OPPOSED} \end{bmatrix} \end{bmatrix}
$$

　　b.　Hand Posture 2

$$
\text{HS:} \begin{bmatrix} +Selected: & \begin{bmatrix} \text{I} \end{bmatrix} \\ & \quad \begin{bmatrix} +\text{BASE}: & \begin{bmatrix} -\text{EXT} \\ -\text{FLEX} \end{bmatrix} \end{bmatrix} \\ & \quad \begin{bmatrix} -\text{BASE}: & \begin{bmatrix} -\text{EXT} \\ -\text{FLEX} \end{bmatrix} \end{bmatrix} \\ -Selected: & \begin{bmatrix} \text{TMRP} \end{bmatrix} \\ & \quad \begin{bmatrix} +\text{BASE}: & \begin{bmatrix} -\text{EXT} \\ +\text{FLEX} \end{bmatrix} \end{bmatrix} \\ & \quad \begin{bmatrix} -\text{BASE}: & \begin{bmatrix} -\text{EXT} \\ +\text{FLEX} \end{bmatrix} \end{bmatrix} \\ Thumb: & \begin{bmatrix} +\text{OPPOSED} \end{bmatrix} \end{bmatrix}
$$

To articulate DREAM the hand changes between the postures in (7a) and (7b). But the hand also moves through space. The organization of information about signing space differs markedly from that of the hand.

1.2.3   Signing Space

The representation of signing space argued for in this thesis is best described as a box in a box in a box, in other words, a set of nested boxes. To characterize this linguistically unusual concept I describe the representation box by box.

The goal of the representation is, quite simply, to specify the position of the hand relative to the signer's body. This requires two pieces of information: (i) its location, or where the hand is, and (ii) its orientation, or which way the hand is facing. For example, in (8) the fingertip is touching the forehead, so the hand is located at the forehead. But in (8a) the palm of the hand faces downward, and in (8b) it faces away from the signer. Hence, to unambiguously specify the position of the hand requires knowing both its location and its relative orientation.

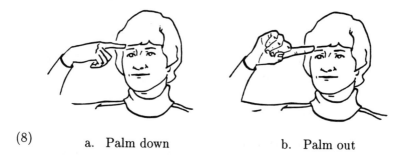

(8)   a. Palm down   b. Palm out

To capture the *location* and *orientation* of the hand, the hand and body are represented as rectangular prisms. Recall from basic geometry that a rectangular prism is a six-sided figure composed of six rectangular faces at right angles to each other. It is helpful to think of each prism as a transparent glass cube.

Location and *orientation* are stated as relations between two nested boxes, where the larger box provides a reference system for the smaller. The *location* of the inner box can be stated in terms of the relation of one of its faces to some position in the outer box. The *orientation* of the inner box can be stated in terms of the relation of its faces to the faces of the outer box.

As an example, consider the position of the hand to articulate DREAM. The parts of the representation are shown in (9). The *hand prism* (HP) is shown in (9a); the *fingertip* of the hand is associated with the *front* of the HP, the *wrist* with the *back* of the HP, the *palm* is associated with the *bottom* of the HP, the *back* of the hand with the *top* of the HP, and the *sides* of the hand are associated with the *sides* of the HP. The special properties of the hand prism are discussed in Chapter 2. The *global signing space* (GSS) is shown in (9c); the *top* of GSS is associated with the top of the signer's head, the *bottom* of GSS with the signer's waist, the *front* of GSS with the front of the signer's body, the *back* of GSS with the signer's back, and the *sides* of GSS with the signer's sides. The *local signing space* (LSS) that mediates between the hand prism and global signing space is shown in (9b). Local signing space expands and contrast to fit the place of articulation of the sign. In this case the place of articulation is the side of the signer's forehead, inducing a long and narrow space. If the sign were articulated on the chest, the proportions of local signing space would shift to accommodate the signing area. The special properties of these representations of signing space are discussed in Chapter 3.

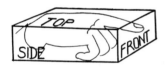

(9) a. Hand Prism
(HP)

b. Local Signing Space
(LSS)

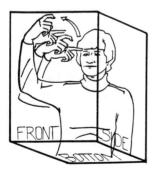

c. Global Signing Space
(GSS)

The abstract representation of the sign is produced by embedding the representation of the manual articulator, the hand prism (HP), in the signing space, local signing space (LSS). Local signing space is then situated in global signing space (GSS), as shown in (10). The location of the hand is specified by noting that the *fingertip* of the hand is associated with the *front* of the hand prism which, in turn, is associated with the *base* of local signing space which is associated with the *side-of-the-forehead* in global signing space. The orientation of the hand is specified by noting that the *fingertip* and *back* of the hand are parallel, respectively, to the *front* and *top* of the hand prism which are, in turn, parallel to the +BASE and +LOCAL sides of local signing space. Because of the topology of the body, the faces of local signing space are not absolutely parallel with the faces of global signing space; however, relatively speaking, the +BASE and +LOCAL sides of local signing space (LSS) are parallel to the *back* and *top* of global signing space (GSS).

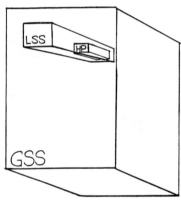

(10)   Representation of DREAM

The notation for the representation in (10) is given in (11). The nested rectangles reflect the nested boxes in (10). The innermost rectangle represents the hand prism (HP), the middle one represents local signing space (LSS), and the outermost represents global signing space (GSS). Note that the specifications for *location* (LOC) and *orientation* (OR) are placed between the boxes they relate. For example, the notation OR [$Front_{HP}$: +BASE$_{LSS}$] outside the HP box but inside the LSS box means that the *front* face of the hand prism is parallel with the *base* of local signing space. The specifications for LOC and OR in the hand prism (HP) mediate between the hand and HP.

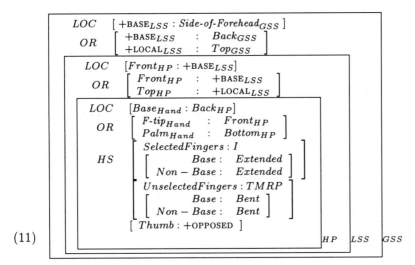

(11)

So the nested prisms in (10) reflect the formal geometric representation of signing space. Furthermore, in geometric terms the hand is a *rigid body*. Roughly speaking, this means that the hand retains the same mass and volume throughout the articulation of a sign. Hence, changes in the position and placement of the hand can be formally represented in geometry as *rigid body transformations.*

The schematic in (12), representing DREAM, depicts how this notion of rigid body transformation can be combined with the geometry-based representation of signing space to capture the properties of a sign. Beginning with the innermost part of the representation, the hand moves through a series of four postures, labeled as HP_a, HP_b, HP_c, and HP_d. In HP_a the hand assumes the handshape $HS1$, in HP_b it assumes handshape $HS2$, in HP_c it assumes handshape $HS1$ again, and in HP_d the sign ends with the handshape $HS2$. Within the local signing space (LSS), the hand starts at location $LOC1$ and ends at $LOC2$. With respect to global signing space (GSS) local signing space is static, so there are no changes.

(12)

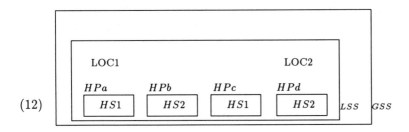

The schematic in (12) captures the spatial relation of the sign gesture, that is to say, the relation between the hand and signing space throughout the articulation of the sign. In the next section I complete the representation of the sign by considering its temporal properties.

1.2.4   Space and Time

Borrowing from computer jargon, the representation in (12) can be described like a computer program, capturing the off-line properties of the sign gesture. It is a step-by-step set of instructions for moving the hand, just as a computer program is a step-by-step set of instructions for running a computer. By turning off the clock of the computer, or "taking the computer off-line", each step of the program can be examined at leisure. This contrasts with the state of affairs when the computer is on-line, and the program runs in real time, executed at the rate dictated by the computer's clock. Signs, too, are articulated in real time, produced to the beat of some internal signing clock. The relation between that clock and the instructions in (12) are represented in (13).

In (13), timelines on either side of the schematic from (12) capture an interval of time from t_i to t_l. For location, the starting location, $LOC1$, associates with time t_i and the ending location, $LOC2$, associates with t_l. For handshape, there are four points of reference at evenly spaced intervals on the timeline, so at the start of the sign HPa associates with time t_i, then HPb associates with t_j, HPc with t_k, and HPd with t_l.

(13)

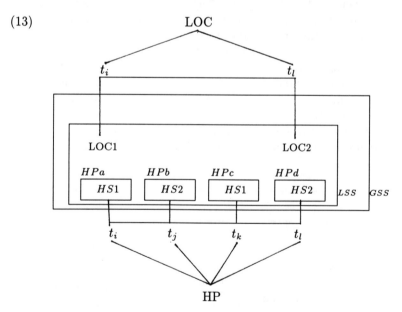

The figure in (14) shows the relation between the timelines in (13).

(14)   LOC1   LOC2
```
       LOC1                 LOC2
        |                    |
       t_i      t_j    t_k     t_l
        |        |      |       |
       HS1      HS2    HS1     HS2
```

1.2.4.1 Phonological Representation

To review, both the timing relations in (14) and the spatial relations in (12) are needed to specify the properties of a sign. In the course of the thesis, the phonological units that I argue for to represent those properties are the *transition unit*, (15), and the *cell*, (16).

The *transition unit* represents a phonological parameter (P) over an interval of time, where the parameter is either *location*, *orientation*, or *handshape*. There are three types of transition units: the parameter can maintain the same value throughout the interval, (15a), it may change once, (15b), or it may change repeatedly, (15b).

(15)   Transition Unit: a. $[\,P\,]$
                             b. $[\,P_i, P_f\,]_\Delta$
                             c. $[\,P_i, P_f\,]_{2\Delta}$

The notation for the *cell* reflects the spatial and temporal properties of the sign gesture. (16) is the skeleton for a morphologically simple sign. Starting from the inside, HS specifies the configuration of the fingers and thumb, HP specifies the location and orientation of the hand inside the hand prism, and the box labeled LSS specifies the location and orientation of the hand prism inside local signing space.

(16)   *Cell* Structure:

$$\begin{bmatrix} LOC \begin{bmatrix} LSS:GSS \\ OR \begin{bmatrix} LSS_1:GSS_1 \\ LSS_2:GSS_2 \end{bmatrix} \end{bmatrix} \\ \begin{bmatrix} LOC \begin{bmatrix} HP:LSS \\ OR \begin{bmatrix} HP_1:LSS_1 \\ HP_2:LSS_2 \end{bmatrix} \end{bmatrix} \\ \begin{bmatrix} HP \begin{bmatrix} LOC \begin{bmatrix} Hand:HP \\ OR \begin{bmatrix} Hand_1:HP_1 \\ Hand_2:HP_2 \end{bmatrix} \end{bmatrix} \\ HS \begin{bmatrix} \ \end{bmatrix} \end{bmatrix}_{HP} \end{bmatrix}_{LSS} \end{bmatrix}_{GSS}$$

The cellular representation for DREAM is given in (17) with hand-shape names used as abbreviated forms for the information specified for the fingers and thumb.

(17)   DREAM:

$$
\left[
\begin{array}{l}
\left[LOC \begin{array}{c} \left[+Base_{LSS} : Side\text{-}of\text{-}Forehead_{GSS} \right] \\ OR \begin{bmatrix} +Base_{LSS} : Back_{GSS} \\ +Local_{LSS} : Top_{GSS} \end{bmatrix} \end{array} \right] \\[3em]
\left[LOC \begin{array}{c} \left[Front_{HP} : +Base_{LSS}, -Base_{LSS} \right]_{\Delta} \\ OR \begin{bmatrix} Front_{HP} : +Base_{LSS} \\ Top_{HP} : +Local_{LSS} \end{bmatrix} \end{array} \right] \\[3em]
\left[HP \begin{array}{c} \left[LOC \begin{bmatrix} Base_{Hand} : Back_{HP} \\ F\text{-}tip_{Hand} : Front_{HP} \\ Back_{Hand} : Top_{HP} \end{bmatrix} \right] \\ OR \\ HS \begin{bmatrix} 1,x \end{bmatrix}_{2\Delta} \end{array} \right]
\end{array}
\right]
$$

From the perspective of spoken language phonology, the representation in (17), and the phonological constructs in (15) and (16) present an unfamiliar organization of linguistic information. For example, phonologists take it for granted that constructs like the segment and syllable are temporally distinct, that is to say, that given any two segments or syllables, one must necessarily precede the other. In contrast, as illustrated by the simultaneous change in location and repeated change in handshape represented in (17), it is clear that two *transition units* may occupy the same interval of time.

In addition to temporal distinctions, the notion of *location* and *orientation* described only briefly in this chapter, are formalized in the thesis as dyadic relations. Furthermore, these relations hold between embedded constructs, specifically between the hand and the hand prism, between the hand prism and local signing space, and local signing space and global signing space. Unlike traditional spoken language features which are formally monadic relations that yield to organization into sets described by feature geometries, the dyadic relations *location* and *orientation* require the development of a hierarchical form of representation. As demonstrated in Chapter 5, once imagined as a hierarchy of nested relations and not as a set of features, *location* and *orientation* yield immediate results for solving puzzles about complex verbal morphology.

1.3   A Guide to the Thesis

The bulk of the thesis is devoted to laying the groundwork for the model of visual phonology.[7] In Chapter 2 I argue for the constructs that represent the hand, and in Chapter 3 I argue for the constructs that represent signing space. Chapter 4 is dedicated to the representation of movement. The results of this chapter are notable because, although movement is treated as a phonological primitive in previous models of sign language, here it emerges as a derivative property of the phonological primitive *handshape*, and the relations *location* and *orientation*. In Chapter 5 I extend the analysis in Chapters 2 through 4, which focus on the lexically simple sign, to include one set of complex signs, namely agreement verbs.

With the basic model of visual phonology in place, in Chapter 6 I review three previously proposed sign language phonologies that are based on the transfer-and-test model of phonology. Perlmutter (1992) presents a Moraic model of signs focused on the syllable, Liddell and Johnson (1989) propose a Movement-Hold model of signs focused on the segment, and Sandler (1989) proposes a Hand Tier model that extends the discussion to include feature geometry. I show that the model of visual phonology proposed here provides a perspective that can simplify the constructs in those models. In addition, the discussion highlights the timing differences between spoken language and sign language phonologies.

In Chapter 7 I summarize the model of visual phonology developed in the thesis and compare the sign language constructs, the *transition unit* and *cell*, with their spoken language counterparts, the *segment* and *syllable*. I show that no clearcut one-to-one mapping between the constructs emerges. Rather, as indicated by the asymmetries between vision and speech noted in this chapter, at a low level of representation the constructs of a spoken language phonology are distinct from the constructs of a visual phonology. It is suggested that the organization of these atomic units into more complex units are, however, likely to follow general principles of organization that are the laws of a theory of universal phonology.

A message about signing. Throughout the thesis, I present data with both pictures and prose. The purpose of this redundancy is to enable the reader to articulate the signs – an activity that is crucial to

---

[7]Arguments in the thesis are based primarily on the characteristics of one-handed signs. Unfortunately, a comprehensive discussion of two-handed signs is beyond the scope of this work. Brief remarks about extending the model to account for two-handed signs are included in Section 5.3.1.

the effective study of visual phonology. If it is true, as I argue, that a theory of phonology requires input from two mode-distinct frameworks, then it will be imperative that linguists interested in developing a theory of universal phonology be familiar with both modes of language. To that end, I hope all readers are able to sign along throughout the thesis. Sign novices will find introductory books such as Humphries, Padden, and O'Rourke (1980), Humphries and Padden (1992), Baker-Shenk and Cokely (1980), and Valli and Lucas (1992), as well as their companion videotapes very helpful. The best resource remains, of course, native intuitions or a signing friend. It is my hope, however, that advances in our field make it the rule rather than the exception that linguists are familiar with visual as well as spoken languages, rendering the descriptive redundancy presented here obsolete.

2

Hand Prism

The hand is central to the articulation of a sign, and is the focus of this chapter. I argue, piece by piece, for each component of its representation. The result is an organization of the parts of the hand similar to those proposed before (Mandel 1981, Sandler 1989, Brentari 1990a, Corina and Sagey 1989, Liddell and Johnson 1989), but with the addition of a hierarchical organization of the joints.

I also argue that handshape by itself is insufficient to account for the distributional facts, and adopt a formal representation of *hand orientation*. Unlike previous proposals in which hand orientation is captured by distinctive features, I define *hand orientation* as a dyadic relation between the hand and a geometric construct I refer to as a *hand prism*. This proposal anticipates a more general property of signs defined in Chapter 3, namely a set of orientation relations that hold between constructs that represent signing space. I start by introducing the set of sign parameters regarded as basic in sign language phonology, and then turn to even more basic concepts such as the *manual articulator* for signs.

2.1 Sign Parameters

Stokoe (1960) was the first to suggest that the gestures of ASL have regular structure. He proposed that the lexically distinctive properties of a sign are the configuration of the hand, or *handshape*, the place where it is articulated, or its *location*, and the nature of its *movement*.[1] Later, Battison (1978) argued that *palm orientation* is also distinctive.

As an illustration of these terms, consider the sign in (1). To articulate it, all the fingers and the thumb are held flat with respect to

---

[1] Stokoe used different terminology to describe *cherology*, the phonology of signs. Handshape is referred to as *dez*, location as *tab*, and movement as *sig*. Those innovations have been abandoned in favor of the more transparent *handshape*, *location*, and *movement*.

the palm. The fingers are held together while the thumb is relaxed and held at about a 45° angle to the fingers. The palm faces the signer and the fingertips point up. To articulate the sign, the fleshy part of the fingertips touch the center of the chin. The hand then moves away from the chin along a straight path and stops a few inches in front of the chin.

(1)   GOOD

In descriptive terms borrowed from Stokoe (1960) and Battison (1978), (1) is articulated with a B-handshape, at the chin, with the palm facing in, and the hand moving away from the chin with a straight outward movement.

In this work I will use terms such as *handshape*, *location*, *movement*, and *palm orientation* as part of the descriptive framework of signs. That is not to be misconstrued however as their acceptance into the theoretical framework as well. Although I will use descriptive terminology without argumentation, each theoretical construct will be explicitly identified and adopted piece by piece as part of the framework. In rare instances, descriptive and theoretical terminology will overlap. For example, the terms *fingers* and *thumb* are used descriptively, but are also adopted as phonological constructs. As much as possible, I will avoid these dualities.

In various previous analyses, *handshape*, *location*, *orientation*, and *movement*, are adopted as phonological constructs and associated with sets of distinctive features (e.g., Liddell and Johnson 1989, Sandler 1989, Brentari 1990). In this work, *handshape* is adopted as a phonological construct, and is the only one that is specified for features. *Location* and *orientation* are recast as dyadic relations that hold between embedded constructs, namely the hand, hand prism, local signing space, and global signing space. *Movement* is not a phonological parameter at all. Rather, it is a derived property of transitions between the values of *handshape*, *location*, and *orientation*.

Over the next four chapters, these "traditional" terms are formalized as constructs of a geometry-based analysis of signs. I begin by examining the properties of the hands.

2.2 Hands that Move

To articulate a sign, a signer moves her hands and arms. But just as the chewing and swallowing gestures of the mouth are irrelevant to speech, so too, the grasping and gripping properties of the hands are extraneous to signs.

For example, to articulate the sign in (2), the signer's non-dominant hand is held in front of the signer with the palm held facing upward. The fingers and the thumb are held flat with respect to the palm, and the fingertips point away from the signer. The thumb and index finger of the signer's dominant hand are bent slightly at the knuckle joint with the non-knuckle joints held straight; the joints of the other fingers are bent so that the fingers are curled against the palm. With the thumb side of the dominant hand resting on the upturned palm of the non-dominant hand, the sign is articulated by bending the index finger at the knuckle joint until the tip of the index finger touches the tip of the thumb.

(2)   PRINT

To articulate the sign in (2), the fingers of the dominant hand are *displaced*, that is, they simply move from one position to another. This property of movement falls under the study of *kinematics*. Another property of the hands is the *kinetics*, or *force* that the muscles can apply. If, for example, an eggshell were placed between the tips of the index finger and the thumb when they make contact as they articulate (2), the fingers could apply enough pressure to break the eggshell. However, a gesture like that would be indistinguishable from (2). So although the hands are capable of applying varying degrees of force, the only physiological function of the hands relevant to signing is the displacement of the hands.

Just as the force exerted by the hand does not matter in signs, neither does the choice of sides. A sign can be articulated with either the right or left hand. In general, a signer will articulate signs with her dominant hand, the hand that she uses to articulate fine motor skills such as writing.

What matters is that the hands move when a sign is articulated. To illustrate, the sign in (2) contrasts with variations of the gesture described in (3). In each case, rather than move, as in (2), the hand is held in a static position.[2]

(3) a. *(hold index finger and thumb open in initial position for PRINT)
     b. *(hold index finger and thumb together in final position of PRINT)

The sign in (2) also contrasts with the physiologically possible gestures described in (4) that include movement, but by themselves are not acceptable signs.

(4) a. *(raise eyebrows, move head forward)
     b. *(squint eyebrows, shake head from side to side)
     c. *(puff cheeks)
     d. *(shrug the shoulders)
     e. *(raise elbow)
     f. *(stick out and wiggle the tongue)

Comparing the well-formed sign in (2) with the ill-formed gestures in (3) shows that movement is a necessary component of a sign. Then comparing (2) with the movements in (4) shows that a sign must be articulated with the hand(s). The proposition in (5) captures the generalization and accounts for this distribution of data, where by *sign gesture* I mean at least a minimally meaningful sign, and by *manual articulator* I mean the displacement properties of the dominant hand(s).[3]

---

[2]When preceding a brief description of a gesture the asterisk (*) denotes a gesture that is an ill-formed sign.

[3]There are two types of signs that involve two hands. If one hand is static, then it is a one-handed sign with the static hand as the place of articulation (Sandler 1989). If both hands mirror a gesture, it is a two-handed sign. I do not explicitly present a representation for two-handed signs, although the representation argued for here can be extended to provide an explanatory account for the symmetry of two-handed signs.

(5) | To articulate a *sign gesture* the *manual articulator* moves. |

(5) correctly rules out gestures like batting the eyelashes or wiggling the ears as signs in ASL.[4] The constructs *manual articulator* and *sign gesture* are crucial to the statement of (5), so both are adopted as constructs of the theoretical framework.

The principle in (5) predicts that only the hand(s) need be present to articulate a sign. Conversely, it predicts that a sign gesture is incomplete if the hands are missing. There is (unfortunate) anecdotal evidence to support the latter prediction. As documented on a BBC program (*See Hear*), a Deaf laborer in England lost both hands in an industrial accident and, though recovered from the accident, has difficulties communicating effectively. Friends rely on cues such as non-manual signals and context to interpret his hand-less gestures. Both predictions could be tested experimentally with a sign synthesizer, or video-editing, to compare signs articulated only with hands or only without hands.

Note, however, that (5) does not rule out non-manual signals, gestures articulated with body parts other than the hands; it simply ensures that the essential part of the sign is present. Non-manual signals are not, by themselves, sufficient to be a sign. In previous work it has been shown that conventionalized facial expressions contribute meaning to gesture (Baker 1976, Liddell 1980). Some non-manual signals are significant at the phrasal level; others appear to be lexical. For example, the gesture described in (4a) is used as a phrasal marker to signal WH-questions. The gesture described in (4b) is a negative marker; when (4c) is added to a gesture it acts as an intensifier meaning "a very large mass of" (Baker-Shenk and Cokely 1980).

Even though non-manual signals are a significant component of the visual grammar, they have received little attention in discussions of phonological representations of signs, and are, unfortunately, also beyond the scope of this discussion. The objective of this work is to characterize the movement of the hand(s) through space.

In the remainder of this chapter I argue for the constructs needed to

---

[4]Two gestures are apparent counterexamples to the principle in (5). In one, signers wrinkle the nose to indicate agreement. This might be regarded as similar to the nodding of the head that accompanies spoken English. Another gesture is used primarily between women to mean *having-one's-menstrual-period*. It is articulated by pressing the tongue against the inside of the cheek to generate a subtle up-and-down movement of the cheek, and is a variant of the manual sign articulated by touching the side of the fist-shaped hand against the cheek twice. The restricted use of the second gesture and the private nature of the subject, along with the para-linguistic nature of the first gesture indicate that, rather than violate (5), these expressions are not part of the system being modeled here.

unambiguously capture the local properties of the hand. I argue for a set of features to specify *handshape*, and for an *orientation* relation that holds between the hand and the *hand prism*, an abstract representation of the articulators.

2.3 Handshape

Handshape has received considerable attention in the work on sign language. There have been several proposals for distinctive feature sets for handshape (Liddell and Johnson 1989, Sandler 1989, Corina and Sagey 1989, Brentari 1990a,b). Those proposals include familiar structures from spoken language phonology such as the hierarchical organization of handshape features into feature geometries (Sandler 1989, Corina and Sagey 1989, Corina 1990) and notions of markedness (Brentari 1990a).

In this section I present a number of patterns that hold for handshapes and argue for a set of constructs to capture those regularities. Parts of the analysis presented here are similar to the proposals that precede it, yet the sum of the representation is broader. For example, whereas four major handshape configurations are accounted for in accounts by Corina and Sagey (1989) and Brentari (1990a), the analysis presented here predicts nine distinct handshape configurations, of which seven are broadly attested in ASL and two occur in more specific contexts.

In rough terms, *handshape* refers to the configuration of the fingers and thumb. Of all the characteristics of the sign, handshape is noteworthy because the hand exhibits considerable versatility. In the realm of signing, the fingers and thumb assume a wide variety of configurations. For example, in one domain of manual communication known as *fingerspelling* there is a one-to-one relation between the shape of the hand and the twenty-six letters of the alphabet, producing a manual alphabet. Although the manual alphabet is often confused with signing, it is not part of natural signs. It is an artificial gesture system designed to allow the transliteration of spoken words into a manual orthography.

In spite of its origins, the manual alphabet enters ASL through *cross-modal borrowings*. There are at least two types of these cross-modal borrowings: (i) the set of "loan signs" described by Battison (1978), and (ii) initialized signs, prescribed for artificial systems like SEE (Signed Exact English) (Gustason, Pfetzing, and Zawolkow 1980). Battison (1978) described a small set of fingerspelled versions of English words that undergo assimilation to conform to the phonological properties of native signs. For example the sequence of handshapes, N and O, (6a), undergo changes to produce the sign that means NO, (6b).

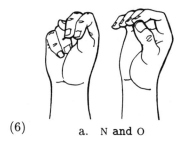
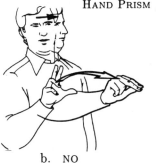

(6)   a. N and O   b. NO

Initialized signs are signs based on a sign from ASL that form a semantic class. For example, the ASL sign for GROUP is articulated with a T-handshape to mean *team*, or with an F-handshape to mean *family*. In this work I exclude these cross-modal borrowings from the analysis. Until the phonology of the target language is well understood, any attempt to characterize the change that borrowings undergo is premature.

Hence, in this section I focus on the distributional asymmetries of native hand configurations that occur in (i) static postures, and (ii) changes in hand posture that occur in simple signs. The phonological constructs that emerge are the *fingers* and *thumb*, *selected* and *nonselected fingers*, and *base* and *non-base joints*.

After arguing for those constructs, I consider a puzzling asymmetry of hand configurations that appear to have the same handshape. I argue that handshape alone is insufficient to capture lexical distinctiveness, and that the *orientation* of the hand, specifically, the orientation of the hand with respect to a construct called the *hand prism* (HP), must be included in a lexically contrastive representation. The net result is a formal representation of the hand as a rigid body whose configuration is specified in terms of the hand prism. This geometric representation anticipates the relation between the hand and signing space, defined in the following chapter. I begin with an examination of the properties of the fingers and thumb.

2.3.1   Fingers and Thumb

Physiologically, the fingers differ significantly from the thumb. The joints of the thumb allow it to oppose the rest of the hand, a capability that sets humans apart from other animals. Physiology aside, distributional patterns in signs provide evidence for representing the fingers and thumb as distinct phonological constructs.

In (7), for example, the fingers and thumb articulate independent movements. In (7a) the index finger and thumb are straight while the rest of the fingers are curled against the palm. The thumb is held at about a 45° angle with respect to the index finger, the tip of the index finger points up, and the palm of the hand faces away from the signer. To articulate the sign, the thumb wiggles back and forth, bending at its end and middle joints while the index finger remains unchanged. In (7b) the index and middle fingers and the thumb are straight while the rest of the fingers are curled against the palm. The thumb is relaxed at the same angle as for (7a).[5] The hand is held near the side of the forehead with the tip of the fingers pointing up, the tip of the thumb hovering near the forehead, and the palm facing to the side. To articulate the sign, the hand moves in small circles perpendicular to the signer, while the middle and end joints of the index and middle fingers bend and extend. The fingers complete one cycle of bending and extending as the hand moves through one circle. The thumb, meanwhile, remains straight.

(7) a. TWENTY-ONE b. MISCHIEVOUS

So (7a) is articulated with the thumb changing position while the fingers are static, and (7b) is articulated with the fingers changing position while the thumb is static. The unison movement of the fingers in (7b) contrasts with the non-occurring gestures described in (8). Moving only one of the extended fingers does not produce a well-formed sign.

(8) a. *(for MISCHIEVOUS, wiggle only the index finger)
  b. *(for MISCHIEVOUS, wiggle only the middle finger)

In addition, only the fingers that are extended participate in the movement. The static status of the non-extended fingers in (7) contrast

---

[5] (7b) is an image from Humphries and Padden, *Learning American Sign Language* (1992) with illustrations by Rob Hills, Daniel W. Renner, and Peggy Swartzel-Lott. Other images from that publication reprinted and adapted by permission of Allyn and Bacon are: APPLE, CONFLICT, FIRE, HOSPITAL, INCOMPETENT, LOCALE, MEET-YOU, MILK, MOTHER, NOW, OLD, PER-CENT, PRINT, RESTAURANT, SHUTDOWN, and TWENTY-ONE.

with the gestures described in (9). If the non-extended fingers move, the gestures are not well-formed signs.

(9)   a.   *(for MISCHIEVOUS, move the ring and pinky)
      b.   *(for TWENTY-ONE, move the middle, ring, and pinky)

The propositions in (10) generalize the differences between the well-formed signs in (7) and the ill-formed gestures described in (8) and (9)

(10) In a well-formed sign:
      (i)   the fingers that move articulate the same movements, and
      (ii) the fingers that do not move maintain the same position throughout the sign.

In some signs the fingers and thumb move at the same time. For example, in (11), both hands are held in front of the signer. The thumb and all of the fingers are straight, slightly spread, and held flat with respect to the palm. The tips of the fingers point away from the signer and the palms of the hands face up. To articulate the sign, the hands move a few inches towards the signer along a straight path while the top two joints of the fingers and thumb bend into a curved position. Both movements start at the same time, and proceed at the same rate so that the bending of the joints and the movement of the hands towards the signer end at the same time.

(11)   WANT

This sign contrasts with the ill-formed gestures described in (12). If only the fingers change posture, (12a), or only the thumb changes, (12b), the sign is ill-formed.

(12) a. *(articulate WANT with only the fingers hooking)
      b. *(articulate WANT with only the thumb hooking)

To summarize, the data in (7) and (11) show, respectively, that the fingers and thumb may move independently, or as a unit. In addition, the fingers may be subdivided into those that move and those that do not, (10). To account for this latter difference, I adopt the terms *selected fingers* and *unselected fingers* from Mandel (1981:82) who noted that the fingers that move, move together, and those that do not move assume either fully extended or fully closed positions, stated here as (13a).[6] Mandel coined the terms *selected fingers* to identify those that move, and *unselected fingers* to identify those that do not. To account for the asymmetries between the fingers and thumb, I add the proposition in (13b).

(13) | a. | The *fingers* function as a unit. |
|---|---|
| | (i) The *selected fingers* articulate the same movement. |
| | (ii) The *unselected fingers* do not move. |
| b. | The *thumb* and *selected fingers* may function as a unit, or as independent units, |
| | (i) If the *thumb* and *selected fingers* are a unit, they articulate the same movement. |
| | (ii) If the *thumb* and *selected fingers* are independent, they need not articulate the same movement. |

The contrasts between the well-formed signs in (7) and the non-occurring gestures described in (8) and (9) are accounted for by the analyses in (14) and (15).

(14) (i)   The *selected fingers* for TWENTY-ONE is the index finger.
      (ii) The *unselected fingers* are the middle, ring, and pinky fingers.
      (iii) By (13a(ii)), the middle, ring, and pinky fingers must not move.

---

[6] "In any HC [hand configuration], the fingers can be exhaustively divided into no more than two groups. One group, the selected fingers, can be in any one of ...[several positions]... but they must all be in the same position. The unselected fingers (or other fingers) may only be all extended or all closed." Mandel (1981:82)

(iv) Therefore, (9b) is ill-formed.

(15) (i) The *selected fingers* for MISCHIEVOUS are the index and middle fingers.

     (ii) The *unselected fingers* are the ring and pinky fingers.

     (iii) By (13a(i)), the index and middle fingers must move together.

     (iv) Therefore, the gestures in (8) are ill-formed.

     (v) By (13a(ii)), the ring and pinky fingers must not move.

     (iv) Therefore, (9a) is ill-formed.

The contrast between the data in (11) and (12) is captured by the analysis in (16).

(16) (i) All fingers are *selected* for WANT.

     (ii) The *selected fingers* and *thumb* are a unit.

     (iii) By (13b(i)), the fingers and thumb must move together.

     (iv) Therefore, the data in (12) are ill-formed.

The constructs *selected fingers*, *unselected fingers*, and *thumb* are crucial to the analyses in (14), (15), and (16), so they are adopted as part of the model. Note that this is one of the instances in which descriptive terms are adopted into the theoretical framework.

Furthermore, the proposition in (13b(ii)) predicts that if the fingers and thumb are independent, then movement is obligatory on the part of the hand that it is assigned to, but not necessarily excluded from the other. The data in (17) indicate that it is acceptable in those cases for movement to be "shared", so (13) also provides a correct account of this data.

(17) a. (TWENTY-ONE articulated with finger bending along with thumb)

     b. (MISCHIEVOUS articulated with thumb bending along with fingers)

Given that there are four fingers, and sixteen logical combinations of selected/unselected fingers, the question now is whether all those possibilities occur in ASL. As discussed in the next section, the answer is negative.

2.3.2 Selected and Unselected Fingers

In addition to the sixteen logically possible combinations of selected and unselected fingers, the unselected fingers may assume one of two different positions: (i) curled, or (ii) straight.

The sign in (18a), described as (2) in the previous section, is an example of the unselected fingers, the middle, ring, and pinky, remaining in a curled position throughout the articulation of the sign. The sign in (18b) is an example of the unselected fingers held in a straight position. In this sign the hand is held in front of the signer with the thumb and all the fingers held straight and slightly spread. The fingertips point away from the signer and the palm faces down. To articulate the sign, two movements are made simultaneously: (i) all the joints of the index finger and thumb bend until the tips of the index finger and thumb touch and form a small circle, and (ii) the hand bends at the wrist, so that at the end of the gesture, the palm of the hand faces away from the signer. Both movements start at the same time and progress at the same rate so that the finger and thumb tips touch at the same time that the palm completes its outward movement.

(18)   a. PRINT   b. CHOOSE

In both signs in (18) the index finger moves, so by (13a), the index finger is selected, and the middle, ring, and pinky fingers are unselected. In (18a) the unselected fingers are curled; in (18b) they are extended. (13a) predicts that even if the unselected fingers are extended, they do not move. The gestures described in (19) confirm that prediction. In both cases, if the unselected fingers move, the gestures are no longer well-formed.

(19)   a.   *(CHOOSE articulated with middle, ring, and pinky fingers bending)

       b.   *(CHOOSE articulated with middle, ring, and pinky fingers curling)

Although the unselected fingers are acceptable curled, as in (18a), or extended, as in (18b), the same is not true for all hand configurations. For example, in (20), the middle and ring fingers are the unselected fingers. In (20a), they are curled, and in (20b), they are extended. (20a) is a hand configuration that occurs in ASL, while (20b) does not occur in well-formed signs in ASL.

(20)   a.   −SEL: curled   b.   *(−SEL:straight)

Similarly, in (21), the middle finger is selected; the index, ring, and pinky fingers are unselected. In (21a), the unselected fingers are curled, and in (21b), the unselected fingers are straight. (21a) is a hand configuration that does not occur in ASL; (21b) does.

(21)   a.   *(−SEL:curled)   b.   SEL:straight

Hence, for some sets of selected fingers the unselected fingers may be either curled or extended, (18), and for other combinations of selected fingers the unselected fingers are obligatorily curled, (20), or obligatorily extended, (21). The combinations of selected and unselected fingers that occur in ASL are listed in (22). A checkmark, √, indicates that the combination occurs, and an asterisk, *, indicates that it does not. (22a), designated as having no selected fingers, could also be stated as all fingers selected (IMRP), with an uninformative assignment of unselected fingers.

(22)

	Selected fingers	Unselected fingers Straight	Curled
a.	none	✓	✓
b.	I	✓	✓
c.	IM	*	✓
d.	IMR	*	✓
e.	IP	*	✓
f.	M	✓	*

To capture the difference between the well-formed and non-occurring hand configurations in (22), consider the organization of the fingers in (23a). Consistent with their physiological organization, the index and pinky fingers are designated "edge" fingers and the middle and ring fingers are "inner" fingers. Based on the designations in (23a), the propositions in (23b) simplify the specification of the possible sets of selected fingers. (23b(i)) captures the pattern of (22a), (22b), (22c), (d22d), and (22e); (23b(ii)) captures (22f).

(23)   a.

```
        e                 e
        d                 d
        g       inner     g
        e                 e

        I    M    R    P
        n    i    i    i
        d    d    n    n
        e    d    g    k
        x    l         y
             e
```

   b.   The sets of selected fingers are:
        (i)   Any set of contiguous fingers that include the In-
               dex finger.
        (ii)   One inner finger.

Given the special status of the index finger in (23b(i)), the patterns of selected fingers suggest the hierarchical organization of fingers in (24).

(24)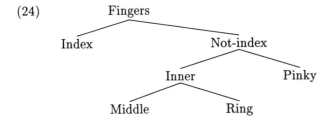

Thus, the set of possible combinations of selected fingers and postures of unselected fingers for ASL can be reduced to the set that meets the stipulations in (25).

(25)   a.   For any combination of selected fingers that includes the index finger, the unselected fingers may be curled.

        b.   If the index finger is not included, then the unselected fingers may only be straight.

        c.   If only the index finger is selected, or no fingers are selected, then the unselected fingers may be straight.

Although these generalizations capture the patterns observed in ASL, they are subject to further cross-linguistic scrutiny. For example, the choice of a selected inner finger may be language dependent. As noted in (22), for ASL the only inner finger that is selected alone is the middle finger. In contrast, in Dutch Sign Language (Nederlands Gebarentaal, or NGT), the ring finger, not the middle finger, is selected in the small set of signs in which only one inner finger is selected.

In addition, as indicated in (22f), extending the middle finger while curling the other fingers does not occur in ASL. That exclusion may, however, reflect cultural bias rather than linguistic status. The hand configuration is taboo in the United States, but in Japan it is often used for pointing. It also occurs in both Taiwan Sign Language and Japanese Sign Language.

Nevertheless, the patterns of selected fingers reflect some sort of underlying organization, tentatively captured for ASL by (25). More specific proposals await further cross-linguistic analysis.

2.3.3 Base/Non-Base Joints

For each of the fingers and thumb, there are three joints, illustrated in (26): (i) the knuckle, the joint that joins the finger to the hand, (ii) the "middle joint", and (iii) the "end joint", the joint at the outermost tip of the fingers and thumb. What corresponds to the knuckle joint for the thumb is not as obvious, but it is the joint at the point where the thumb seems to attach to the hand.[7]

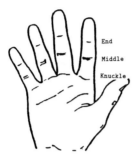

(26)   Joints

Although each finger and thumb has three joints, they do not move independently.[8] Recall the pronunciation of the signs MISCHIEVOUS, (7b), and PRINT, (2). To articulate MISCHIEVOUS the middle and end joints bend while the knuckle joint is straight. To articulate PRINT the index finger and thumb bend only at their knuckle joints; the middle and end joints remain straight.

The configurations of the fingers and thumb used to articulate either MISCHIEVOUS or PRINT contrast with the ill-formed gestures described in (27). Although some people are able to articulate (27a), most people find the gesture impossible or, at best, difficult. Similarly, bending only the middle joint is possible for some people, nearly impossible for others, and usually simpler if the knuckle joint is also bent. Independent of the physiological challenge they pose, the gestures described in (27) do not occur in well-formed signs.

(27)   a.   *(bend only the end joint)
        b.   *(bend only the middle joint)

The contrast between the gestures in (27) and the well-formed signs, MISCHIEVOUS and PRINT, is captured by the proposition in (28).

---

[7] Although the thumb is constructed of joints that are more complex than the other joints in the fingers, that difference is not of direct consequence. However, it does provide some phonetic grounding for the distinction between the fingers and thumb discussed in the next section.

[8] Ann (1993) presents this same observation based on the physiology of the hands.

(28)   In well-formed signs, the middle and end joints bend together.

The organization of the joints is simplified by the proposition in (29).

(29)   a.   The *base joint* is the knuckle joint.
       b.   The *non-base joints* are the middle and end joints.

The tree in (30) reflects the organization of the joints suggested here. To simplify the reference to the joints, I adopt the binary feature [BASE], where [+BASE] refers to the base joint, and [−BASE] to the non-base joints.

(30)

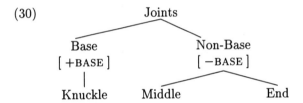

In the next section, I argue for a set of features for the base and non-base joints that captures the properties of the set of well-formed handshapes in ASL.

2.3.4   Joint Values

The sign in (31a) is an example of what has been referred to in the literature as "finger spreading" (Corina and Sagey 1989). In (31a), the fingers and thumb are straight, and slightly separated from each other. At the start of the gesture, the hand is held a few inches from the chin with the tip of the thumb pointing towards the signer and the palm facing to the side. To articulate the sign, the hand moves in a straight line towards the chin until the tip of the thumb touches the center of the chin.[9] In contrast, to articulate (31b), presented earlier as (1), the fingers are held together throughout the gesture.

---

[9]There are at least two other pronunciations of this sign: (i) hold hand at chin and wiggle fingers, (ii) move hand toward chin and touch chin repeatedly. The model of visual phonology proposed here also accounts for these pronunciations.

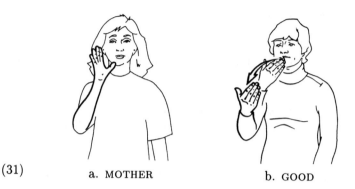

(31)   a. MOTHER   b. GOOD

In previous analyses, the spreading of the fingers is treated as a phonological property and assigned the feature [SPREAD] (Corina and Sagey 1989). In this section I argue that the spreading (or absence of spreading) of the fingers is a predictable property of signs. I present a puzzle in which three different positions of the knuckles produce three different patterns of finger spread, and propose a solution in which I adopt three distinctive joint positions: (i) *extended*, or what I have been referring to as "straight", (ii) *neutral*, or "curved", and (iii) *flexed*, or "curled". Not only does this capture the distribution of finger spreading, it also provides the theoretical machinery to state constraints on handshape change.

The joint features proposed here are similar to the binary features proposed by Corina and Sagey (1989): (i) [+/ − BENT], that specifies bending or straightness of the knuckle, and (ii) [+/ − HOOK], that specifies bending or straightness of the other joints. But whereas Corina and Sagey account for four major handshape configurations, I argue that there are nine distinct handshapes to account for in ASL. Hence, the need for a richer set of joint features.

The first data set of interest for this three part puzzle are the signs in (31). Both are articulated with the fingers and thumb straight, but as described above, in (31a) the fingers are spread and in (31b) they are not. It is possible, however, for (31a) to be articulated with the fingers together. Although the gesture looks odd, it is not distinct from (31a). Likewise, the sign in (31b) can be articulated with the fingers spread. Again, it is odd looking, but not distinct from (31b).

In contrast, in the second piece of the puzzle, in (32), finger spread is obligatory. At the start of the gesture, the fingers and thumb are bent slightly at the knuckle, and the middle and end joints are straight. The tips of the fingers and the palm face away from the signer. To articulate the sign, the fingers and thumb bend at the knuckles until the finger and thumbtips touch.

(32)   SHUTDOWN

To articulate (32), as the tips of the fingers and thumb move closer together, the fingers also move together. But at the start of the sign, the fingers are obligatorily spread, in contrast with the gesture described in (33) which is distinct from (32).[10]

(33)   *(SHUTDOWN with fingers held together throughout the sign)

The last piece of the puzzle is a sign that excludes spreading. In (34) the end and middle joints of the fingers are straight; the fingers bend at the knuckles to form a right angle with the palm of the hand. The thumbs are held at about a 45° angle at the side of the palm. The tips of the fingers and the palm both face up. Both hands are held about a foot in front of the signer's upper chest. To articulate the sign, both hands move down in a straight line for a few inches.

---

[10]The gesture in (33) can be interpreted as a form of a classifier meaning "something large deflates". However, the focus in this work is on lexicalized signs. A discussion about the relation between the classifier system and the set of lexicalized signs is, unfortunately, beyond the scope of this discussion (Supalla 1978, 1982, 1986, Schick 1990).

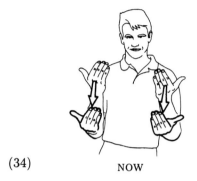

(34)   NOW

The sign in (34) contrasts with the ill-formed gesture described in (35).

(35)   *(NOW with fingers spread)

The chart in (36) summarizes the puzzle presented by the data described in (31) through (35). Knuckle position is described on the left side of the chart, and finger position on the right side. The signs are listed in the column that describes the spread or non-spread state of the fingers. A checkmark, √, means that the alternative is acceptable, and an asterisk, *, means that it is not.

(36)

| | Finger position: | |
Knuckles	Spread	Not spread
straight	MOTHER √	√ GOOD
slightly bent	SHUTDOWN	*
bent at right angle	*	NOW

To account for this asymmetric distribution of finger spreading, I adopt the joint features in (37).

(37)   Joint Feature   Joint Posture
   a.   EXTENDED   straight
   b.   NEUTRAL   slightly bent
   c.   FLEXED   bent to right angle

Given the features in (37), the propositions in (38) capture the distribution of spreading in (36).[11]

(38)	a.	If the *base joint* is EXTENDED, the fingers may or may not spread.
	b.	If the *base joint* is NEUTRAL, the fingers obligatorily spread.
	c.	If the *base joint* is FLEXED, finger spreading is excluded.

The results of this analysis of finger spreading are discussed below: (i) it explains the association between finger spreading and *fingerwiggling*, a specific type of movement in ASL, (ii) the joint features provide the theoretical machinery to capture a constraint on handshape change, and (iii) the combination of joints and joint features produce the inventory of handshapes that occur in ASL.

Fingerwiggling. The sign in (39) is articulated with a movement that has been dubbed *fingerwiggling*. In fact, the movement might more accurately be described as "fingerwaving" because the fingers execute a wavelike motion.

To articulate the sign in (39), the signer holds her non-dominant hand in front of her with the fingers and thumb straight, fingers together and the thumb at a 45° angle to the side of the index finger. The tips of the fingers point to the side and the palm of the hand faces the signer.[12] The

---

[11]There are two exceptions to (38a). First, handshapes used for numbers, e.g., 2, 3, 4, and 5, are articulated with extended fingers that are obligatorily spread. I propose that these handshapes, like the manual alphabet, are exceptions to the general principles of signs that are native to ASL. Second, Corina (1993) notes a small set of signs that are articulated with handshapes that alternate spread fingers and fingers together, e.g., SCISSORS, CRAB. I propose that those type of signs are lexicalized forms of gestures that originate in the classifier system and, as such, may import non-native properties like alternating spreading. In both these cases, spreading must be stipulated. Barring evidence to the contrary in the native signs from other sign languages, these may be the only stipulations required with respect to the claims made here.

[12](39) is reprinted by permission of the publisher from *The Signs of Language* by Edward Klima and Ursula Bellugi, Cambridge, Mass.: Harvard University Press, Copyright (c) 1979 by the President and Fellows of Harvard College. Other images

hand maintains this position for the duration of the sign. The dominant
hand hovers about two inches above the static hand, with the fingers
and thumb straight and the fingers slightly spread. The fingertips are at
right angles with respect to the static hand, and the palm of the hand
faces downward. The thumb is at a 45° angle to the side of the index
finger and is static throughout the sign. The wave starts with the pinky
bending forward slightly at the knuckle. The ring finger follows, then
the middle finger, and finally the index finger; each one bending slightly
at the knuckle. As soon as the pinky has bent forward (and even while
the ring finger is just starting its first movement), it moves back to its
original upright position; the ring finger, then the middle finger, and
finally the index finger follow suit. The effect is a wavelike motion of the
fingers that starts with the pinky.[13] In signs like (39), fingerwiggling is
usually articulated with two or three cycles of these "finger waves".

(39)   STUDY

In rapid signing, the movement may be reduced to a wave that involves only the index and non-index fingers moving back and forth, producing a trilling effect. Nevertheless, a careful articulation of fingerwiggling is produced by a full wave that engages all four fingers.

The fingerwiggling in (39) contrasts with the non-occurring gesture
described in (40).

---

from that publication are CHILDREN, DRY, SUMMER, THING, UGLY, articulatory space,
and various handshapes.

[13]In Japanese Sign Language it appears that *fingerwiggling* is articulated with a
wave-like motion that starts with the index finger. Although the movement feels odd
to Americans, in hearing Japanese culture a similar movement occurs in a counting
gesture. The fingers start in an extended position, then one by one, from the index
to the pinky finger, each finger is bent towards the palm. This observation raises two
interesting questions: (i) Is fingerwiggling universal? If so, how is it articulated? and
(ii) What influence/overlap is there between the native sign language of an area and
the gesture system of the associated spoken language?

(40) *(hold fingers together and wiggle fingers)

The analysis in (41) provides an explanation for the ill-formed gesture in (40).

(41) To wiggle the fingers, the *base joints* alternate between EXTENDED and NEUTRAL positions.
    (i) Although by (38a) finger spread is optional, because the joints are in the NEUTRAL position, by (38b) finger spread is obligatory.
    (ii) To comply with (38b), fingers are spread.

Handshape change constraint. Recall the signs for PRINT, (2), and MISCHIEVOUS, (7b). To articulate MISCHIEVOUS all joints of the selected fingers are straight, then the end and middle joints bend. To articulate PRINT the index finger is bent slightly at the knuckle and straight at the end and middle joints. The index finger bends at the knuckle to touch the tip of the thumb. In contrast to these well-formed gestures, the combination of the initial configuration of the index finger in PRINT with the final configuration of the index finger in MISCHIEVOUS is an unattested handshape change in ASL. There is also no well-formed sign in which the fingers are bent at the base joint while the non-base joints change from an extended to a neutral position. These possible and impossible sequences of combinations are represented in (42). (42a) represents the change used to articulate the well-formed sign MISCHIEVOUS. (42b) represents the non-occurring combination of the initial configuration from PRINT and the final configuration of MISCHIEVOUS, and (42c) represents the third change described above.

(42) a. $\left\{ \begin{array}{l} +\text{BASE}: extended \\ -\text{BASE}: extended \end{array} \right\} \longrightarrow \left\{ \begin{array}{l} +\text{BASE}: extended \\ -\text{BASE}: neutral \end{array} \right\}$

    b. $*\left\{ \begin{array}{l} +\text{BASE}: neutral \\ -\text{BASE}: extended \end{array} \right\} \longrightarrow \left\{ \begin{array}{l} +\text{BASE}: neutral \\ -\text{BASE}: neutral \end{array} \right\}$

    c. $*\left\{ \begin{array}{l} +\text{BASE}: flex \\ -\text{BASE}: extended \end{array} \right\} \longrightarrow \left\{ \begin{array}{l} +\text{BASE}: flex \\ -\text{BASE}: neutral \end{array} \right\}$

The set of constraints in (42) can be stated more simply as a single constraint on the base joint: if the base joint is not extended, then the non-base joints cannot articulate a change from an extended to a neutral position. From this perspective, the model can be simplified by re-stating the feature values as the binary features in (43). If the joint is [+EXT] and [−FLEX], then it is extended, (43a); if it is [−EXT] and [−FLEX], then it is in the neutral position, (43b); and if it is [−EXT] and [+FLEX], then it is flexed, (43c). A joint cannot be extended and flexed at the same time, so the combination in (43d) is ruled out on the basis of its physiological impossibility.

(43)

		EXTENDED (EXT)	FLEXED (FLEX)
a.	*extended*	+	−
b.	*neutral*	−	−
c.	*flexed*	−	+
d.	* (impossible)	+	+

Adopting the features in (43), the observations from (42) can be re-stated as constraints in (44).

(44) a.
$$\left\{ \begin{array}{l} +Base : \left[\begin{array}{l} +\text{EXT} \\ -\text{FLEX} \end{array} \right] \\ -Base : \left[\begin{array}{l} +\text{EXT} \\ -\text{FLEX} \end{array} \right] \end{array} \right\} \longrightarrow \left\{ \begin{array}{l} +Base : \left[\begin{array}{l} +\text{EXT} \\ -\text{FLEX} \end{array} \right] \\ -Base : \left[\begin{array}{l} -\text{EXT} \\ -\text{FLEX} \end{array} \right] \end{array} \right\}$$

b. *
$$\left\{ \begin{array}{l} +Base : \left[\begin{array}{l} -\text{EXT} \\ -\text{FLEX} \end{array} \right] \\ -Base : \left[\begin{array}{l} +\text{EXT} \\ -\text{FLEX} \end{array} \right] \end{array} \right\} \longrightarrow \left\{ \begin{array}{l} +Base : \left[\begin{array}{l} -\text{EXT} \\ -\text{FLEX} \end{array} \right] \\ -Base : \left[\begin{array}{l} -\text{EXT} \\ -\text{FLEX} \end{array} \right] \end{array} \right\}$$

c. *
$$\left\{ \begin{array}{l} +Base : \left[\begin{array}{l} -\text{EXT} \\ +\text{FLEX} \end{array} \right] \\ -Base : \left[\begin{array}{l} +\text{EXT} \\ -\text{FLEX} \end{array} \right] \end{array} \right\} \longrightarrow \left\{ \begin{array}{l} +Base : \left[\begin{array}{l} -\text{EXT} \\ +\text{FLEX} \end{array} \right] \\ -Base : \left[\begin{array}{l} -\text{EXT} \\ -\text{FLEX} \end{array} \right] \end{array} \right\}$$

The set of constraints in (44) can be simplified to (45).

(45) If [+Base : −EXT],
then $* \left\{ -Base : \left[\begin{array}{l} +\text{EXT} \\ -\text{FLEX} \end{array} \right] \right\} \longrightarrow \left\{ -Base : \left[\begin{array}{l} -\text{EXT} \\ -\text{FLEX} \end{array} \right] \right\}$.

So the feature set in (43) provides a way to capture constraints on sequences of handshapes. They will be discussed more in Chapter 4.

Inventory of handshapes. The feature set in (43) produces the set of logical possible combinations in (46).

(46)

Base Joint	Non-Base Joints		
	$\begin{bmatrix} + & flex \\ - & ext \end{bmatrix}$	$\begin{bmatrix} - & flex \\ - & ext \end{bmatrix}$	$\begin{bmatrix} - & flex \\ + & ext \end{bmatrix}$
$\begin{bmatrix} + & flex \\ - & ext \end{bmatrix}$	CLOSED	CURVED-CLOSED	FLAT-CLOSED
$\begin{bmatrix} - & flex \\ - & ext \end{bmatrix}$	$restricted_1$	CURVED	FLAT
$\begin{bmatrix} - & flex \\ + & ext \end{bmatrix}$	$restricted_2$	FLAT-CURVED	OPEN

Seven of the possibilities are common in ASL, (47). The names are adopted from descriptive work on ASL except for the *open-curved* handshape, (47g), not previously characterized as a distinct handshape.[14]

(47)

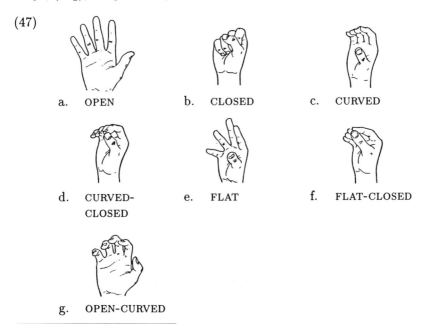

a. OPEN   b. CLOSED   c. CURVED

d. CURVED-   e. FLAT   f. FLAT-CLOSED
   CLOSED

g. OPEN-CURVED

---

[14]In Chapter 4, the *open-curved* handshape is shown to be distinctive with respect to handshape change.

The hand configurations marked *restricted₁* and *restricted₂* occur in ASL, but under restricted conditions. For example, as in (48a), ASL has a configuration like *restricted₁* in which the *base joint* is in the *neutral* position and the *non-base joints* are *flexed*. However, this configuration occurs only when the index finger is selected. A configuration like *restricted₂* is the handshape adopted to represent the letter *x* in the manual alphabet.

(48)   a. APPLE   b. X

So, as predicted by the feature set, the *restricted₁* and *restricted₂* handshapes occur in ASL, even if only under specific conditions. Hence, the joint and feature system proposed here accounts for the data in ASL. Whether similar claims can be made about handshape inventories in other signed languages is a task left for future work.

2.3.5   Opposed Thumb

As mentioned above, the joint specifications in (43) apply to the thumb as well as the fingers. However, as illustrated in (49), the thumb can assume one of three positions. In each configuration in (49) the index finger is extended and the other fingers are curled against the palm; only the position of the thumb varies. In (49a) the thumb is wrapped around the folded fingers, in (49b) the thumb is held flat with respect to the palm approximately at right angles with respect to the index finger, and in (49c) the thumb is opposite the index finger. (49a) occurs in signs like DREAM, described in Chapter 1, (49b) occurs in signs like TWENTY-ONE, (7a), and (49c) occurs in signs like PRINT, (2). Hence, there is evidence that at least three thumb positions should be included in the model.

  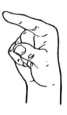

(49) a. 1   b. L   c. BENT-L

In the data described in this chapter the thumb exhibits a variety of patterns with respect to the fingers. In some signs it patterns with the selected fingers, in others with the unselected fingers, and in still others the thumb acts independently.

For the signs WANT, (11), and CHOOSE, (18b), the thumb articulates the same movement as the fingers. To articulate CHOOSE it mirrors the movement of the index finger, that is to say, the thumb is held opposite the index finger and mimics it as it changes from a straight to a curved posture. In contrast, to articulate WANT, the thumb makes the same change as the fingers, namely from a straight to a flat-curved shape. However, in this case the thumb does not oppose the fingers. Rather, it is in the same plane as the fingers. In both cases, the thumb movement with the fingers is obligatory, as illustrated by the ill-formed gestures described in (50).

(50) a. *(CHOOSE with thumb by the side of the hand)
      b. *(CHOOSE with thumb curved against the palm of the hand)
      c. *(WANT with thumb opposite to and mirroring the fingers)
      d. *(WANT with thumb on the side but not moving)

The difference between the well-formed signs and the gestures in (50) is captured by the observation that the thumb is included with the set of selected fingers. However, the distinct positioning of the thumb, specifically that it is opposite from the index finger in CHOOSE but in the same plane as the index finger for WANT, is puzzling. The pattern of articulation for two other signs helps solve this puzzle.

Recall the signs DREAM, described in Chapter 1, and STUDY, presented earlier as (39). To articulate DREAM, the index finger is extended, while the other fingers are curled against the palm of the hand and the thumb rests across them. In this case the thumb patterns with the uns-elected fingers. To articulate STUDY, the fingers move while the thumb is extended at the side of the hand and does not move. In this pro-nunciation the thumb appears to be unselected. However, an optional pronunciation of STUDY is to articulate it with the thumb resting against the side of the palm. To contrast with these possibilities, the gestures described in (51) are not acceptable signs.

(51) a. *(DREAM with thumb to the side)
      b. *(DREAM with thumb opposite the extended index finger)
      c. *(STUDY with thumb opposite the extended fingers)

In fact, two characteristics of the thumb are salient in the pattern of these signs: (i) whether it is selected, and (ii) whether it opposes the fingers. For example, CHOOSE and WANT pattern together, but CHOOSE and DREAM also pattern together. For CHOOSE and WANT the thumb patterns with the selected fingers. For CHOOSE the thumb patterns with the selected fingers, and for DREAM it patterns with the unselected fingers, but in both cases it is held in a position opposite to the fingers it patterns with. STUDY patterns with DREAM in that the thumb is not selected, but it has the peculiar property of being either open or closed, thus varying between the two options for the unselected fingers. The set of logical possibilities and the patterning of the data is captured in (52).[15]

(52)

Selected	Opposed	
	+	−
+	a. CHOOSE	b. WANT
−	c. DREAM	d. STUDY

Thus, if the thumb is selected, it assumes the same posture as the selected fingers, (52a) and (52b), but if it is not selected and opposed

---

[15]Liddell and Johnson (1989) include the feature *opposed* to capture the variety of positions of the thumb. Thanks to Diane Brentari for pointing out that the opposition of the thumb might solve the puzzle that signs like VIDEOTAPE and DENVER-BOOT pose when only fingers and joints are considered.

to the unselected fingers, (52c), it will be folded against the palm. Only if the thumb is not selected and not forced to be in opposition to the relevant set of fingers is it free to vary between postures, (52d).

2.3.6 Handshape

In sum, in this section I have argued for a formal representation of *handshape*. During the course of the discussion, the dominance relations represented by the tree structures in (53) and (54) have been suggested. The tree in (53) captures the relations between the five appendages of the hand. In (53) any of the appendages below the Hand node are subject to selectedness, but only the thumb is subject to opposition so it is represented on a branch separate from the fingers. Within the set of fingers, the index finger is singled out in describing patterns of selected fingers in well-formed handshapes, hence, the finger node branches to differentiate the index finger from the other fingers. In the set of non-index fingers, data from Dutch Sign Language (NGT) suggests that the inner fingers are interchangeable, so they are on a branch separate from the pinky which, as an edge finger, patterns with the index finger.

(53)

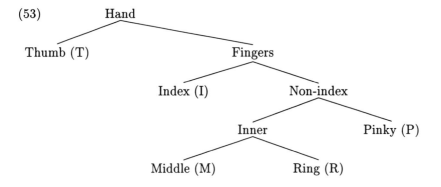

The tree in (54) captures the organization of the joints of each appendage into base and non-base joints.

(54)

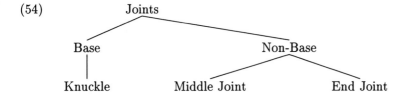

The representation of a handshape thus requires two pieces of information: (i) the joint values of selected and unselected fingers, $[\,+/-\text{EXT}\,]$ and $[\,+/-\text{FLEX}\,]$, and (ii) the opposition of the thumb, $[\,+/-\text{OPPOSED}\,]$. The frame in (55) presents a skeleton for capturing this. The sets of possible values are indicated in parentheses. To illustrate the use of this notation, the representation for the hand configuration in (56a) is given in (56b).

$$
(55)\quad \text{HS:}\quad
\begin{bmatrix}
+Selected: & \begin{bmatrix} [\,(TIMRP)\,] \\[4pt] \begin{bmatrix} +\text{BASE}: & \begin{bmatrix} (+/-)\text{EXT} \\ (+/-)\text{FLEX} \end{bmatrix} \end{bmatrix} \\[12pt] \begin{bmatrix} -\text{BASE}: & \begin{bmatrix} (+/-)\text{EXT} \\ (+/-)\text{FLEX} \end{bmatrix} \end{bmatrix} \end{bmatrix} \\[40pt]
-Selected: & \begin{bmatrix} [\,(TIMRP)\,] \\[4pt] \begin{bmatrix} +\text{BASE}: & \begin{bmatrix} (+/-)\text{EXT} \\ (+/-)\text{FLEX} \end{bmatrix} \end{bmatrix} \\[12pt] \begin{bmatrix} -\text{BASE}: & \begin{bmatrix} (+/-)\text{EXT} \\ (+/-)\text{FLEX} \end{bmatrix} \end{bmatrix} \end{bmatrix} \\[40pt]
Thumb: & [\,(+/-)\text{OPPOSED}\,]
\end{bmatrix}
$$

$$
(56)\quad
\begin{bmatrix}
+SEL: & \begin{bmatrix} [\,I\,] \\[4pt] \begin{bmatrix} +\text{BASE}: & \begin{bmatrix} +\text{EXT} \\ -\text{FLEX} \end{bmatrix} \end{bmatrix} \\[12pt] \begin{bmatrix} -\text{BASE}: & \begin{bmatrix} +\text{EXT} \\ -\text{FLEX} \end{bmatrix} \end{bmatrix} \end{bmatrix} \\[40pt]
-SEL: & \begin{bmatrix} [\,TMRP\,] \\[4pt] \begin{bmatrix} +\text{BASE}: & \begin{bmatrix} -\text{EXT} \\ +\text{FLEX} \end{bmatrix} \end{bmatrix} \\[12pt] \begin{bmatrix} -\text{BASE}: & \begin{bmatrix} -\text{EXT} \\ +\text{FLEX} \end{bmatrix} \end{bmatrix} \end{bmatrix} \\[40pt]
THUMB: & [\,+\text{OPPOSED}\,]
\end{bmatrix}
$$

a. Handshape   b. Representation of Handshape

For the hand configuration in (56a) the index finger is selected; all of its joints are extended, so the finger is straight. The rest of the fingers and the thumb are unselected; all of their joints are bent, so they are curled against the palm of the hand. The thumb is opposed to the fingers, so it rests against the bent fingers and will not alternate with an open position. However, as discussed in the next section, the representation in (56b) is ambiguous because the orientation of the hand is also distinctive.

2.4   Hand Orientation

The signs in (57) are ostensibly articulated with the same handshape. Both signs are articulated with two hands. The index finger of both hands are straight while the other fingers are curled against the palms of the hands and tucked under the thumbs. In both cases, the hands are held in front of the signer. In (57a) the tips of the fingers point away from the signer and the palms of the hands face the sides. At the start of the gesture the hands are a few inches apart. To articulate the sign the hands move towards each other along a straight path. As the hands meet, the fingers cross so that the hands stop moving when the knuckles of the middle fingers touch. In (57b) one hand is held still while the other moves towards it. Both hands are held so the fingertips point up. The palm of the static hand faces the signer and the palm of the moving hand faces away from the signer. The moving hand starts a few inches from the static hand. It then moves towards the static hand along a straight path until the front of the folded fingers touch.

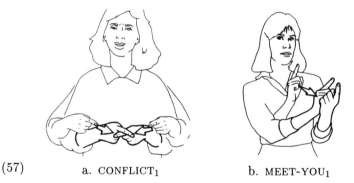

(57)   a. CONFLICT₁   b. MEET-YOU₁

Slightly altering the handshape of the signs in (57) presents an interesting contrast. (58a) illustrates an overhead view of the final position of the hands in (57a). In (58b) the handshape is changed so that the index finger bends at the knuckle to form a 90° angle with the palm while the middle and end joints of the index finger are still straight. The result is an acceptable variation of the sign in (57a). The difference between (58a) and (58b) is minor. In contrast, if (57b) is articulated with the modified handshape, the sign is ill-formed, (58b). So for (57a) the handshapes may vary, but for (57b) the handshapes are distinctive.

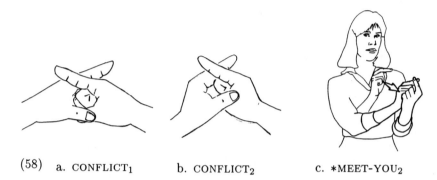

(58) a. CONFLICT₁   b. CONFLICT₂   c. *MEET-YOU₂

A hint towards understanding this pattern is to notice the part of the hand that seems to lead the movement. In (57a) and (58b) the hands move along the direction that the fingertip points. In contrast, in (57b) the hands move along the direction that the palms face. If we take the front of the hand as leading the movement, then one way to differentiate between the signs is to identify when the fingertip acts as the front of the hand and when the palm acts as the front of the hand. In other words, relative to some system of reference, it is necessary to be able to specify the facingness, or orientation, of the hand. The reference system I propose is based on rectangular geometry.

2.4.1 Hand Prism

I start by proposing an abstraction of the hand in terms of its six sides. Holding all the fingers straight, it is possible to identify three pairs of opposing sides: (i) the *palm* and *back* of the hand, (ii) the *fingertips* and *base* of the hand, and (iii) the *thumb-side* and *pinky-side* of the hand. For this representation of the hand each of the sides is roughly parallel to its opposing side and perpendicular to its adjoining sides, as in (59a).

To specify the orientation of the hand, I adopt the reference system in (59b) – the *hand prism*.[16] The hand prism (HP) is a rectangular prism that represents the space immediately around the hand. For con-

---

[16]This discussion anticipates the formalization of the term *orientation*. In Chapter 3 it is defined as a dyadic relation between two constructs. In this case orientation is defined in terms of the relation between the *hand* and HP.

venience, the sides of the hand prism are named *front*, *back*, *top*, *bottom*, *contralateral side*, and *ipsilateral side*. The ipsilateral side refers to the same side as the hand being represented, and contralateral side refers to the opposite side as the hand being represented.

As illustrated in (59b), the relative orientation of the hand can be specified by placing the hand inside the hand prism (HP). The position of the *hand* in HP can be unambiguously stated by specifying the association of two adjoining sides of the hand with the respective sides of HP. In this example the *palm* of the hand is parallel to the *front* of HP, and the *fingertips* of the hand are parallel to the *top* of HP.[17]

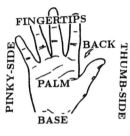

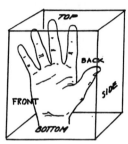

(59) a. *Hand*   b. *Hand Prism* (HP)

With these constructs the hand configuration used to articulate (57a) can be differentiated from the configuration used to articulate (57b).

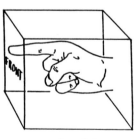

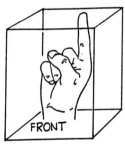

(60)   a. G-handshape   b. 1-handshape

The hand configuration used to articulate (57a) is given in (60a), and the configuration used to articulate (57b) is given in (60b). In

---

[17]Note that only two of the six relations between faces of the prisms need to be specified. Specifying the relation between two faces of the *hand* and HP that are at right angles to each other is the same as specifying the orientation of two dimensions of the hand in HP. The relation between the three dimensions, represented in coordinate geometry as the X-, Y-, and Z-axes, is predetermined so that specifying the orientation along two of the axes necessarily determines the orientation of the third.

(60a), the *palm* and *fingertips* of the *hand* are associated with the *side* and *front* of the hand prism, respectively; in (60b), they are associated with the *front* and *top* of the hand prism. For ease of discussion I refer to the former as the G-handshape and the latter as the 1-handshape. This follows Sandler (1989) who recognizes the distinction between these configurations.

Adding this information to the specification for handshape provides the distinct representations for each of the hand configurations. (61) is the notation for the G-handshape, and (62) is the notation for the 1-handshape. The specification for hand prism (HP) includes information about the handshape (HS), as well as the location (LOC) and orientation (OR) of the hand in the hand prism. The location of the hand in the hand prism is captured by associating the center of one prism with the center of the other.[18] The orientation of the hand in the hand prism is captured by specifying the associations of the fingertips and palm to the relevant faces of the hand prism.

(61)   G-handshape:

$$
HP \begin{bmatrix} LOC \; [\; Base_{Hand} \; : \; Back_{HP} \;] \\[4pt] OR \begin{bmatrix} Palm_{Hand} & : & Contra\text{-}Side_{HP} \\ Fingertips_{Hand} & : & Front_{HP} \end{bmatrix} \\[6pt] HS \begin{bmatrix} +SEL: \; [\,I\,] \\ \quad +Base: \begin{bmatrix} +\text{EXT} \\ -\text{FLEX} \end{bmatrix} \\ \quad -Base: \begin{bmatrix} +\text{EXT} \\ -\text{FLEX} \end{bmatrix} \\[6pt] -SEL: \; [\,TMRP\,] \\ \quad +Base: \begin{bmatrix} -\text{EXT} \\ +\text{FLEX} \end{bmatrix} \\ \quad -Base: \begin{bmatrix} -\text{EXT} \\ +\text{FLEX} \end{bmatrix} \\[6pt] THUMB: \; [\,+\text{OPPOSED}\,] \end{bmatrix} \end{bmatrix}
$$

---

[18]In Chapter 3 *location* is formally defined as a dyadic relation between two constructs. The location relation between the *hand* and *hand prism* is assumed to be static, and is specified by associating one face of the hand, usually the *base*, with a face of the *hand prism*, usually the *bottom*.

The minimal difference between these hand configurations is the specification of orientation. In (61) the *fingertips* are associated with the *front* of the hand prism and the *palm* is associated with the *side* of the hand prism. In contrast, in (62) the *fingertips* are associated with the *top* of the hand prism and the *palm* is associated with the *front* of the hand prism.

(62)   1-handshape:

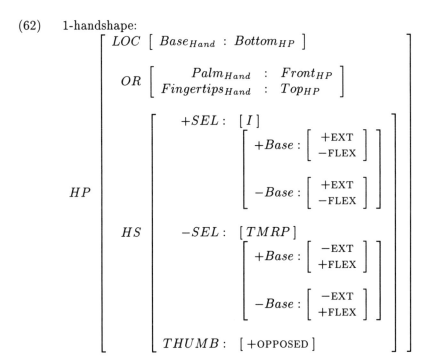

Hence, the difference between the data in (57) is accounted for by the complete representation of the *hand* captured by the *hand prism*. Specifically, the representation includes not only the configuration of the fingers and thumb, but also the orientation of the hand with respect to the hand prism. In the next chapter, I discuss the relation of the hand prism to signing space.

3

Signing Space

In this chapter I argue for a formal representation of signing space as a set of nested rectangular prisms, (1). The *hand prism* (HP) from the previous chapter is nested in *local signing space* (LSS), a construct that represents the space corresponding to the lexical sign. Local signing space is, in turn, nested in *global signing space* (GSS), a construct that represents the space corresponding to the level of an utterance. And global signing space is nested in *discourse signing space* (DSS), a construct that constrains the use of space at the level of discourse.

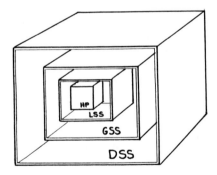

(1)   Signing Space

The result is a formal representation of signing space in which the position of the articulators can be unambiguously stated in terms of the relative positions of these nested spatial constructs. In this chapter *location* and *orientation* are formalized as dyadic relations between adjacent prisms.

3.1 Local Signing Space

In this section I argue for *local signing space*, a construct that represents the space in which a simple sign is articulated. I start by presenting observations that have been described in previous studies of signs (e.g., Klima and Bellugi 1979), namely that a simple sign is articulated in a localized area, and that the hand(s) are constrained to a two-dimensional space that is, in general, either parallel to or perpendicular with respect to the signer's body. I then describe variations in the size of the gesture that demonstrate that, although the hand moves along only two dimensions to articulate a sign, the size of lexical space varies along all three dimensions of space. I propose that the appropriate formalism for modeling these properties is coordinate geometry. In particular, I adopt a six-sided representation of the lexical signing space I call *local signing space*. I start by arguing for a *plane of articulation* that constrains the type of movement referred to in previous analyses as "path movement" (e.g., Liddell and Johnson 1989).

3.1.1 Planar Movements

As illustrated by the data in (2), there are three basic shapes that the path of the hand follows: straight, circular, and arc-shaped.[1] (2a) is articulated with a straight path movement, (2b) with circular path movement, and (2c) with an arc-shaped path movement.

In (2a) all of the fingers are held straight and together; the thumb is tucked against the palm. The fingertips point to the side, and the palm faces down. The side of the tip of the index finger starts at the same side of the chin as the hand that is articulating the sign. To articulate the sign, the hand moves across the chin in a straight line. The side of the index finger is always in contact with the side of the chin. The gesture stops when the knuckle of the index finger reaches the other side of the chin.

In (2b) the fingers are curled against the palm and the thumb is held against the side of the index finger. With the palm facing towards the signer, the middle part of the fingers touch the middle of the chest. To articulate the sign, the hand makes a large circle at the chest while the hand maintains contact with the chest. The gesture ends at the same point that it starts – at the middle of the upper chest.

In (2c) the index finger is straight while the rest of the fingers are curled against the palm with the thumb held across them. The tip of the index finger points up and the palm of the hand faces away from the

---

[1]Other path shapes that can be attributed to sequences of straight and circular path movements are described in Chapter 4, Section 4.1.3.3.

signer. To articulate the sign, the tip of the index finger starts near the upper part of the cheek. The hand moves in a straight line towards the face until the tip of the index finger touches the cheek. The hand then moves along an arc-shaped path and touches the lower part of the cheek. It is also possible to articulate the sign by first touching the lower part of the cheek and then touching the upper part of the cheek.

(2) a. LIE   b. SORRY₁   c. DEAF

These data illustrate two properties of the sign gesture: (i) the path of the gesture is confined to two-dimensional space, and (ii) the shape of the path of the gesture is restricted. The first property is accounted for in this section; the second property is discussed in Chapter 4.

In each of the signs in (2) the movement of the hand is confined to a two-dimensional space. To articulate (2a) the hand moves along a line that is parallel to the front of the face, to articulate (2b) the hand moves along a circle parallel to the chest, and to articulate (2c) the hand moves along an arc that is perpendicular to the cheek. These well-formed gestures contrast with the physiologically possible gestures described in (3) that do not occur in ASL.

(3) a. *(Hand moves in spiral while moving upward)
  b. *(Hand moves in spiral while moving downward)
  c. *(Hand moves downward in front of signer, then in a circle perpendicular to the signer)

In each gesture described in (3) the hand moves along three dimensions of space. In contrast, to articulate the well-formed signs in (2) the hand moves along only two dimensions of space. In other words, whereas it is possible to trace the patterns articulated in (2) on the surface of a table, the gestures described in (3) require the hand to move outside of the two dimensional surface defined by a table top. This observation is generalized in (4).

(4)   In a sign gesture, the hand moves from one place to another in a single flat area.

A "flat area" like a table top is, in formal geometric terms, a *plane.* Referring to the plane that the hand moves in to articulate a sign as a *plane of articulation*, the generalization in (4) can be stated formally as (5).

(5) | In a well-formed sign, the manual articulator moves along a single *plane of articulation.* |
    | --- |

Because the gestures described in (3) are articulated in three-dimensional space, they are correctly ruled out by the proposition in (5). The construct *plane of articulation* is crucial to the statement of (5), therefore it is adopted into the model.

For a sign articulated in the space in front of the body, as in (6), the properties of movement are more specific. The fingers and thumbs of both hands are held in fists so the back of the hands face the signer and the palms face away from the signer. To articulate the sign, the hands move along parallel circles at the same rate, but are 180° out of phase with each other. In other words, when one hand reaches the highest point of its circle, the other hand is at the lowest point of its circle. The hands make two or three circling movements to articulate the sign.

(6)   BICYCLE

In this sign the hands are parallel to each other throughout the articulation of the sign. This contrasts with the physiologically possible but non-occurring gestures described in (7).

(7)   a.   *(BICYCLE with hands moving along circles at 45° with respect to each other)

          b.   *(one hand moves in a circle that is perpendicular to the signer; the other hand moves in a circle that is horizontal with respect to the signer)

The difference between the well-formed sign in (6) and the gestures described in (7) is that the hands move in parallel circles in the former and in non-parallel circles in the latter. This observation is captured by the generalization in (8). The generalization captures a property of signs that must be captured by the model.[2]

(8)   In a two-handed sign, the hands move along parallel paths.

Another property of signs that must be accounted for is illustrated by the sign in (9). In formal terms a *plane of articulation* represents an infinite set of parallel lines. The sign in (9) provides evidence that it is not the entire plane, but only a portion of it that is relevant. Recall from sign (1) in Chapter 2 that (9) is articulated at the chin, and that to articulate the sign the hand moves away and slightly downward from the chin along a straight path, stopping a few inches in front of the chin.

(9)   GOOD

The well-formed sign in (9) contrasts with the gestures described in (10) which differ from (9) in the distance that the hand travels from the chin. In (10a) the hand moves much farther than in (9), and in (10b) the hand moves much less than in (9). As discussed in Section 3.1.2.1, the

---

[2]A complete discussion of two-handed signs is beyond the scope of this discussion. See Section 5.3.1 for a brief discussion of two-handed signs in a transition-based model.

pronunciations in (10a) and (10b) are possible, but only under special circumstances, as indicated by the hash mark (#) that precedes them. (10c) is very odd, to the point of being an ill-formed version of the gesture in (9).

(10)   a.   #(GOOD articulated with hand moving a foot and a half away from chin)

             b.   #(GOOD articulated with hand moving one inch from chin)

             c.   *(GOOD with hand moving away until arm is maximally extended)

Similarly, the physiologically possible gestures described in (11) are ill-formed variations of the signs in (2a) and (2c).

(11)   a.   *(LIE articulated with hand starting near shoulder, moving across chin, and continuing as far as hand can reach)

             b.   *(DEAF with hand moving along arc that extends as far as the arm can reach)

The difference between the well-formed signs in (2) and (9), and their variations in (10) and (11), is captured by the generalization in (12).

(12)   The movement of a simple sign starts and ends in the same general vicinity.

In formal terms, the hand is confined to only a small part of the potentially infinite area of the plane of articulation. This is stated in (13).

(13)   The *plane of articulation* is finite.

(13) is a formal property that will be incorporated into the representation after considering other properties of signs relevant to the plane of articulation.

Recall that LIE, (2a), is articulated by moving the hand in a straight line parallel to the front of the chin, SORRY, (2b), by moving the hand along a circle that is parallel to the chest, DEAF, (2c), by moving the hand along an arc that is perpendicular to the cheek, and GOOD, (9), by moving the hand along a straight path perpendicular to the chin. These gestures are either parallel or perpendicular with respect to the body, and contrast with the gestures described in (14).

(14)   a.   *(LIE articulated by holding the palm of the hand at a
               45° angle with respect to the front of the face)
        b.   *(SORRY articulated with a circular movement at a 30°
               angle with respect to the chest)
        c.   *(DEAF articulated with an arc along a 20° angle with
               respect to the face)
        d.   *(GOOD articulated with the hand moving along a 45°
               angle with respect to the face)

The gestures described in (14) contrast with their well-formed counterparts in that the signs are articulated with movements of the hand
that are either parallel or perpendicular to the body. In a mix of formal
and informal terms, this observation can be generalized as (15).

(15)   The *plane of articulation* is parallel or perpendicular to the signer's
        body.

(15), along with (13), are properties that must be accounted for in a
formal representation of the sign.

3.1.2 Proportional Gestures

In this section, I consider two factors that affect the relative size of
signing gestures: (i) the place they are articulated, and (ii) the utterance
they are articulated in.

3.1.2.1 Different Places

The signs in (16) are articulated at different parts of the body. (16a) is
articulated at the nose and (16b) at the chest. Although the gestures
used to articulate the signs are similar, the one at the nose is smaller
than the one at the chest.

For both signs, the fingers and thumb are extended with the fingers
are held together and the thumb is held against the side of the index
finger. The fingertips point up and the palm of the hand faces the side.
At the start of the sign, the thumb side of the hand is held against the
same side of the body as the hand articulating the gesture. At the end
of the gesture, the pinky side of the hand is held against the opposite
side of the body. To move from the initial to the final positions of the
gesture, the hand moves along an arc-shaped path while the fingertips
maintain their upward position. During the movement the palm shifts
so that at the end of the gesture it faces the side opposite from the one
it faces at the beginning of the sign. The signs differ only in that (16a)
is articulated by moving the hand from one side of the nose to the other

and (16b) is articulated by moving the hand from one side of the chest to the other.

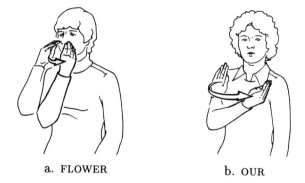

(16)   a. FLOWER   b. OUR

The significance of the size of the gesture relative to the place that it is articulated is easily seen by considering the possible but ill-formed gestures described in (17). Imagine, for example, articulating (16b) with the same size of gesture used for (16a), as described in (17a), or vice versa, articulating (16a) with the size of gesture used for (16b), as described in (17b). The results are unacceptable variations of the signs in (16).

(17)   a.   *(gesture for FLOWER articulated at the chest)
        b.   *(gesture for OUR articulated at the nose)

The generalization in (18) captures the difference between the signs in (16) and the ill-formed gestures described in (17).

(18)   The *plane of articulation* is proportional to the size of the place that a sign is articulated.

This presents another property of the plane of articulation to be captured in the formal representation of the signing space.

3.1.2.2   Different Purposes

Not only the place of articulation, but also the purpose of the articulation affects the size of the gesture, as illustrated by the scenario described here.

In the Spring of 1988, there was an outcry by students at Gallaudet University when the Board of Trustees appointed a hearing person as the seventh president of the only accredited university in the world to service Deaf students (Gannon 1989). For one week the students shut down the university as protesters rallied on campus, in the streets, and on the steps of the Capitol chanting DEAF PRESIDENT NOW!

The signs used for this protest are given in (19). The forms shown are typical of their pronunciation in an unmarked discourse situation. Recall from (2c) that (19a) is articulated by moving the hand along an arc-shaped path at the cheek. For (19b), the hands are held on either side of the forehead with the fingers and thumb open and extended.[3]

The tips of the fingers point up and the palms of the hands face away from the signer. To articulate the sign, the hands move along straight paths away from the side of the forehead while the fingers and thumb simultaneously curl into the palms of the hands to form fists. In (19c) the pinky and thumb are extended while the index, middle, and ring fingers are folded against the palm. The palms of the hands face upward as both hands are held about a foot in front of the signer's upper chest. To articulate the sign, both hands move downward in a straight line.

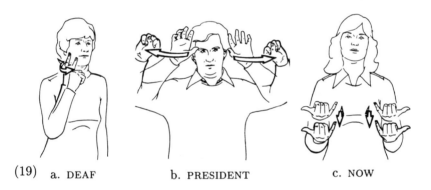

(19)   a. DEAF   b. PRESIDENT   c. NOW

On the steps of the Capitol during the highly charged Gallaudet protest, the sequence of signs DEAF PRESIDENT NOW! was articulated in an emphatic style that extended the movements of the hands into the space beyond the illustrations in (19). (19a) was articulated with a large arc-shaped movement at the cheek in which the hand moved as far as a foot or more from the cheek. The gesture for (19b) extended

---

[3](19b) is reprinted by permission of the publisher and authors, Charlotte Baker-Shenk and Dennis Cokely, of *American Sign Language: A Teacher's Resource Text on Grammar and Culture* (1980). Washington, DC: Clerc Books, an imprint of Gallaudet University Press. Copyright (c) 1980 by Gallaudet University. Illustrated by Frank A. Paul. Other images from this publication are FIGHT, IT'S-NOTHING, LIAR, LOOK-AT$_{over-time}$, and LOOK-AT$_{over-and-over-again}$.

above and away from the signer's head as far as the arms could reach. The downward movement of (19c) began near the forehead where (19b) ended, with the arms extended outward, and ended with the arms as low as they would go.[4] In some cases, protesters would bend over far enough for their hands to reach their knees as they emphatically articulated the last part of the slogan.

To contrast with this public protest, one could imagine that the same situation arose in a police state that banned public protest. In that situation, students might signal their support for a Deaf president by articulating the same slogan, but with small, discrete gestures hidden from the view of the omnipresent state police. In this hypothetical situation the size of the gestures would occupy a fraction of the space in (19). (19a) would be articulated with a short arc-shaped movement close to the cheek, (19b) would be articulated with the hands moving below the top of the head in front of the forehead, and (19c) would be articulated with a short movement that starts level with the nose and ends level with the chin. To maximize discretion, the two-handed signs, (19b) and (19c), could be articulated with only one hand. In sharp contrast to the version of the utterance in public protest that occupied as much space as the hands could cover, the articulation of this phrase would be compressed into the space in front of the face.

In each situation described above, the size of the space used to articulate the protest slogan varies with the function of the discourse. As summarized in (20), a small, private exchange is articulated in a small space, a standard conversation in a moderate space, and a public statement in the maximum space available. In each case, changing the volume of the space in which the hands move does not change the meaning of the signs. The more private the situation, the smaller the space used; the more public the situation, the larger the space used.[5]

---

[4] Tenseness and speed of a gesture also vary. However, they are independent of the changes in size of the gesture, and are not considered here.

[5] The smaller signing space might be interpreted as being analogous to whispering and the larger signing space to shouting, so that the three-dimensional volume of signing space seems to parallel the loudness of speech. But just as loudness in spoken language is the result of a combination of factors, there are variations of muscle tension and speed of gesture that also need to be considered in the analysis of variations of sign *volume*. All of these factors need to be considered when examining the gesture-based correlates of "loudness".

(20)

	Discourse Situation	Utterance	Size of Gestures
a.	Private	DEAF PRESIDENT NOW!	small
b.	Unmarked	DEAF PRESIDENT NOW!	medium
c.	Public	DEAF PRESIDENT NOW!	large

Of particular interest here is the expansion and contraction of the size of the gesture as the nature of the utterance varies. This can be illustrated by considering the type of physiologically possible gestures that do not occur. Taking the sign NOW as an example, two ill-formed variations are described in (21). In (21a) the space between the hands is much smaller than the distance that the hands travel to articulate the sign. (21b) describes the opposite situation; the distance between the hands is disproportionately wider than the distance that they move to articulate the sign.

(21)   a.   *(NOW articulated with two inches of space between the hands; gesture starts in front of the face and ends at the waist)

         b.   *(NOW articulated with two feet of space between the hands; gesture starts level with the shoulder and moves downward four inches)

Neither gesture in (21) is well-formed. Rather, as the size of the gesture changes, the space between the hands and the length of the movement to articulate the sign vary proportionally, as schematized in (22).

(22)   a. NOW$_{public}$ b. NOW   c. NOW$_{private}$

The generalization in (23), stated in terms of the plane of articulation, summarizes the observations of the data in (21) and (22).

(23)   The dimensions of the *plane of articulation* vary proportionally as the size of the sign varies.

Hence, the formal representation of signing space must also include some mechanism for dealing with the proportional use of space in signs.

3.1.3   Contrastive Direction

As I demonstrate in this section, the direction of movement is also significant, but only for straight movement. The direction of circular and arc-shaped movements may vary without affecting the meaning of the sign. The asymmetry between straight, circular, and arc-shaped movements is a puzzle that is addressed in Chapter 4. Of specific concern to the current discussion is the need to specify the direction of movement in the plane of articulation.

Recall that LIE, (2a), is articulated by moving the hand in a straight line, SORRY, (2b), by moving the hand in a circle, and DEAF, (2c), by moving the hand along an arc-shaped path. Specifically, to articulate (2a) the hand moves from the same side of the chin as the hand used to articulate the gesture to the opposite side of the chin. To articulate (2b) the hand moves along the circle in a clockwise direction, and to articulate (2c) the hand starts at the top of the cheek and ends at the bottom of the cheek. The gestures described in (24) are variations of the signs in (2); in each case, the direction of movement of the well-formed sign is reversed.

(24)   a.   (articulate LIE starting at opposite side of chin from hand articulating the sign; end at same side of chin as hand)
       b.   (articulate SORRY with a counter-clockwise circle)
       c.   (articulate DEAF starting at the lower part of the cheek; end at the upper part of the cheek)

All of the gestures in (24) are possible well-formed signs. In fact, (24b) and (24c) are possible variations of the signs in (2b) and (2c), respectively. Changing the direction that the hand circles does not change the meaning of the sign. And, as noted by Johnson (1986), the order of contact for most signs articulated with arc-shaped path movement is variable.[6] [7] In contrast, the gesture in (24a) is not a variation of (2a), nor is it an ill-formed gesture. Rather, it is contrastive. The generalization that emerges from this data is stated in (25).

(25) a. Direction of a gesture is contrastive for straight movement.
      b. Direction of a gesture is non-contrastive for circular or arc-shaped movement.

In terms of the plane of articulation, the generalization in (25) can be restated as (26).

(26) The direction of straight movement in the *plane of articulation* is contrastive.

3.1.3.1 Center and Sides

Finally, it is important to note that signs like FLOWER, (16a), and OUR, (16b), are articulated by moving from side to side at the nose or chest, whereas a sign like GOOD, (9), is articulated at the center of the chin. Signs like FLOWER and OUR contrast with gestures like those described in (27).

(27) a. *(articulate OUR by starting at one side of the chest and ending at the center of the chest)
      b. *(articulate FLOWER by starting at the center of the nose and ending at the side of the nose)

Whereas signs are articulated by moving from one side to the other, they are not articulated by moving from the center to the side or vice versa. The generalization in (28) captures this observation.

(28) The sides and center of a *plane of articulation* are distinct.

---

[6]Johnson (1986), and Liddell and Johnson (1989) propose that the variation is conditioned by the preceding sign. Lucas (1993) presents an alternative statistical analysis challenging this explanation.

[7]Some signs articulated with arc-shaped path movement do not have variable pronunciations, e.g., CHILDREN is articulated with the flat hand, palm down, moving from the center of the space in front of the signer along an arc-shaped path to the side of the space. Moving the hand from the side of the space to the center is not a well-formed alternation of the sign. I suspect that this property of the sign is affected by the bilateral symmetry of the body. For example, in its citation form, the right hand moves from left (center) to right (side) to articulate the sign; moving from right (side) to left (center) is the ill-formed variant. However, if the right hand is held so that it crosses the body, i.e., it is on the left side of the body, the pronunciation of the sign from right to left is more acceptable. The solution to this puzzle is left for future work.

3.1.4 Local Signing Space

In this section I develop a formal representation to account for the properties of the sign gesture identified above, and summarized in (29).

(29) a. In a two-handed sign, the hands move along parallel paths. (8)
      b. The movement of a simple sign starts and ends in the same general vicinity. (12)
      c. The *plane of articulation* is finite. (13)
      d. The *plane of articulation* is parallel or perpendicular to the signer's body. (15)
      e. The *plane of articulation* is proportional to the size of the place that a sign is articulated. (18)
      f. The dimensions of the *plane of articulation* vary proportionally as the size of the sign varies. (23)
      g. The direction of straight movement in the *plane of articulation* is contrastive. (26)
      h. The sides and center of a *plane of articulation* are distinct. (28)

Taking the *plane of articulation* as a starting point for discussion, I use the properties in (29) to build, step by step, a formal structure for representing signing space.

Recall from proposition (5) that the manual articulator moves along the plane of articulation. Also recall from observation (29c), that the plane is finite. Given the three path shapes presented by the data in (2), the first step in building a representation of signing space is the simple, finite plane in (30). I refer to this as the *base plane*. (30a) captures the straight path that the hand moves along to articulate LIE, and (30b) captures the circle that the hand moves along to articulate SORRY. To represent LIE, the base plane in (30a) will be parallel to the signer's chin; to represent SORRY, the base plane in (30b) will be parallel to the signer's chest.

(30)

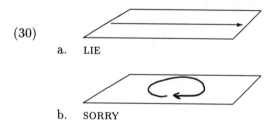

a. LIE

b. SORRY

From (29d) the plane of articulation is not only parallel to the signer's body, but also needs to be perpendicular to the signer's body. The image in (31) captures the articulation of the sign in (2c). Here the base plane will be parallel to the side of the face, so that the arc-shaped path that the hand follows to articulate DEAF is perpendicular to the face.

(31)

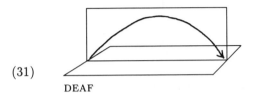

DEAF

From (29e) the size of the plane varies with the size of the place that the sign is articulated. As indicated by the images in (32), the representation of the space can vary to accommodate those differences. Imagine that the base plane of (32a) is held parallel to the nose and that the base plane of (32b) is held parallel to the chest. (32a) represents the dimensions of the nose where FLOWER is articulated, and (32b) represents the chest where OUR is articulated.

(32)

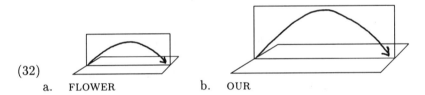

   a.   FLOWER   b.   OUR

From (29f) the dimensions vary as the size of the sign varies, and from (29a), two-handed signs are articulated along paths that are parallel. Hence, each hand of the two-handed sign NOW is assigned a distinct plane in (33). (33a) represents the articulation of NOW when it is whispered in a secret police state, and (33b) represents it when it is shouted during public protest.

(33)

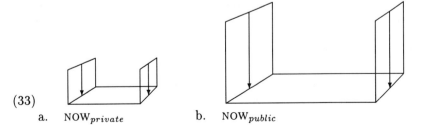

   a.   NOW$_{private}$ b.   NOW$_{public}$

The configuration of planes that has been proposed up to now defines three-dimensions of a space. Specifically, a space with height, length, and width, (34).

(34)

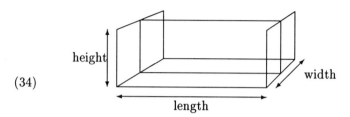

The dimensions of the space in (34) can be related to account for proportional variations like that depicted in (33). The ratio in (35) captures the relation between the dimensions of the space, where k is a proportionality constant. The relation in (35) ensures that if one dimension of the space varies, the others will also vary to maintain the same proportions. So, for example, if the proportions of the base change, as in (32), to fit a different place, the height is adjusted accordingly, (35a). Similarly, as the overall size of the space changes, as for (33), the distance between the hands relative to the length of the gesture is maintained, (35).

(35) Constant Proportions: $k = h : w : l$
  a. Width (w) and length (l) may vary to accommodate different places of articulation.
  b. The proportions of the space fit the dimensions of a discourse situation.

Finally, recall from (29g) that the direction of a straight movement is contrastive. (36a) shows the direction of the gesture used to articulate LIE if the bottom plane were parallel to the chin. Similarly, (36b) captures the direction that the hand moves to articulate GOOD if the bottom plane is parallel to the chin. As noted in (29h) the center is distinct from the sides, so (36b) includes a center plane of articulation, labeled *center*. To specify the direction the hand moves, the planes of articulation are named. To capture the side to side movement in (36a), the side that is on the same side as the hand articulating the gesture is referred to as the *ipsilateral side* and the side that is opposite from the hand is referred to as the *contralateral side*. To capture the direction of movement in (36b), I refer to the bottom plane as the *base* plane (+BASE), and the opposite side as the *non-base* plane (-BASE).

(36)

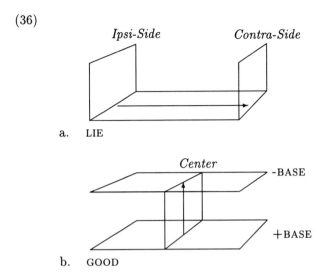

a. LIE

b. GOOD

In sum, the properties of signs described in the previous section converge on the single formal representation of signing space in (37). I refer to this set of planes as *local signing space*. The resulting object is a six-sided figure with parallel faces adjoined at right angles – in geometric terms, a rectangular prism. The names of the outer faces of the prism that have been discussed are the *base* and *non-base*, and the *ipsi-side* and *contra-side*. To complete the identification of the six sides, I refer to the remaining sides as the *local* and *non-local* faces of local signing space. These faces are useful for specifying orientation, as discussed in Section 3.4.2.

(37)

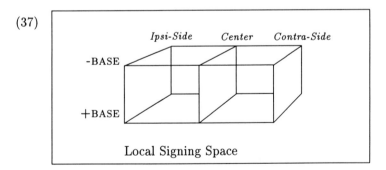

Local Signing Space

In combination with the proposition in (38), the construct *local signing space* accounts for the properties of the data described above. The planes are finite, and parallel or perpendicular to each other. The sides are distinct from the center. The dimensions of the space can be related to specify proportionality relations between signs. And the organization of the planes provide points of reference that can be used to specify the direction of straight movement.

(38) | The *planes of articulation* of *local signing space* are the *base plane, side planes,* and *center plane.*

The relation of local signing space to the signer's body is discussed at more length at the end of this chapter. The representation of the direction of movement is discussed in Chapter 4.

3.2   Global Signing Space

Moving beyond a single sign, a string of signs that contribute to a longer utterance is articulated in a finite area about the signer that Klima and Bellugi (1979) refer to as "articulatory space". In this section I formalize the representation of articulatory space as a rectangular prism called *global signing space.*

The well-formed signs introduced in the previous section contrast with the physiologically possible gestures described in (39).

(39)   a.   *(move hand in area above head)
        b.   *(move hand in the area to the far side of the body)
        c.   *(move hand near the knees or feet)
        d.   *(move hand behind the head)

Gestures like those in (39) are not well-formed signs and, therefore, should be excluded by the model. This can be accomplished by specifying the space about the body in which signs are articulated. The articulatory space Klima and Bellugi (1979:51) describe is shown in (40). They characterize the space as a sphere about the signer. In the unmarked case, the height of the space extends roughly between the top of the head and the waist. The width of the space is the distance between the elbows when they are lifted slightly from the side of the body. The depth of the space extends approximately an arm's length in front of the signer when the elbows are bent.

In unmarked conversation the area described in (40) adequately identifies the boundaries that separate the set of well-formed signs from the set of physiologically possible gestures. However, (40) fails to account for the properties of well-formed utterances that occur in more marked discourse situations.

(40)   Articulatory Space (Klima and Bellugi 1979:51)

Size of signing space varies. Recall the scenarios presented in the previous section describing the DEAF PRESIDENT NOW! protest. During the protest signers often violated the articulatory space circumscribed in (40) as they extended their hands high above their heads to articulate PRESIDENT and outward and downward as far as possible to articulate NOW. In contrast, in a whispered version of the same utterance, the gestures occupy only a fraction of the space in (40), keeping within the area around the face.

In these situations the space used to articulate the utterance varies with the function of the discourse. The gestures for a private exchange occupies a small space, for a conversation they occupy a medium size space, and for a public protest they occupy the maximum space available. These observations are summarized in (41). (41a) and (41c) represent the extreme cases. (41b) represents the unmarked case, though variations are expected along a continuum between the two extremes.

(41)	Discourse Situation	Utterance	Size of Signing Space
a.	Discrete	DEAF PRESIDENT NOW!	small
b.	Unmarked	DEAF PRESIDENT NOW!	medium
c.	Public	DEAF PRESIDENT NOW!	large

Even though the size of gestures may vary, as shown by the data in (42) the size of signs is consistent within an utterance. (42a) represents the large gestures of a public protest, and (42c) represents the small gestures of a secret exchange. (42b) and (42d) are physiologically possible but odd (#) due to the inconsistent size of the individual signs in the utterance. In (42b) the second sign is articulated in a smaller space than the signs surrounding it. In (42d) the articulation of the middle sign is much larger than the rest of the utterance.

(42)   Public: a.   DEAF PRESIDENT NOW!
                 b.   #(DEAF PRESIDENT NOW!)
       Private: c.   DEAF PRESIDENT NOW!
                 d.   #(DEAF PRESIDENT NOW!)

The generalizations in (43) capture these observations.

(43)   a.   The size of space in which signs are articulated varies with the function of the discourse.
       b.   The sizes of individual signs are proportional to the size of the utterance.

The generalizations in (43) can be accounted for by adopting a representation of signing space whose proportions vary with that of the lexical units articulated in it. To that end, I represent articulatory space as a finite three-dimensional space, *global signing space* (GSS), that subsumes local signing space. Like local signing space, global signing space is represented as a finite rectangular prism. To account for the properties of signing observed at the utterance level, global signing space associates with the signer's body as shown in (44). For ease of discussion, the faces of the prism are labeled *front, back, top, bottom,* and *sides.*

(44)

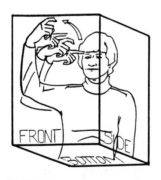

Global Signing Space (GSS)

The propositions in (45) define the relation between local and global signing space. (45a) specifies the relation of global signing space to the signer, and (45b) associates global signing space to the utterance level. (45c) establishes a hierarchical relation between local and global signing space such that local signing space is embedded in global signing space. (45d), in combination with the rest of the propositions, links the proportions of local signing space to the proportions of global signing space to ensure that the size of individual signs is consistent across an utterance.

(45)
a. *Global signing space* (GSS) associates with the signer's body so that the origin of GSS is congruent with the center of the signer's body at the level of the signer's waist.
b. An utterance is articulated in GSS.
c. *Local signing space* (LSS) is a subspace of GSS.
d. $K_{GSS} \; \alpha \; k_{LSS}$,
where K_{GSS} is the proportionality constant of GSS and varies with the function of the discourse.

It follows from (45c) that signs are articulated within the confines of articulatory space. And (45d) guarantees that signs articulated in an utterance maintain the same proportion. Therefore, this set of propositions accounts for the properties of signs that are problematic for the simple notion of articulatory space in (40).

Furthermore, as discussed in the following section, this notion of global signing space provides a construct for modeling discourse level phenomena.

3.3 Discourse Signing Space

In this section I examine two characteristics of ASL discourse: (i) *role-playing*, a common narrative device in ASL in which the signer shifts her body (or eyegaze) to express direct discourse or describe a character's actions, and (ii) spatial agreement between two signers.

3.3.1 Role Playing

The images in (46) illustrate a situation that Baker-Shenk and Cokely (1980:272-273) refer to as direct address. In this example, the signer relates an incident in which a boy wanted to pick a fight with her. During this narrative the signer assumes the role of the boy as well as of herself.

Earlier in the narrative the signer establishes that the boy is represented by the area on her right, and she is represented by the area on her left. In the course of the narrative, the signer articulates the sequence of signs in (46). As depicted in (46a), the signer shifts her body slightly to the right and articulates the sign shown. By shifting her body to the right, the signer takes on the role of the boy signs so that the gesture means *The boy asks, "You wanna fight?"*. Then, as in (46b), the signer shifts to the left and articulates the sign shown. The shift to the right signals that the signer is representing herself, so the gesture means *I replied, "Hah?! You're not worth it"*.

(46)   a.   (shift right) $\overline{\text{FIGHT}}^{\text{Q}}$ b.   (shift left) NOTHING-TO-IT

The scenario in (46) contrasts with a situation in which the signer articulates the same sequence of gestures but without shifting her body. In that situation, the first sign would be interpreted as a rhetorical question, and the second sign would be interpreted as "something having no worth", so the sequence of signs would mean "Fighting? – it's not worth it." Thus, body shift between distinct areas of space is crucial to the interpretation of the discourse. The generalization in (47) captures this observation.

(47)   A signer may change the discourse function of an utterance without changing the meaning of lexical items by shifting the position of her body.

Given that, by proposition (45b), global signing space is associated with an utterance and that, by proposition (45a), it is associated with a specific position of the body, it follows that by shifting the body and articulating an utterance, the signer may establish a new instance of a global signing space. Following this logic, the proposition in (48) accounts for the generalization in (47).

(48)   A signer may invoke more than one *global signing space*.

Although the maximum number of global signing spaces that a signer may invoke is left unspecified, there would appear to be a practical upper bound to the number of referents a signer can express through body shift. Specifying such a boundary remains a question for future work.

Independent of that issue, the combination of propositions in (45) and (48) predict that a signer can articulate a role-play in which one referent makes large gestures in a large global signing space while another referent makes small gestures, demanding only a small global signing space. Indeed, in a narrative depicting an interaction between a father and his toddler son, the signer would contrast the two by using large gestures to portray the father, and small gestures to portray the son. Thus, the model makes the correct predictions for a single signer's use of signing space.

To account for multiple instantiations of global signing space required by (48), I introduce *discourse signing space* (DSS), defined by the set of propositions in (49).

(49)

(i)	Sequences of utterances are articulated in *discourse signing space* (DSS).
(ii)	*Global signing space* is a subspace of *discourse signing space*.
(iii)	Multiple instances of *global signing space* may be invoked in *discourse signing space*.

Unfortunately an in-depth examination of discourse signing space is beyond the scope of this work. However, the scenario described below provides an indication of the type of properties that the construct can account for when the study of visual phonology extends beyond the bounds of the utterance and of global signing space.

3.3.2   Spatial Agreement Between Signers

In a discussion about the function of space in ASL, Liddell (1990a) describes the alternation between pronunciations of the agreement verb meaning *to ask*.[8] As shown in (50), to articulate the sign the trajectory of the hand starts near the subject of the verb, in this case the signer herself, and ends near the object of the verb, in this case the addressee, so that the gesture means *I ask you*. (50a) and (50b) are acceptable

---

[8]The articulation of an agreement verb can be accompanied with a movement from the subject towards the object. See Chapter 5.

variations, but (51) is not. In (50a) the signer and addressee are about
the same height and the gesture is articulated along a plane horizontal
to the ground. In (50b) the signer is shorter than the addressee and
the gesture is articulated at an upward angle relative to the ground. In
contrast, the gesture in (51) is unacceptable because the signer's hand
moves along a plane horizontal to the ground in a situation in which the
addressee's height demands an upward oriented gesture as in (50b).

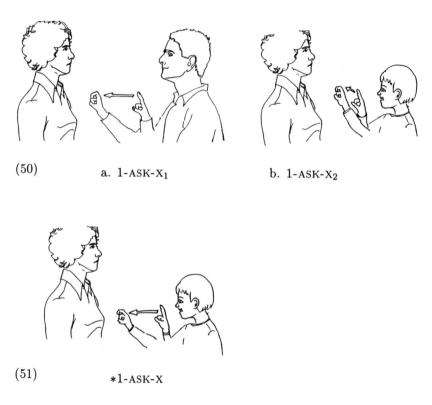

(50) a. 1-ASK-X$_1$ b. 1-ASK-X$_2$

(51) *1-ASK-X

To account for the data in (51), Liddell proposes that some agreement
verbs are lexically specified for a height relative to the characteristics of
the addressee. In essence, the posture of the signer's body is affected
by discourse specific situations. As for the role shift described in the
previous section, the signer physically accommodates to the position
of the discourse referent by tilting the whole body, tilting the face or,
more subtly in some cases, by shifting her eyegaze. The concept of a
global signing space associated with a specific utterance, embedded in a

larger signing space representing discourse provides a formal system for representing the properties observed by Liddell.

Just as global signing space provides a frame of reference for local signing space, so too, discourse signing space provides a frame of reference for global signing space. The evidence from role playing and spatial agreement between signers is suggestive of relations between global and discourse signing space. Formalization of those properties is, however, beyond the scope of this work, and remains an area for further study. I continue now with discussion that focuses on the relation between global signing space, local signing space, the hand prism, and the hand.

3.4 Location and Orientation

To summarize the discussion of signing space thus far, I have argued for a construct, *local signing space* (LSS), to capture the properties of simple signs and proposed that a simple sign is, in turn, articulated in *global signing space* (GSS). Strings of signs form utterances that are represented at the level of global signing space. Global signing space is embedded in *discourse signing space* (DSS) which represents signing at the discourse level. At the heart of signing space are the articulators, represented by the *hand prism* (HP), argued for in Chapter 2. The schematic in (52) captures this notion of a box in a box in a box in a box representation of the hand in signing space.

(52)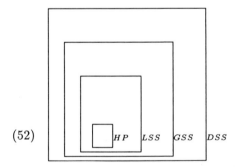

This idealization of signing space provides a representation in which the location and orientation of each construct can be stated in terms of the construct it is nested in. If this is done at each level of the representation, the net results are relative definitions of location and orientation. In other words, the orientation of the hand is stated in terms of its relation to the hand prism which, in turn, is stated in terms of its relation to local signing space whose orientation is stated in terms of its relation to global signing space, and so on.

In this section I argue for relations that hold between the spatial constructs: (i) a *location* relation that specifies the placement of the target prism relative to its adjacent prism, and (ii) an *orientation* relation that specifies the relation of the faces of the target prism relative to the faces of the adjacent prism. The relation between 'target' and 'adjacent prism' is specified so that the target prism is immediately embedded in its adjacent prism.

In this discussion only local relations are significant. I do not consider, for example, interactions between global signing space and the hand prism. The study of non-local relations between levels of signing space is left for future work. I argue first for the *location* relations between the hand prism and local signing space (HP in LSS), and between local and global signing space (LSS in GSS). I then argue for the *orientation* relations between the hand prism and local signing (HP in LSS), between local and global signing space (LSS in GSS), and between global signing space and discourse signing space (GSS in DSS).

3.4.1 Location

Stokoe (1960) was the first to recognize that the place a sign is articulated is lexically distinctive. For example, the signs in (53) are articulated with the same gesture. They differ only in where they are articulated.

At the start of the signs in (53) the index finger is straight. The other fingers are curled against the palm and tucked under the thumb. The tip of the index finger points to the side and the palm of the hand faces down. The hand starts on the opposite side of the face with the side of the index finger knuckle near the face. To articulate the sign, the hand moves along a straight path towards the same side of the face as the hand while the middle and end joints of the index finger bend. During the articulation of the sign, the hand brushes against the face. The movement across the face and the curling of the index finger start at the same time and are articulated at the same rate, so the index finger finishes bending at the same time that the hand stops moving. (53a) is articulated at the forehead, (53b) below the nose but above the upper lip, and (53c) at the chin.

Stokoe adopted the term TAB to refer to places of articulation like the forehead, chin, and upper lip, but "location" is the more commonly accepted term. In generative accounts of signs, *location* is characterized by sets of distinctive features (e.g., Liddell and Johnson 1989, Sandler 1989, Brentari 1990b). Sandler (1989) argues for a hierarchical organization of the location features and goes as far as to elevate location to the status of a timing segment (as discussed in Section 6.3).

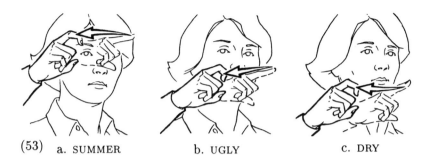

(53) a. SUMMER   b. UGLY   c. DRY

In previous models, location is stated in terms of absolute position relative to the signer's body. Here, location is stated in relative terms.

Consider, for example, the data in (53). As noted above, the signs are articulated with the identical gesture, but with distinct placement of the hand. In terms of the model of visual phonology, the common side to side movement of the hand in these signs can be captured by specifying the same location relation between the hand prism and local signing space. The distinct placement of the gestures can be captured by specifying distinct location relations between local and global signing space.

3.4.1.1 Hand Prism in Local Signing Space

In this section I focus on specifying static postures of the hand. The representation of the movement of the hand will be discussed in more detail in Chapter 4.

As schematized in (54), the movement of the hand from one side of the face to the other can be represented as a path that starts at one point in the local signing space and ends at the other. The small box represents the hand prism (HP) and the planes represent the base and sides of local signing space. Imagining that the base plane of local signing space is parallel to the signer's face, the change in position of the index finger relative to the face is captured by the images in (54). At the start of the sign the hand is at the opposite side of the face from the hand that articulates it. This is represented in (54a) as the hand prism on the base plane at the contralateral side of local signing space. At the end of the sign the hand is at the same side of the face as the hand that articulates it. This is captured in (54b) with the hand prism at the ipsilateral side of local signing space.

(54)

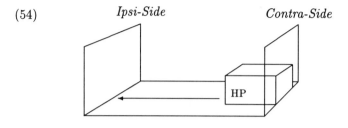

a.   Start of gesture for SUMMER, UGLY, DRY.

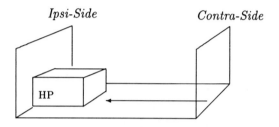

b.   End of gesture for SUMMER, UGLY, DRY.

The relation between the hand prism and local signing space in (54) is formalized by the definition of *location* given in (55).

(55) | There is a *location* relation, $Location(A_x, B_y)$, where x is a signing space contained in signing space y such that plane A in space x is positioned at place B in space y.

The notation for the representations in (54) is given in (56). The dyadic location relation (LOC) is represented by an ordered pair of positions separated by a colon and enclosed by brackets. The first member of the pair specifies a face of the inner construct, and the second member of the pair specifies a place in the outer construct. (56a) represents the association between the side face of the hand prism and the contra-lateral side of the base plane of local signing space. The notation +BASE(*Contra-Side*) represents a function that applies to the base plane to choose the contralateral side of the plane. (56b) represents the association between the side face of the hand prism and the ipsi-lateral side of the base plane of local signing space where +BASE(*Ipsi-Side*) is a function that identifies the ipsilateral side of the plane.

(56)   a.   At the start of the gesture:
           LOC $[Bottom_{HP} : +\text{BASE}(Contra\text{-}Side)_{LSS}]$

       b.   At the end of the gesture:
           LOC $[Bottom_{HP} : +\text{BASE}(Ipsi\text{-}Side)_{LSS}]$

The notation in (56) captures the relation between the hand prism and local signing space for all three signs in (53). The location relation between local and global signing space captures the differences between them.

3.4.1.2   Local Signing Space in Global Signing Space

The signs in (53) are articulated at three distinct places on the face: the forehead, above the upper lip, and the chin. Those places contrast with the places described in (57). Even though it is physiologically possible, no signs in ASL are articulated there.[9]

(57)   a.   *(gesture for SUMMER articulated inside elbow)
       b.   *(gesture for SUMMER articulated at armpit)
       c.   *(gesture for SUMMER at center of stomach)

So even though a wide range of places is available, only some are possible sites for sign gestures. This observation is generalized in (58).

(58)   A well-formed sign is articulated at specific places.

Returning to the data in (53), recall that the gestures differ only in hand placement; everything else about them is identical. The generalization in (59) captures that observation.

(59)   The place where a gesture is articulated affects the meaning of the sign.

Using the location relation in (55), the propositions in (60) account for the generalizations in (58) and (59). The inventory of locations for ASL, given in (60iii), includes the anatomical landmarks on the body as well as the neutral signing space and the non-dominant hand (H2). Explicit arguments for each of the anatomically identified locations is left

---

[9]It is possible to articulate a sign such as HURT-AT-X at any of these locations. However, that is a complex sign. Lexically simple signs are not articulated at the positions in (57).

for work that includes a cross-linguistic analysis. Besides being relevant to lexically simple signs, other properties of neutral signing space emerge in discussions about complex signs. Some properties are discussed in Chapter 5; other properties of neutral signing space are left for future work.

Similarly, properties of the non-dominant hand require more investigation. Following Sandler (1989), the hand, H2, is included here as a place of articulation. A complete representation for a sign articulated with H2 will include the specification of a distinct hand prism, as well as its location and orientation with respect to local signing space. As argued by Brentari and Goldsmith (1993), those values will be more constrained than those for the moving hand. Further elaboration of the representation of H2 is left for future work.[10]

(60)

(i) The location relation between local signing space (LSS) and global signing space (GSS), $Location(A_{LSS}, B_{GSS})$, is specified so that B_{GSS} is from the inventory of possible locations in global signing space, in (iii).

(ii) The location relations $Location(A_{LSS}, B1_{GSS})$ and $Location(A_{LSS}, B2_{GSS})$, such that $B1 \neq B2$, are lexically distinct.

(iii) Inventory of places in Global Signing Space:

face	forehead	cheek
nose	above-lip	throat
upper-arm	lower-arm	shoulder
upper-chest	lower-chest	chin
ear	neutral (area in front of signer)	
waist	H2 (non-dominant hand)	

Applying the propositions in (60) to the data in (53) and (57) produces the analysis in (61).

---

[10]In particular, an analysis of the properties of two-handed signs will lead to improved understanding of both neutral signing space and H2. See Section 5.3.1 for a brief note on two-handed signs.

(61)   a.   The location relations for the gestures in (53) are:

           SUMMER: $LOC\ [+Base_{LSS} : Forehead_{GSS}]$

           UGLY: $LOC\ [+Base_{LSS} : Above\text{-}Lip_{GSS}]$

           DRY: $LOC\ [+Base_{LSS} : Chin_{GSS}]$

      b.   The location relations for (57) are:

           (57a): $LOC\ [+Base_{LSS} : Inside\text{-}Elbow_{GSS}]$

           (57b): $LOC\ [+Base_{LSS} : Armpit_{GSS}]$

           (57c): $LOC\ [+Base_{LSS} : Stomach_{GSS}]$

      c.   The values *Inside-Elbow*, *Armpit*, and *Stomach* are not part of the inventory of possible locations in (60iii). Therefore, by (60i), the gestures in (b) are ill-formed.

      d.   By (60i), the gestures in (a) are well-formed; by (60ii), they are lexically distinct.

The analysis in (61) provides the correct account for the data. The *location* relation and the propositions in (60) are crucial to the analysis, therefore they are adopted into the model.

3.4.2   Orientation

Just as location is defined in other models as a parameter with feature values, so too orientation is represented as a parameter of signs and assigned a set of feature values. Battison (1978) adopts palm orientation as a contrastive property of signs, while Klima and Bellugi (1979) classify orientation as a minor parameter of hand configuration, a proposal that is echoed in Sandler's (1989) argument for the organization of features for hand configuration where palm orientation is dominated by handshape. Liddell and Johnson (1989) and Brentari (1990) also include inventories of orientation features.

However, just as *location* can be recast as a dyadic relation, in this section *orientation* also follows as a dyadic relation. The discussion here focuses on the orientation relation between the hand prism and local signing space, and the orientation relation between local signing space and global signing space.

3.4.2.1   Hand Prism in Local Signing Space

The signs in (62) are articulated with gestures that are identical except for the direction that the palm faces. In both signs the fingers and thumb of the hand are straight. The fingers are held together while the thumb rests at a 45° angle with respect to the side of the index finger. The hand is held in front of the signer with the tips of the fingers pointing away from the signer. To articulate (62a) the palm of the hand faces up and the hand moves along an arc-shaped path from a point towards the center of the signer to a point to the side of the signer. To articulate (62b) the palm of the hand faces down and the hand moves in the same way as for (62a), along an arc-shaped path from the center of the signer to the side of the signer.

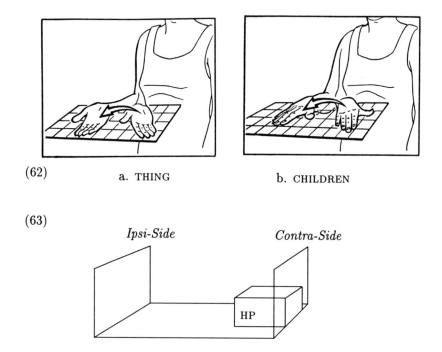

(62)

a. THING

b. CHILDREN

(63)

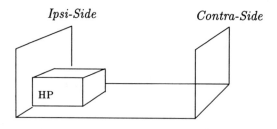

a.   Start of gesture for THING and CHILDREN.

b.   End of gesture for THING and CHILDREN

The location relations for the signs are the same. As schematized in (63a), at the start of the signs the hand prism is at the base plane on the contralateral side of the signing space. At the end of the signs the hand prism is on the ipsilateral side of local signing space, as in (63b).

The notation for the location relations is given in (64). The relations between the hand prism and local signing space are given in (64a), and the location relations between local and global signing space in (64b). They are identical for both signs. Hence, by the location relations alone, the signs in (62) are indistinguishable.

(64)   a.   (i)   At the start of the gesture:
$$LOC \; [Bottom_{HP} : +\text{BASE}(Contra\text{-}Side)_{LSS}]$$

            (ii)   At the end of the gesture:
$$LOC \; [Bottom_{HP} : +\text{BASE}(Ipsi\text{-}Side)_{LSS}]$$

    b. $LOC \; [+\text{BASE}_{LSS} : Neutral_{GSS}]$

Based on the descriptions of the data in (62), the crucial difference between the signs is the direction the palms face. To capture that distinction, I define *orientation* in terms of the dyadic relation in (65).

(65)   There is an orientation relation, $Orientation(x, y)$, where x and y are rectangular prisms that represent signing space, and x is a sub-space of y such that the faces of x are in a one-to-one parallel relation with the faces of y.

In (65) orientation is defined so that each of the six faces of the inner spatial construct are parallel to the faces of the construct it is embedded in. So, for example, recall from Chapter 2 that the hand is represented as a six-sided object embedded in the hand prism (HP). As illustrated in (66a), the fingertips of the hand are parallel to the front of the hand prism, and the back of the hand is parallel to the top of the hand prism. Note that specifying the relation between two non-parallel faces of the prism uniquely determines the relation between the other four faces. This reduction is easily understood by considering the geometry of the situation. In effect, there are only three dimensions of space. Specifying the relation between two non-parallel faces fixes two of the three dimensions; the third dimension can be deduced from the other two. The notation for specifying the orientation relation schematized in (66a) is given in (66b).

(66)

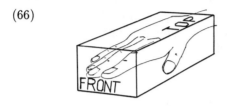

    a.   Hand in Hand Prism (HP)

    b.   OR $\begin{bmatrix} Fingertips_{Hand} & : & Front_{HP} \\ Back_{Hand} & : & Top_{HP} \end{bmatrix}$

With the orientation relation between the hand and hand prism in (66), the orientation relation between the hand prism and local signing space is specified in (67). (67a) captures the relative position of the hand prism with respect to local signing space at the start of the gesture for THING, and (67c) captures the relative position of the hand prism with respect to local signing space at the start of CHILDREN. The notations for the orientation relations are given in (67b) and (67d), respectively.

(67)

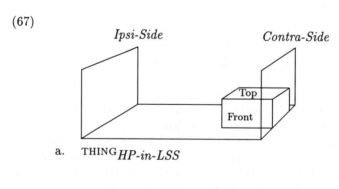

    a.   THING $_{HP\text{-}in\text{-}LSS}$

    b.   OR $\begin{bmatrix} Front_{HP} & : & -Local_{LSS} \\ Top_{HP} & : & -Base_{LSS} \end{bmatrix}$

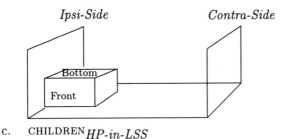

c.　CHILDREN $HP\text{-}in\text{-}LSS$

d.　OR $\begin{bmatrix} Front_{HP} & : & -Local_{LSS} \\ Top_{HP} & : & +Base_{LSS} \end{bmatrix}$

Note that the *non-local* face of local signing space is represented by the feature -LOCAL and the *local* face is represented by the feature +LOCAL. Recall from Section 3.1.4 that the *local* and *non-local* faces are not planes of articulation but are, rather, reference planes to complete the six sides of local signing space.

From both the schematized images and the notation in (67), it is easy to see that the orientation relation for THING, in (67b), is minimally contrastive with the orientation relation for CHILDREN, in (67d). The *orientation* relation defined in (65) is crucial to this distinction, so it is adopted into the model.

3.4.2.2　Local Signing Space in Global Signing Space

The orientation relation also holds between local and global signing space. However, at this level of relations, differences between morphologically simple and morphologically complex signs start to emerge. In particular, for lexically simple signs there are default specifications for the orientation relation between local and global signing space. The default specification for a simple sign depends on whether it is articulated at the body or in the neutral space in front of the body.

If a sign is articulated at a place on the body it is referred to as an *anchored* local signing space. In that case the base plane of local signing space associates with the body location and the local plane is parallel to the top plane of global signing space. In contrast, if a sign is articulated in the neutral signing space, it is referred to as a *floating* local signing space. The base plane of a floating local signing space is parallel to the bottom of global signing space and the local plane is parallel to the front of the signer's body.

The diagram in (68) illustrates the difference between these two classes of local signing space. The signer is profiled so that the top of her head is parallel to the top plane of global signing space (GSS), her front is parallel to the front plane of GSS, her waist is parallel to the bottom plane of GSS, and her back is parallel to the back plane of GSS. Here, the anchored local signing space is associated with the signer's face. The floating local signing space is in the neutral signing space.

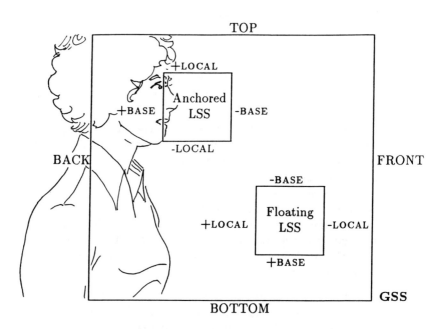

(68)   Anchored and Floating Local Signing Space

The notation for these default orientations are given in (69).

(69)   a.   Anchored Local Signing Space

$$OR \begin{bmatrix} +Base_{LSS} & : & Back_{GSS} \\ +Local_{HP} & : & Top_{GSS} \end{bmatrix}$$

   b.   Floating Local Signing Space

$$OR \begin{bmatrix} +Base_{LSS} & : & Bottom_{GSS} \\ +Local_{HP} & : & Back_{GSS} \end{bmatrix}$$

Simple signs receive the default orientation relations in (69). In contrast, as discussed in Chapter 5, more detailed specifications of places in global signing space are required to account for the syntactic use of space in complex signs like agreement verbs. The orientation relation between local and global signing space is crucial to the interpretation of those signs.

3.4.3 Notation for Static Hand Posture

To summarize, the box in a box in a box in a box relation described at the start of the chapter is repeated as (70), where the boxes are the hand prism (HP), local signing space (LSS), global signing space (GSS), and discourse signing space (DSS).

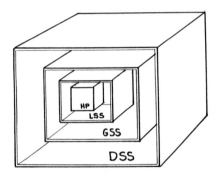

(70)   HP in LSS in GSS in DSS

Each box represents a level of signing space. The position of each box relative to its adjacent box, that is, the box that it is embedded in, is specified by two dyadic relations, *location* and *orientation*. Location specifies the placement of one level of space within its adjacent space, and orientation specifies the facingness of the inner space relative to the adjacent outer space.

Based on the notation proposed to capture the location and orientation relations, the generic representation for a static hand posture is given in (71). Starting at the center of the notation, the specifications for the hand prism, namely its handshape (HS), and location (LOC) and orientation (OR) relations with respect to the hand, are enclosed in a box labeled *HP*. Working outward, the notation for the hand prism is embedded in a box representing local signing space, labeled *LSS*, within which the location and orientation relations between the hand prism and local signing space are specified. At the next level of the representation, the notation for local signing space is embedded in a box representing global signing space, labeled GSS, with the location and orientation relations between local and global signing space specified. The relations between global and discourse signing space are left, as indicated before, for future work, though it is anticipated that the location and orientation relations between them will parallel those shown for the other spatial constructs.

(71) Representation of Manual Articulator in Signing Space

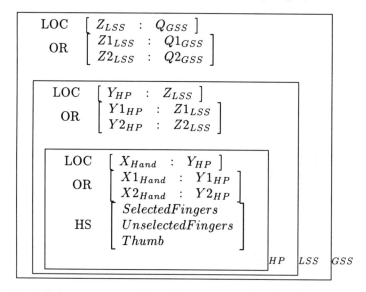

Based on the notational schema in (71), the difference between the initial positions of the hand for SUMMER, UGLY, and DRY, (53), can be specified as in (72). In (72a) the complete notation is given for the initial hand position for SUMMER. Handshape (HS) is specified for an extended index finger with the rest of the fingers bent and tucked under the thumb. The tip of the index finger is associated with the front of HP, and the back of the hand is associated with the top of HP. The front of HP is associated with the opposite side of LSS than the hand being used to articulate the sign, and the top of HP is associated with the local plane of LSS which in turn is associated with the top of global signing space because local signing space in this case is anchored.

The details of the notation for (72b) and (72c) are identical to (72a). The only difference between them is the location relation between local and global signing space. For (72a) LSS is associated with the forehead, for (72b) LSS is associated with the area above the lip, and for (72c) LSS is associated with the chin. All other characteristics of the hand posture are the same.

(72)   a. SUMMER:

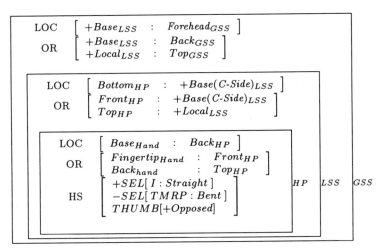

b. UGLY:

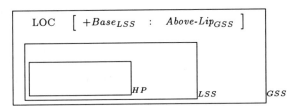

c. DRY:

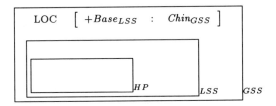

Similarly, the only difference between the initial positions of the hand for THING and CHILDREN, (61), is the orientation relation between the hand prism (HP) and local signing space (LSS), as highlighted by the representations in (73). (73a) completely specifies the properties of the initial hand posture for THING. The fingers and thumb are straight with the thumb unopposed to the fingers. The fingertips are associated with the front of HP and the back of the hand is associated with the top of HP. The front of HP is associated with the non-local plane of LSS and the top of HP is associated with the base plane of LSS. Because local signing space is floating, the net result of the orientation relations is that the back of the hand faces downward.

In contrast, as captured by the reduced representation in (73b), the only difference between the initial hand postures for THING and CHILDREN is the orientation relation between HP and LSS. In (73b) the top of HP is associated with the non-base face of LSS. The net result of the orientation relations in this case is that the back of the hand faces upward. Hence, the representation captures the crucial difference between these two hand postures.

(73) a. THING:

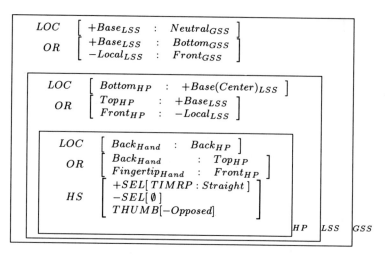

b. CHILDREN:

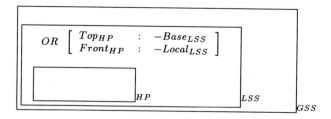

3.5 Signing Space, Location, and Orientation

In this chapter I have argued for a geometry-based representation of signing space. Specifically, I have adopted three spatial constructs into the model: *local signing space*, *global signing space*, and *discourse signing space*. The *hand prism*, adopted in Chapter 2, is nested at the center of signing space. It is embedded in local signing space which is embedded in global signing space which, in turn, is embedded in discourse signing space. At each level of embeddedness the relation between the constructs is captured by the *location* and *orientation* relations.

The novelty of the model of signing space presented here is twofold. First, in previous models signing space is treated as a unified entity. Here, I introduce the notion that space is divided into hierarchically related embedded units. Second, in previous models *location* and *orientation* are treated as parameters with their values captured by monadic features. The hierarchical treatment of signing space leads, however, to a much different conclusion. *Location* and *orientation* are recast here as dyadic relations that hold between the spatial constructs. As a result, the relation between the hand and signing space can be specified in completely relative terms.

The full impact of adopting a relative specification is explored more fully in the discussion of complex signs in Chapter 5. But first I continue by arguing for a representation of the dynamic properties of signs based on the groundwork layed thus far.

4

The Transition Unit

In this chapter I argue for a formal representation of "movement". Continuing with the analysis of the hand as a rigid body in space, the formal representation for "movement" is the displacement of the rigid body, or parts of the rigid body, in three-dimensional space. Capturing these displacements as *rigid body transformations* provides the basis for the phonological construct that is the focal point of the chapter – the *transition unit*. The *transition unit* provides a unified account for the changes in handshape, location, and orientation that contribute to the movement of the hand during a sign gesture. Unlike previous models of signs, the surprising conclusion of this chapter is that *movement* itself does not emerge as a phonological construct of the model.

4.1 Change in Location

In this section I focus on signs that are articulated by moving the whole hand through space, a phenomenon referred to as "path movement". I start by reviewing the three shapes of path movements described in Chapter 3: straight, circular, and arc-shaped.

In previous analyses, path shape is represented as a distinctive feature with unique values for each path shape (Liddell and Johnson 1989, Brentari 1990b, Sandler 1989).[1] Path shape has been invoked as one of the primary arguments to favor movement as a phonological construct. Yet, as described here, there are puzzling asymmetries between straight and circular movement on the one hand, and arc-shaped movement on the other that have no explanation in a feature-based analysis of path shape. To account for this puzzle I will argue that arc-shaped path is not a phonological property of signs. Rather, it is predictable from other

---

[1]Although Sandler (1989) adopts only one shape feature, *arc*; straight movement is the default and circular movement is represented as a sequence of concave/convex arcs.

characteristics of a model in which only straight and circular paths are represented.

In this section I present a formal representation of movement that combines the rigid body representation of the hand from Chapter 2 with the three-dimensional representation of signing space from Chapter 3 into a *transition unit*. The *transition unit* captures both the temporal and spatial properties of path movement, and provides the basis for the analysis of repeated movement ("secondary movement" in previous analyses) and arc-shaped path movement. I conclude the section by demonstrating that a transition-based analysis not only provides better coverage of the data, but also provides an explanation for the asymmetries between path shapes.

4.1.1   The Data

The data from the Chapter 3, example (2), are presented again in (1). Recall that to articulate (1a) the hand moves along a straight line, for (1b) it moves in a circle, and in (1c) it moves along an arc-shaped path.

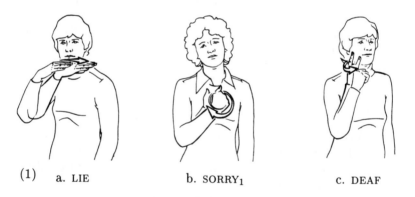

(1)   a. LIE   b. SORRY₁   c. DEAF

In (1a) all of the fingers are held straight and together; the thumb is tucked against the palm. The fingertips point to the side, and the palm faces down. The side of the tip of the index finger starts at the same side of the chin as the hand that is articulating the sign. To articulate the sign the hand moves across the chin in a straight line while the side of the index finger maintains contact with the chin. The gesture stops when the knuckle of the index finger reaches the other side of the chin.

In (1b) the fingers are curled against the palm to form a fist with the thumb held against the side of the index finger. With the palm facing the signer, the middle part of the fingers touch the middle of the chest. To articulate the sign the hand makes a large circle at the chest while maintaining contact with it. The gesture ends at the same point that it starts – at the middle of the upper chest.

In (1c) the index finger is straight while the rest of the fingers are curled against the palm with the thumb held across them. The tip of the index finger points up and the palm of the hand faces away from the signer. To articulate the sign the tip of the index finger starts near the upper part of the cheek. The hand moves in a straight line towards the face until the tip of the index finger touches the cheek. The hand then moves along an arc-shaped path and touches the lower part of the cheek. It is also possible to articulate the sign by first touching the lower part of the cheek and then touching the upper part of the cheek.

4.1.2 Line, Circle, Arc

Recall from Chapter 3 that the movement of the hand is confined to a plane of articulation. Yet physiologically, even within the confines of a plane, the hand is free to trace an infinite number of shapes. The data in (1) represent only three of those possible shapes: a line, circle, and arc. In contrast, paths following shapes like those described in (2) do not contribute to well-formed monomorphemic lexical signs.

(2)   a.   *(hand moves back and forth along a zig-zag path)
       b.   *(hand makes a figure eight)
       c.   *(hand moves along a two-dimensional spiral)
       d.   *(hand traces a square)

The difference between the well-formed signs in (1) and the gestures described in (2) are the shapes of the paths traced by the hand. In the well-formed signs, only straight, circular, or arc-shaped paths occur. This observation is generalized as (3).

(3)   In a sign gesture, the hand traces a straight, circular, or arc-shaped path.

4.1.3 The Asymmetries

In addition to being restricted to the set of shapes in (3), there are three asymmetries exhibited in the set of ASL signs. First, whereas the initial and final positions of the hand are contrastive for straight movement and irrelevant for circular movement (that starts and stops at the same place), the initial and final positions for arc-shaped movement may be interchanged. Second, straight and circular movements may be repeated in a simple sign, but arc-shaped movement is not. Finally, straight and circular movement occur in a small set of simple signs articulated with sequences of movements, but arc-shaped movement does not.

4.1.3.1 Direction

To illustrate the first type of asymmetry consider that, as described in Section 3.1.3, the direction the hand moves to articulate LIE, (1a), is contrastive. Moving the hand from the same side of the body as the hand articulating the sign to the opposite side as in (1a) produces a well-formed sign. Reversing the gesture so the hand starts on the opposite side of the body from the hand articulating the gesture and moves in the opposite direction from that in (1a) produces a non-interpretable gesture in ASL.[2]

In contrast, the direction of articulation for DEAF, (1c), may change. The sign can be pronounced by first touching the top of the cheek and then the lower part of the cheek. Alternatively, it can be articulated by first touching the lower part of the cheek and then touching the upper part of the cheek. This non-contrastive alternation has been described as a form of metathesis by Johnson (1986) and Liddell and Johnson (1989).

Similarly, the circular movement in SORRY, (1b), may be articulated in either a clockwise or counter-clockwise direction. These observations are generalized in (4).

(4)   a.   Direction of a gesture is contrastive for straight movement.

        b.   Direction of a gesture is non-contrastive for circular or arc-shaped movement.

4.1.3.2 Repeated Movements

Some signs are articulated with repeated movements. The repetition of movements in a lexical sign is referred to variously as "micro movement" (Friedman 1976), "hand-internal movement" (Klima and Bellugi 1979, Sandler 1989), "local movement" (Klima and Bellugi 1979, Liddell and Johnson 1989), "secondary movement" (Perlmutter 1992), and "secondary path movement" (Brentari 1990b). The movements are characterized by repeated articulations of the same gesture that are smaller than their singly articulated counterparts. Although repeated movements are characterized as being able to be repeated uncountably, extra repetitions are not without consequence. As will be discussed, the number of repetitions affect the interpretation of the gesture.

---

[2]There are minimal pairs of signs in which changing the direction of the movement changes the meaning of the sign, e.g., SHOW-UP, and DISAPPEAR.

(5a) is similar to (1a) except that it is articulated with a sequence of two movements at the chin. Rather than move the full length of the chin from one side to the other, the hand articulates two short identical straight movements at the center of the chin. The duration of the repeated movement is impressionistically the same as the time it takes to articulate the single movement in (1a). (5b) is similar to (1b), but articulated with repeated circular movement. Rather than circle once, as for (1b), the sign has the pronunciation in (5b) in which the hand moves in two small circles, one on top of the other. Just as for (5a) and (1a), (5b) and (1b) take about the same amount of time to articulate. In contrast to (5a) and (5b), repeated arc-shaped movement does not contribute to a well-formed sign, (5c).[3]

(5)   a. LIAR   b. SORRY₂   c. *ARC

The pattern of well-formedness illustrated by the data in (5) is generalized in (6).

(6)   Well-formed signs may be articulated with repeated straight or repeated circular movements, but not repeated arc-shaped movements.

With respect to the number of iterations that can be articulated when a sign is repeated, note that (1a) is a verbal form meaning "to lie", while

---

[3]It has been suggested that signs like GRANDMOTHER/GRANDFATHER and FAR-INTO-THE-FUTURE may be counter-examples to this observation. However, these signs differ from the gesture in (5c) in that they are articulated as linear sequences of arc-shaped movement in the signing space. Furthermore, they are arguably complex signs. The gesture of interest here is one that is repeated in the same space, and is morphologically simple. Therefore, these are not counterexamples to the conclusions of this discussion. Thank you to Jean Ann for bringing these potential counter-examples to my attention.

(5a) is a nominal form meaning "liar". This is an example of the noun-verb pairs described in Supalla and Newport (1978) in which the nominal form of the verb is characterized by repeated, reduced articulation of the same gesture used to articulate the verb. Note, however, that if the basic gesture in (5a) is repeated more than twice, it is likely to receive a verbal interpretation. Similarly, (5b) can be articulated more than twice, but it too will be interpreted differently. In this case repetition acts as an intensifier. Other characteristics of the repetitions, such as the path of movement of the hand between the repetitions, will also affect the meaning of the gesture (Klima and Bellugi 1979).

Hence word class is a factor in determining the acceptability of repetitions. A complete examination of ASL morphology is, unfortunately, beyond the scope of this discussion, but given the contrast between a single iteration, a doubled iteration, and greater numbers of iterations, I adopt the position that lexically only two types of movements need to be represented: (i) a single iteration of a movement, and (ii) a doubled iteration of a movement.[4] This follows Stack's (1988) proposal that *secondary movements* are repeated versions of *primary movements*, movements that are articulated once. As will be seen, the analysis that explains the unacceptability of the repeated arc-shaped movement in (5c) (Section 4.1.6) is consistent with the representation of secondary movement as doubled movement.

4.1.3.3 Sequences of Movements

The third asymmetry between path shapes emerges in a small set of signs which are articulated with a sequence of movements. There are only four patterns, referred to as 7, ?, X, and + path shapes for reasons that will become clear from the data in (7) and (8). The sequences of movements are constrained in two significant ways: (i) each pattern can be described as a sequence of only two movements, and (ii) each pattern is a combination of only straight and circular movements. Arc-shaped movements do not occur in this set of phonologically complex signs.

(7a) is an example of the 7 pattern. To articulate (7a) the fingertips and thumbtip touch to form a flattened looking handshape. The palm faces outward as the hand first moves along a straight path that is horizontal with respect to the signer and then moves along a vertical path while the palm shifts to face downward. This sequence of movements traces a shape that resembles the number seven and is thus referred to as a '7 movement'.

---

[4] Preliminary work by Chris Miller (p.c.) indicates that the number of repetitions of movement is context-sensitive. More work in this area is required to sort out the factors that affect repeated movement.

(7b) is an example of the question mark pattern. To articulate (7b), the fingers and thumbs of both hands are curled into a fist. The static hand is held with the palm down in front of the signer. The other hand moves first in a small circle a few inches above the back of the static hand, and then moves downward in a straight line until it contacts the static hand. The outline of this sequence of movements resembles a question mark.

(7) a. 7: PER-CENT b. ?: APPOINTMENT

(8a), an example of the X pattern, is articulated with the index finger of the moving hand extended while the other fingers are curled against the palm and tucked under the thumb. The other hand is held static in front of the signer with the fingers and thumb straight, the palm facing the signer, and the fingertips pointing towards the side. First the tip of the index finger of the moving hand traces a straight line on the palm of the hand starting at one of the upper corners of the palm and ending at the corner of the palm caddy-corner to the first. The hand then moves to the opposite upper corner of the palm and the fingertip traces another line that ends at the corner of the palm caddy-corner to it. The result is a sequence of movements that traces an x-shaped path.

(8b) is an example of the + pattern and is articulated with the index and middle fingers straight while the other fingers are curled against the palm with the thumb across them. At the start of the sign, the tips of the fingers point to the side and the palm faces the signer. First the tips of the extended fingers trace a short horizontal path across the upper arm. Then the hand shifts so the fingertips point up and the palm faces away from the signer. After shifting to the new position the fingertips trace a short vertical path that bisects the first path. The combination of the movements trace the outline of a +-sign on the signer's upper arm.

(8)   a. X: CRITICIZE   b. +: HOSPITAL

As mentioned above, these sets of signs are small. Other examples of signs with these patterns are:

7 END, NEVER, ORDER, CHICAGO, BOSTON, PHILADELPHIA, and other city names

? CENTER, HABIT, RESERVATION/ESTABLISH, PERFECT, WHEN, NATU-RALLY/NATIONAL, INCLUDE, GRADUATE, ENGAGEMENT, POLITI-CAL, GOVERNMENT, ATTITUDE

x CANCEL

+ SCHEDULE, CATHOLIC, PEPSI

In addition, the sources for three of the four patterns, namely the 7, x, and +, may be iconic. For example, the shape of (7a) resembles the outline of the *per-cent* sign, the shape of (8a) resembles the outline of an X, a shape associated with crossing something off of a list or schedule, and the shape of (8b) resembles the red crosses worn by hospital personnel. Furthermore, these patterns of sequences of movements may not be universal. For example, they appear to be absent in Dutch Sign Language (Els van der Kooij, p.c.). These properties of this small set of signs deserve more attention, but for the purposes of this discussion it is sufficient to note the characteristics of the movements that contribute to these patterns.

The movement in (7b) is a combination of a circular movement followed by a straight movement. All the other patterns in this set of signs are generated by a sequence of straight movements. Curiously, those combinations do not include arc-shaped movement, as demonstrated by the physiologically possible but non-occurring gestures described in (9). None of these gestures contribute to well-formed signs.

(9) a. *(arc-shaped movement followed by straight movement) or
          *(straight movement followed by arc-shaped movement)

     b. *(circular movement followed by arc-shaped movement) or
          *(arc-shaped movement followed by circular movement)

The generalization in (10) captures this pattern of distribution.

(10) Straight and circular movements occur in sequences of gestures in
      monomorphemic sign gestures; arc-shaped movements do not.

4.1.3.4 Asymmetries in Review

The asymmetries described in this section are summarized in (11). (11b)
and (11c) are asymmetries that set arc-shaped movement apart from the
other two. Although the asymmetry in (11a) does not follow the same
pattern as (b) and (c), it, too, has implications for differentiating arc-
shaped movement from the others. As indicated by (11a), the initial and
final points of movement are significant. For straight movement, the endpoints are distinct; for circular movement, the endpoints are the same.
Because straight movement is directional, the order of the endpoints
must be specified. Even though this is trivial for circular movement,
arc-shaped movement is the odd one out – as described above, the order
of its endpoints may alternate without changing the meaning of the sign.

		Straight	Circle	Arc
(11)				
a.	Direction is contrastive:	YES	NO	NO
b.	Repeated movement in signs:	YES	YES	NO
c.	Occurs in complex monomorphemic signs.	YES	YES	NO

In the remainder of this section I argue for a formal representation
of movement based on a rigid body analysis of the hand. I start with
straight and circular movements and then argue that arc-shaped movement is derived from a specific representation of straight movement, thus
accounting for the asymmetries in (11).

4.1.4   Straight and Circular Movement

In the signs presented thus far, the description of movement is straightforward: to articulate a path movement, the hand starts at one place, moves, then stops at another place. The anatomy of a movement is as presented in (12).

(12)   Movement: (i)   Start
                    (ii)   Transition
                    (iii) End

Setting arc-shaped movements aside for the moment, and noting that the endpoints are distinct for straight paths but the same for circular paths, it is possible to derive the shape of the transition from the spatial relation between the endpoints. If the endpoints are the same then the transition is circular, but if the endpoints are distinct then the transition is linear. This is the reasoning that leads to the proposal for the *transition unit.*

4.1.4.1   Straight Movement

Recall from Chapter 3 that a sign gesture is articulated in a plane of articulation, and that the following planes of articulation have been specified: *base* and *non-base, contralateral-side, ipsilateral-side,* and *center.* Well-formed signs articulated with straight movement are articulated in the base plane (LIE), the side planes (NOW), and the center plane (GOOD). The schematic in (13) illustrates, relative to the planes of articulation, the set of straight paths that contribute to well-formed signs.

(13)   Paths of Well-formed Signs

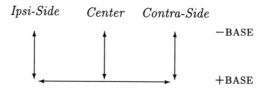

The paths of well-formed signs contrast with the paths of logically possible gestures like those described in (14).

(14) a. *(gesture for LIE articulated parallel to chin, but a few
inches in front of the chin)
   b. *(gesture for LIE that starts at the center of the chin and
moves to the side)
   c. *(gesture for LIE that starts at the side of the chin and
ends at the center of the chin)

The gestures described in (14) do not occur in well-formed signs.
The paths they follow are schematized in (15).

(15) *Ipsi-Side*   *Center*   *Contra-Side*

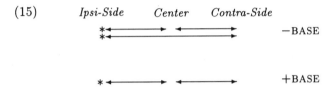

With reference to the constructs of signing space, the contrast between the paths in (13) and (15) can be generalized as (16).

(16) a. Gestures articulated parallel to, but a few inches from the
body are not well-formed signs.
   b. Gestures that start at the center and end at the side, or
start at the side and end at the center, are not well-formed
signs.

With respect to the generalization in (16b), consider the data in (17).
Both signs are articulated with the fingers straight and pointing upward,
the thumb folded against the palm and the palm facing towards the side.
The hand is held in front of the chin so the side of the index finger is a
few inches in front of the chin. To articulate (17a), the hand starts in
front of the center of the chin, moving towards the chin until the side
of the index finger touches it. The gesture is repeated twice. The same
repeated gesture is used to articulate (17b), except that it is articulated
on the side of the chin.[5]

---

[5]The handshape used to articulate these signs corresponds to the handshape from
the manual alphabet that represents the letter *B*. These signs are, therefore, arguably
loan signs from Signed Exact English. Nevertheless, they conform to the other properties of native signs, and are used here to illustrate the distinction between the side
and center of a location. That few minimal pairs of native signs take advantage of the
distinction between these two parts of location is a question for future consideration.

(17)   a. BITCH   b. BREAKFAST

The difference between the signs in (17) is the position of the hand. (17a) is articulated at the center of the chin and (17b) at the side. To articulate the signs the hand need not contact either the center or the side precisely. However, if a signer intends to articulate (17b) and the gesture wanders too far to the middle of the chin, it will be interpreted as (17a) and vice versa.

The sign in (17b) may also alternate between the left and right side of the chin. In general, a right-handed signer will articulate (17b) on the right side of the chin, and a left-handed signer will articulate it on the left. But the other logical possibilities are also interpretable. For example, a right-handed signer could articulate (17b) on the left side of the chin, or a left-handed signer could articulate it on the right side of the chin. Although the addressee may find these gestures odd, they do not affect the meaning of the sign (Uyechi 1992). The generalization in (18) captures these observations.[6]

(18)   Articulating a sign on the right or left side of the body does not change the meaning of a sign.

The proposition in (19) accounts not only for the generalization in (18), but also for the contrast between the paths in (13) and (15).

---

[6]A possible exception is the pair PHILADELPHIA and LEATHER, for which side may be distinctive. To account for such a distinction, $SIDE_{ipsi}$ and $SIDE_{contra}$ can be specified in the representation of the signs. The difference may, however, be regional and bears further investigation.

(19) (i) Signs are articulated in the *base, center, side*$_{ipsi}$ and *side*$_{contra}$ planes.
      (ii) In a well-formed sign with distinct starting and ending points, the hand moves from one side of the plane to the other side to the extent of local signing space.

The propositions in (19) not only rule out the non-occurring gestures described in (14), but also ensure the exclusion of gestures articulated by moving the hand to any of the medial points of the plane. Hence, they are adopted into the model. Further work is required, however, to determine if (19i), which stipulates the exclusion of the non-base plane, can be derived from more general principles.

4.1.4.2 Circular Movement

Like straight movement, circular movement is also subject to constraints that can be stated in terms of local signing space. Consider, for example, the signs in (20). To articulate (20a) the index finger is straight while the rest of the fingers are curled against the palm with the thumb folded across them. The tip of the finger points up and the palm faces the side. The hand moves along a circular path perpendicular to the chin so that the side of the index finger brushes against the center of the chin as it passes by. Recall from (1b) that (20b) is articulated by moving the hand in a circle while touching the chest.

(20)   a. LONELY   b. SORRY

The circular movement that characterizes the well-formed signs in (20) contrast with the gestures described in (21).

(21) a. *(move hand in circle parallel to but not touching the chest)
      b. *(move hand in circle at 45° angle with respect to chest)

The circular movement of well-formed signs is either perpendicular to the body or parallel to it. In either case, the hand touches the body while articulating the circle – once per circle when the path is perpendicular to the body, or throughout the circle when the path is parallel to the body. Using the formalism of local signing space, the proposition in (22) captures this observation.

(22) | Circular movement starts and ends in the *base plane*. |

This proposition predicts that circular movements not articulated in contact with the body will be either perpendicular to or horizontal with respect to the signer's body, because when local signing space is in neutral space the base plane is horizontal with respect to the body. The data in (23) and (24) confirm that prediction.

To articulate (23a) both hands are held in fists with the palms facing downward and the knuckles of the hands pointing away from the signer. The hands alternate along circular paths that are perpendicular to the signer's body as though pumping the pedals of a bicycle. In (23b) the fingers and thumb of the hand are straight and flat with respect to the palm. The palm faces downward and the fingertips point away from the signer. To articulate the sign the hand moves along a circular path that is horizontal with respect to the signer's body while keeping the palm face down.

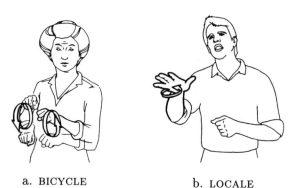

(23)   a. BICYCLE   b. LOCALE

The gestures in (23) comply with the constraint in (22) and are, as predicted, well-formed signs. In contrast, the gestures described in (24) violate the proposition in (22) and, as predicted, do not occur in well-formed signs.

(24)   a.   *(BICYCLE articulated with hands moving at 45° angle with respect to the upright position of the signer's
body)

b.   *(LOCALE articulated with palm facing body and fingertips forming 30° angle with respect to the floor)

4.1.5   Transition Unit

In this section I combine the geometry-based representation of signing
space developed in Chapter 3 with a representation of the hand as a *rigid
body*, a mathematical abstraction for an object that retains its form as
it changes position. Within this formalism the movement of the hand
is characterized as a *rigid body transformation* in rectangular space. I
argue that the properties relevant to movement can be represented by
a construct I call a *transition unit*. The mathematical basis of this new
construct not only accounts for the properties of movements described
thus far, but also presents a foundation for capturing properties such as
variations in the speed and tenseness of pronunciations of signs.

4.1.5.1   Rigid Body and Transformations

As described in Chapter 2 the hand is capable of a number of configurations. In all of those possible configurations it retains the same form.
That is, the length and size of the fingers and thumb are invariant. In
geometry an object that retains its form even as it changes position is
called a *rigid body*. A movement of a rigid body is represented by a *rigid
body transformation* where, as Stewart and Golubitsky (1992) put it, a
transformation is a "recipe for moving things around".

In two-dimensional, or planar, space there are four transformations
that can be applied to a rigid body. Three are of interest here: *translation, rotation*, and *reflection*.[7] They are represented in (25) using a
two-dimensional triangle to represent the rigid body.

In each diagram the rigid body has two positions: position A represents the start of the transformation, and position B represents its
end. A *translation*, (25a), is simply a movement of the body from one
point to another. A simple linear translation like the one illustrated in
(25a) is similar to moving the hand along a straight path. A *rotation*
is implemented by twisting the rigid body through some angle about
a fixed point. In (25b) the rigid body rotates forward through a 90°
angle. This transformation is like pivoting the hand about the wrist.
Finally, a *reflection* is a transformation that flips the rigid body about
a line, (25c). The result is a mirror-image of Position A with respect
to Position B. Although this transformation is not relevant to the rep-

---

[7]The fourth transformation is a *glide reflection*.

resentation of the movement of a hand through space, it is crucial for capturing the symmetry conditions on signs articulated with two hands. In the remainder of the section the discussion will focus on translation and rotation.

(25)

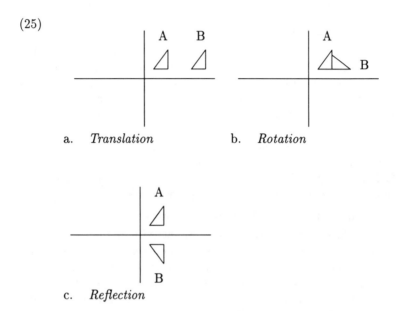

a. *Translation*   b. *Rotation*

c. *Reflection*

Movements of the whole hand can be captured by treating it as a single body and describing its translations and rotations. Movements of parts of the hand, such as flexing or extending the fingers, can be captured by treating parts of the hands, for example a single finger, as a single body and describing its rotation. I begin by discussing the movement of the whole hand.

4.1.5.2 A Movement Function

A translation, as described in (25), captures only the initial position and the final position of the rigid body. To get from point A to point B the rigid body may follow any path. For example, the triangle in (25a) may start in position A, be lifted from the page, dance around the desk, circle the room, and then finally come to rest in position B. The path it takes from A to B is irrelevant.

But in sign language the path is crucial. The functions in (26) each represent a set of points. (26a) captures the set of points that correspond to a line, and (26b) captures the set of points that correspond to a circle.

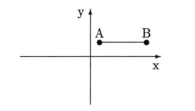 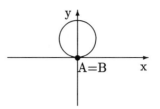

(26)

a.   Line: b.   Circle:
$$M_l(x,y) = (x + k_x, y + k_y)$$ $$M_c(x,y) = x^2 + y^2 = K$$

To apply these functions to the movement of the hand, assume that the hand starts at position A and moves along the path described by M_l until it reaches position B. This is represented by the notation in (27a). If, however, the hand starts at position A and moves along a path described by the circle function, M_c, then it ends at the same position, as captured by the notation in (27b).

(27)   a.   Straight: $\vec{M_l}(x,y)_{initial} = LOC_A$
                        $\vec{M_l}(x,y)_{final} = LOC_B$

       b.   Circular : $\vec{M_c}(x,y)_{initial} = LOC_A$
                        $\vec{M_c}(x,y)_{final} = LOC_A$

Thus it is possible to differentiate a straight path from a circular path by comparing the endpoints of the vector functions. Adopting a convention in which an ordered pair represents the initial and final endpoints of the transition produces the notation in (28).

(28)   Given the ordered pair of positions, [LOC_x, LOC_y],
       (i)   If $x \neq y$, then path is $\vec{M_l}$.
       (ii)   If $x = y$, then path is $\vec{M_c}$.

The ordered pair in (28) captures the spatial properties of a gesture. Movements also have a temporal component. To articulate a well-formed unmarked sign, the hand moves at a steady rate from its initial to its final position. The overall rate that the hand moves may increase or decrease without changing the basic lexical meaning of a sign. However, as illustrated by the possible gestures described in (29) which do not contribute to well-formed signs, changes within a single gesture are unacceptable.

(29)   a.   *(articulate LIE so that second half of the gesture is twice
                as fast as the first half of the gesture)
         b.   *(articulate SORRY so that the second half of the gesture
                is half as slow as the first half of the gesture)

To account for the contrast between the well-formed versions of LIE
and SORRY and the gestures described in (29), the formal representation
of movement, the *transition unit* is defined in (30). The transition unit
relates the spatial and temporal properties of a gesture, in particular
ensuring that the rate of change is controlled. The default rate of change
is specified by the Principle of Proportionality, defined in (30iii).

(30) | A *transition unit* consists of a *time unit*, T, associated with a *spatial unit*, S.

 (i)   The *time unit*, T, represents a duration of time that starts at time t_i and ends at t_f.

 (ii)   The *spatial unit*, S, represents the space that is spanned by a *rigid body translation*, whose initial position is P_i, whose final position is P_f, and whose path is determined by *movement vector*, $\vec{M}_l$ or $\vec{M}_c$.

 (iii) *Time unit*, T, and *spatial unit*, S, are associated so that the *manual articulator* assumes position P_i at time t_i and position P_f at time t_f. Unless otherwise stated, the rate of change is determined by the *Principle of Proportionality*:
         In the absence of any other specification, the hand moves through space such that
         $$\frac{P_f - P_i}{t_f - t_i} = \frac{\Delta P}{\Delta t} = speed_{constant}$$

The Principle of Proportionality, (30iii), sets the stage for representing varying rates of movement. For example, as noted by Klima and
Bellugi (1979), the speed (and acceleration) of the hand may affect the
meaning of a sign. So (30) not only rules out ill-formed gestures, it also
anticipates the crucial role that the relation between time and space
plays in the morpho-phonology of signs.

The notation I adopt to capture the relations specified in (30) is illustrated in (31). The square brackets represent the time unit associated

with the spatial unit, the ordered pair of parameter values, P, represent the spatial unit, and the subscripts represent the initial and final values of the movement function. The Greek symbol *delta*, Δ, represents a transition between two points. Straight and circular movement need not be specified explicitly. That information is derived from the relation between the endpoints. For straight movement, they are distinct; for circular movement, they are the same.

(31)

Notation for the *Transition Unit*
Straight Movement: $[\,P_i, P_f\,]_\Delta$
Circular Movement: $[\,P_i, P_i\,]_\Delta$

The fully specified notation for the path movements used to articulate LIE and SORRY are given in (32). Only the relevant location information is included. Of the three large brackets, the outermost represent global signing space, the middle represent local signing space, and the innermost represent the hand prism. In each case the change in location is specified at the level of local signing space, capturing the change of position of the *hand prism* with respect to *local signing space*.

(32) a. LIE

$$\left[\, LOC \quad [+Base_{LSS} : Chin_{GSS}] \quad \left[\, LOC \quad [Side_{HP} : I\text{-}Side_{LSS}, C\text{-}Side_{LSS}]_\Delta \quad \left[\, LOC \quad [T\text{-}Side_{Hand} : Side_{HP}] \,\right] \,\right] \,\right]$$

b. SORRY

$$\left[\, LOC \quad [+Base_{LSS} : Chest_{GSS}] \quad \left[\, LOC \quad [Front_{HP} : Center_{LSS}, Center_{LSS}]_\Delta \quad \left[\, LOC \quad [Palm_{Hand} : Front_{HP}] \,\right] \,\right] \,\right]$$

A condensed form of the notation in (32) is given in (33).

(33) a. LIE:
$$LOC_{LSS} \; [Base_{LSS}(Chin_{GSS}) : I\text{-}Side, C\text{-}Side]_{\Delta}$$

b. SORRY:
$$LOC_{LSS} \; [Base_{LSS}(Chest_{GSS}) : Center, Center]_{\Delta}$$

The representation of the movements for LIE and SORRY in (33), in combination with the propositions in (30), account for the well-formedness of the gestures in (1a) and (1b). The gestures described in (29) are ruled out by the Principle of Proportionality, (30iii). Hence the analysis provides a correct account of the data. The *transition unit* and the Principle of Proportionality are crucial to this analysis and, therefore, are adopted into the model.

In sum, the *transition unit* is a phonological construct that represents a unit of movement. In the next section I extend the coverage of the transition unit to include repeated movement, and then show that it explains the puzzling asymmetries between path shapes described above.

4.1.5.3 Doubled Transition Unit

The well-formed signs for LIAR and SORRY, (5a) and (5b), contrast with the physiologically possible gestures described in (34). (34a) resembles the verbal form LIE, (1a), but is odd because the length of the gesture is shorter because it is only half of the repeated gesture used to articulate (5a). (34b) is not interpretable as the nominal form meaning *liar*. (34c) and (34d) are possible variations of the sign in (5b), but they would be accompanied with other characteristics. For example, (34c) could be acceptable with a tensing of the gesture, but would not have an unmarked interpretation.[8]

(34) a. *(gesture for LIAR articulated once)
      b. *(gesture for LIAR articulated three times)
      c. ♮(gesture for SORRY articulated once)
      d. ♮(gesture for SORRY articulated three times)

So the well-formed signs in (5) are articulated with two repetitions of a gesture that occurs in other signs, whereas the ill-formed or odd

---

[8]Note that LIAR is a noun and SORRY is an adjectival predicate, i.e., *to be sorry*. The unacceptability of (34a) and (34b) reflect the constrained environment for nouns; the variations in (34c) and (34d) reflect the adverbial type of modulations applicable to other classes of signs.

gestures in (34) are articulated with more or fewer than two gestures. The statement in captures (35) this observation.[9]

(35) When a sign gesture is repeated in a monomorphemic sign, it is articulated twice.

The diagrams in (36) represent the properties of the single sign gesture with the repeated sign gesture. (36a) represents the paths the hands follow to articulate the signs with a single path movement, and (36b) represents the paths of the repeated gestures. The repeated gestures in (36b) are roughly half the size of the single iterations of the gestures in (36a). In addition, all four signs take roughly the same amount of time to articulate.

(36) a. LIE   SORRY$_1$

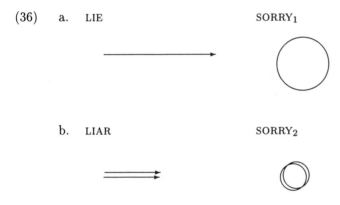

b. LIAR   SORRY$_2$

The diagrams in (37) illustrate physiologically possible, but non-occurring versions of the gestures in (36b). Repeated gestures are ill-formed if they are different sizes, (37a) and (37b), or if they are articulated at different rates, (37c).

---

[9]This is not to say, however, that signs with repeated gestures are always articulated with two-and-only-two repetitions. Rather, just as the speed and tenseness of articulation may vary for a sign, so too, may the number of repetitions. Precise bounds on the number of repetitions may be negotiated between the phonology and phonetics of a sign. With respect to the phonology, I adopt a representation based on two repetitions. A better understanding of the environments that induce variations in the number of articulations of a gesture is crucial to continued work on this topic.

(37)   *LIAR   *SORRY₂

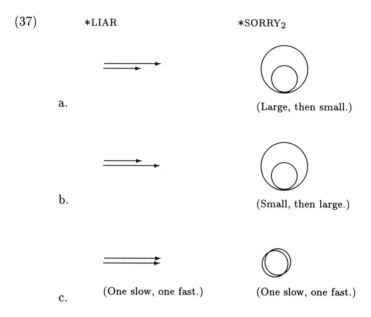

a.   (Large, then small.)

b.   (Small, then large.)

c.   (One slow, one fast.)   (One slow, one fast.)

The difference between the well-formed patterns in (36b) and the unacceptable patterns in (37) is that each iteration of a well-formed repeated gesture is roughly the same size and takes about the same amount of time to articulate. The characteristics of the repeated gesture observed in (36) and (37) are summarized in (38).

(38)   a.   In a well-formed monomorphemic sign, a repeated gesture is about half the size and takes roughly half the time to articulate as a similar gesture in a sign that is articulated with a single iteration of the gesture.

        b.   A well-formed repeated gesture is articulated with two identical gestures.

The two to one relation between singly iterated and doubly iterated sign gestures described in (38) is reinforced by the patterns of alternations represented in (39). As the "loudness" of a sign changes, the characteristics of a sign articulated with a double gesture changes accordingly. (39b) represents a moderate volume of signing the doubly articulated gestures, (39a) represents reduced volume, and (39c) represents increased volume. In each case, even though the size of the gesture varies, the repeated gesture maintains the same dimensions as the first gesture. With respect to a singly iterated sign articulated at the same volume, the size of the single gesture is always roughly twice that of a single iteration of the re-articulated gesture.

(39)   LIAR   SORRY$_2$

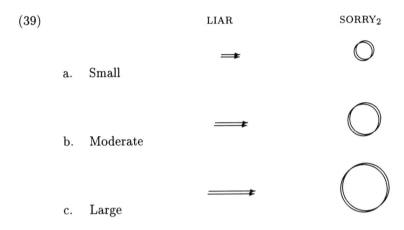

    a.   Small

    b.   Moderate

    c.   Large

To capture the generalizations in (38) and to account for alternations like (39), I adopt the formalism in (40). The doubling function $Double(x)$, in (40), takes as its input a movement function, $\vec{M}(x)$, and outputs a repeated version of the input. When $\vec{M}(x)$ is spelled out, the doubling function is represented as a repeated sequence of initial and final positions, x_i and x_f, the endpoints of a single iteration of the repeated gesture.

(40) | Doubling Function:
$$Double(\,\vec{M}(x)\,) = \vec{M}(x)\vec{M}(x) = (x_i, x_f, x_i, x_f)$$

The output of the doubling function is a repeated movement that contributes to the *doubled transition unit*, defined in (41). The units of time (T) and space (S) are the same as for the *transition unit*, (30). In combination with the Principle of Proportionality, as specified before as (30iii), the doubled transition unit ensures that the uniform relation between space and time is conserved. The result is that the repeated gestures are adjusted so that a single iteration of a doubled transition is half the size and half the duration of a standard transition unit.

(41) A *doubled transition unit* consists of a *time unit*, T, associated with a *spatial unit*, S.

    (i)   The *time unit*, T, represents a duration of time that starts at time t_i and ends at t_f.

    (ii)   The *spatial unit*, S, represents the space spanned by a *rigid body translation*, whose initial position is P_i, whose final position is P_f, and whose path is specified by a the *doubling function, Double($\vec{M_l}$)* or *Double($\vec{M_c}$)*.

    (iii)   *Time unit*, T, and *spatial unit*, S, are associated so that the *manual articulator* assumes position P_i at time t_i and position P_f at time t_f. The repeated positions are related evenly to time and, unless otherwise stated, the rate of change is determined by the *Principle of Proportionality*.

The notation for the doubled transition unit is given in (42). The subscript 2Δ represents the doubling of the spatial movement function.

(42) Notation for the *Doubled Transition Unit*

    Straight Movement: $[\, P_i, P_f\,]_{2\Delta l}$
    Circular Movement: $[\, P_i, P_i\,]_{2\Delta c}$

The fully specified notation for the repeated path movements used to articulate LIAR and SORRY₂ are given in (43). Only the relevant location information is included. Just as for the singly iterated path movements, in each case the change in location is specified at the level of local signing space, capturing the change of position of the *hand prism* with respect to *local signing space*.

(43) a.   LIAR

$$\begin{bmatrix} LOC & [+Base_{LSS} : Chin_{GSS}] & \\ & \begin{bmatrix} LOC & [Side_{HP} : \textit{I-Side}_{LSS}, \textit{C-Side}_{LSS}]_{2\Delta} \\ & \begin{bmatrix} LOC & [\textit{T-Side}_{Hand} : Side_{HP}] \end{bmatrix} \end{bmatrix} \end{bmatrix}$$

b. SORRY₂

$$\left[\begin{array}{l} LOC \quad [+Base_{LSS} : Chest_{GSS}] \\[4pt] \left[\begin{array}{l} LOC \quad [Front_{HP} : Center_{LSS}, Center_{LSS}]_{2\Delta} \\[4pt] \left[\begin{array}{l} LOC \quad [Palm_{Hand} : Front_{HP}] \end{array} \right] \end{array} \right] \end{array} \right]$$

A condensed form of the notation in (43) is given in (44).

(44) a. LIAR:

$LOC_{LSS} \; [Base_{LSS}(Chin_{GSS}) : I\text{-}Side, C\text{-}Side]_{2\Delta}$

b. SORRY₂:

$LOC_{LSS} \; [Base_{LSS}(Chest_{GSS}) : Center, Center]_{2\Delta}$

The representations in (44), in combination with the propositions in (41), and the doubling function in (40), account for the well-formed characteristics of repeated movement schematized in (36b). The principle of proportionality invoked by (41iii) rules out the non-occurring gestures represented in (37). The *doubled unit transition* and the *doubling function* provide a correct account of the data, therefore I adopt both into the model of signs.

The relation between the transition unit and doubled transition unit are similar to the proposal by Stack (1988), who observed that primary movements, or single iterations of change, are related to secondary movements, or doubled iterations of change. The model proposed here is similar to Stack's in that both models account for properties of repeated movements without adopting the feature-based analysis of Liddell (1990b), Sandler (1993c), or Perlmutter (1992).[10] The models differ, however, in that Stack (1988) operates within the framework of spoken language phonology, appealing to a syllabic template to account for constraints on the sign gesture. In the model proposed here the transition unit states the properties of the sign in formal mathematical terms, capturing the relation between the spatial and temporal properties of the sign explicitly. The analysis of arc-shaped movement presented in the next section demonstrates the advantage of a transition-based account.

---

[10]Liddell (1990) adopts the feature *oscillating* [OSC] for the Movement-Hold model, Sandler (1993c) adopts the feature *trill* feature for the Hand Tier model, and Perlmutter (1992) uses *wiggling* in the Moraic model. These models are discussed in more detail in Chapter 6.

4.1.6   Arc-Shaped Movement

With the transition-based representation of repeated movement, a surprising analysis of arc-shaped path movement emerges – an arc-shaped path is a by-product of repeated straight movement.

Recall the signs LIAR, (5a), BITCH, (17a), and BREAKFAST, (17b), whose movements are schematized in (45). All three are articulated with doubled straight movement. The movement for LIAR is articulated by moving the hand repeatedly from one side of the chin to the other, (45a). To articulate BITCH the hand moves repeatedly in a straight movement from near the center of the chin to touch the center of the chin, (45b). To articulate BREAKFAST the hand moves repeatedly from near the side of the chin to touch the side of the chin, and can be articulated on either side of the chin, (45c) or (45d).

(45)

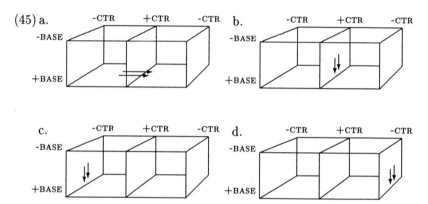

The diagrams in (45) represent all but one of the logically possible combinations of repeated straight movements. Because the non-center planes of articulation are phonologically equivalent but physically split between two places, a doubled gesture may be articulated first at one side and then the other side of local signing space, as in (46). It is this combination of repeated gestures that I propose is the source of the arc-shaped movement used to articulate a sign like DEAF, (1c).

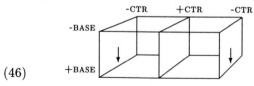

(46)

Consider the characteristics of the movement needed to articulate the repeated straight movements in (46). (47a) shows the idealized target movement, a straight movement at one side followed by a straight movement at the other side. In reality, to get from one side of the space to the other requires an epenthetic movement from the end of the first movement to the start of the next. This is idealized in (47b). When the sequence of movements in (47b) is articulated in real time, the result is the smoothed path in (47c) – an arc-shaped path.

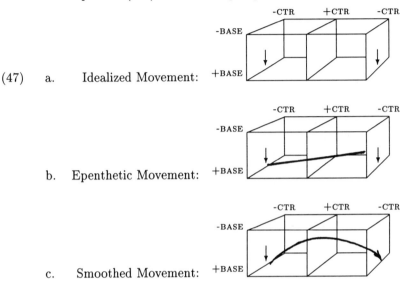

(47)   a.   Idealized Movement:

       b.   Epenthetic Movement:

       c.   Smoothed Movement:

By this account arc-shaped path movement is represented by the transition unit in (48). The gesture is articulated at both non-center sides, so a full specification of the doubled transition unit is necessary.

(48)   "Arc-shaped" Doubled Transition Unit

$$LOC_{LSS} \begin{bmatrix} X_{LSS}(Y_{GSS} : Side_a(-Base), \\ X_{LSS}(Y_{GSS} : Side_a(+Base), \\ X_{LSS}(Y_{GSS} : Side_b(-Base), \\ X_{LSS}(Y_{GSS} : Side_b(+Base) \end{bmatrix}_{2\Delta}$$

This analysis predicts that an arc-shaped gesture is preceded by a straight downward movement. The set of physiologically possible gestures in (49) represent other possible directions of "downbeats" to an arc-shaped movement. None of those occur in well-formed signs.[11]

---

[11]Note that when local signing space is associated with the body, (49b) is physiologically impossible.

(49) a.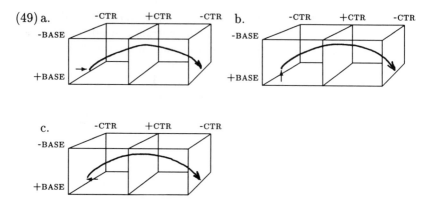

c.

This analysis also predicts that the downbeat will occur even in sequences of signs where there is an opportunity to forego the downbeat. For example, (50) is articulated with an arc-shaped movement. It is an initialized sign that borrows the handshape used for the letter r in the manual alphabet. The index and middle fingers are straight and crossed with the middle finger resting on top of the index finger. The other fingers are curled against the palm of the hand with the thumb resting on top of them. The hand is held so the fingertips point up and the palm faces the signer. To articulate the sign the front top pad of the index finger touches one side of the chin then moves along an arc-shaped path to touch the other side of the chin.

(50)   RESTAURANT

If the signs DEAF and RESTAURANT are articulated in sequence, as in (51), the analysis for arc-shaped movement predicts that the hand will follow the paths shown in (51a) so that at the end of the first sign the hand moves away from the face before articulating the second sign. If, as illustrated in (51b), the hand moves directly from the end of the first sign to the arc-shaped path of the second sign without the intermediate move towards the face, then the sequence is unacceptable. Preliminary evidence confirms this expectation.

(51)   a. DEAF RESTAURANT   b. *DEAF RESTAURANT

In sum, when straight movement is repeated, all logical combinations of gestures available, subject to the constraints of local signing space, appear in well-formed signs. Arc-shaped path movement is a side effect of one of those combinations.[12]

4.1.7 Asymmetries Revisited

The summary of asymmetries from (11) is repeated in (52). All three asymmetries can now be explained in terms of the analysis of straight, circular, and arc-shaped movement based on the transition unit.

(52)			Straight	Circle	Arc
	a.	Direction is contrastive:	YES	NO	NO
	b.	Repeated movement in signs:	YES	YES	NO
	c.	Occurs in complex monomorphemic signs.	YES	YES	NO

---

[12]Liddell and Johnson (1989) proposed a similar analysis. The timing structure they propose for DEAF (1989:244) is MHMMH. The first MH represents a straight downward movement, the next M represents an arc-shaped movement to the starting point for the final MH that represents a final downward movement. This explicit representation of arc-shaped movement in the phonology differs significantly, however, from its derivative status in the model of visual phonology presented here.

The representation of the transition unit which includes the initial and final endpoints of the gesture provides an account for asymmetry (a). For straight movement the endpoints are distinct, so the direction of the movement is contrastive. For circular movement the endpoints are co-located, so direction is not phonologically contrastive. For a different reason the direction of arc-shaped movement is also not contrastive. Arc-shaped movement is represented as repeated movements in phonologically equivalent, but physically distinct, locations. So phonetically the gesture may be articulated starting on either side of the location. Phonologically, the representation is the same, accounting for the non-contrastive properties of the direction of movement.

Asymmetry (b) has a straightforward explanation in this analysis. As argued here, at most two repetitions of a gesture are allowed in a simple sign. Because arc-shaped movement is articulated with repeated straight movement, two repeated arc-shaped movements would introduce four repeated straight movements in a simple sign, thus violating the maximum number of repetitions allowed. Straight and circular movement are, on the other hand, each articulated with a single gesture and therefore can be repeated in a simple sign.

The explanation for asymmetry (c) is related to the explanation for asymmetry (b). A simple sign can only accommodate a maximum of two gestures. So if one of the gestures in a monomorphemic sign articulated with a sequence of gestures is an arc-shaped movement, the total number of gestures would exceed the ceiling of two. Combinations of straight and circular movement are allowed because each of those movements contribute a single gesture.

In sum, the transition unit, the doubled transition unit, and the related propositions of the model provide a set of logically consistent explanations for the asymmetries between path movements. And as will be presented in the following sections, the transition unit unifies the properties of changes in handshape and orientation. But before continuing this discussion, it is important to digress and note that the line and circle emerge in this analysis as the only underlying shapes of the transition function. The finding is mathematically significant.

4.1.8 Symmetry

The line and circle are special. A circle is the simplest geometric form with rotational symmetry. In other words, it has the same form regardless of how it is rotated. A(n infinite) line is the simplest geometric form with translational symmetry. That is to say that it has the same form regardless of how it is translated. It is significant that these two shapes emerge from the set of all physiologically possible shapes for path movements because their properties of symmetry, or sameness, are consistent with other properties of bilateral symmetry that have been recognized in signs.

For example, Frishberg (1976) notes that the line of bilateral symmetry running vertically through the signer's body is relevant to historical change. Gestures show a tendency to move towards the center of the body. And when a sign is articulated with two independently moving hands, they tend to be positioned on either side of the center of the body. Thus as signs undergo change, they appear to respect the bilateral symmetry of the body.

In addition, as discussed here and in Chapter 2, there is a lack of contrastiveness between the right and left hands or the right and left sides of the body. These observations reflect "the symmetry of left and right, which is so conspicuous in the structure of the higher animals, especially the human body," and "is strictly geometric and ... an absolutely precise concept" (Weyl 1969).

So the emergence of path shapes that exhibit perfect symmetry in one dimension (line) and two dimensions (circle) is consistent with the inherent symmetry of the body. Furthermore, this observation links the sign system to other natural systems that exhibit and exploit bilateral symmetry. Stewart and Golubitsky (1992), for example, present examples of bilateral symmetry in nature that range from the formation of crystal structures to the gaits of multi-pedal animals. The discussion here strongly suggests that a similar consideration might also be extended to sign language.

The analysis presented here, therefore, differs crucially from previous proposals. By formalizing the properties of the system in geometric terms, the model builds links beyond language to other natural systems. In contrast, previous models of signs which have been based on the constructs from spoken language phonology build links to the structure of spoken languages while missing the broader organizational principles underlying signs. For example, the constructs for signing space provide the basis for formalizing the symmetry that Battison (1978) observes in two-handed signs. Although two-handed signs are beyond the scope of the current discussion, it is a logical extension of the work presented here. A more complete discussion of the formal symmetric properties of two-handed signs is likely to strengthen the ties to other natural systems that is suggested here by the emergence of the line and circle as the only underlying path shapes of signs.[13]

If symmetry does indeed play a key role in the representation of

---

[13]See Section 5.3.1.

signs, then it will raise new questions related to a theory of universal phonology: Is symmetry reflected in the phonology of spoken language? If so, how? And if not, why not? If a similar symmetry does not exist, then it provides more evidence to argue for distinct frameworks of visual phonology and spoken language phonology, but it would raise an even more fundamental question: Why the (phonological) asymmetry between visual and spoken language?

4.2 Change in Handshape

In this section I show that the *transition unit* also accounts for changes in hand posture, or handshape change. In previous accounts of handshape change a single handshape change constraint is proposed (Sandler 1989, Brentari 1990a). Following Sandler (1989), I exclude fingerspelled loan signs from the analysis of handshape change. But in contrast to Sandler and Brentari, I propose that not one, but a set of constraints on handshape change are required to capture the distributional asymmetries of handshape change.

In another account of handshape change, Corina (1993) represents handshape change in the context of spoken language feature geometry as sequences of root nodes, or non-branching contours. He treats handshape change as a sequence of two distinct but related handshapes. Similarly, in this analysis handshape change is represented as a sequence of handshapes. Unlike previous analyses, however, a transition-based analysis of handshape change links it to changes in location.

I argue for a movement function that applies to the hand. The movement function in this case applies not to a single rigid body, as for the transition of the hand between two places, but to a system of rigid bodies defined by the organization of the components of the hand presented in Chapter 2. I start by describing some characteristics of handshape change. I then describe the specific type of rigid body transition that applies to the hand, and then argue that the transition unit, as defined in the previous section, is applicable to handshape change.

4.2.1 The Data

The sign in (53) is articulated with only a change in handshape. At the start of the sign all the fingers are curled against the palm of the hand with the thumb resting across them. The hand is held near the side of the forehead with the palm facing towards the signer and the tops of the knuckles facing up. To articulate the sign the index finger uncurls until it is straight. The hand stays in the same position throughout the change in the index finger.

(53)   UNDERSTAND

The well-formed sign in (53) contrasts with the gestures described in (54). Unlike the gesture described in (54a), the change from the first hand position to the second in (53) is direct – the index finger changes directly from folded to straight. And unlike the gesture described in (54b), the change in (53) is smooth – the unbending of the joints occur simultaneously.

(54)   Starting from closed initial position,
       a.   *(the middle and end joints extend while knuckle re-
            mains at 90° angle, then index finger straightens at
            knuckle)
       b.   *(knuckle of index finger straightens, pauses, then mid-
            dle and end joint straighten)

In short, the change from the initial to the final position of the index finger in (53) is articulated with a smooth transition accomplished by the simultaneous movement of the joints. To exclude gestures like those in (54) from the representation of signs, I propose to model the hand as a set of rigid bodies.

4.2.2   Rigid Body and Angular Translations

In the discussion about change in location, the hand was modeled as a single rigid body. In a similar fashion, each of the bone segments of the finger can be modeled as a rigid body. As shown in (55a), the finger is composed of three bone segments: (i) between the knuckle and the middle joint, (ii) between the middle and end joint, and (iii) from the end joint to the finger tip. As schematized in (55b), each bone segment can be represented as a rigid body and each joint as a pivot point.

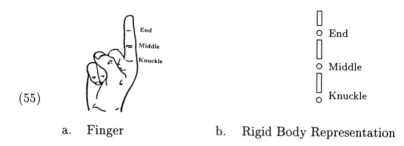

a. Finger   b. Rigid Body Representation

(55)

Using the representation from (55b), the movement in (53) can be characterized as a change from a posture in which the finger segments are all bent, (56a), to one in which the segments are all straight, (56b).

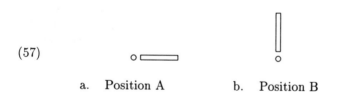

(56)

a. HS_1 b. HS_2

The movement of a single bone segment can be formalized as a rigid body rotation. For example, the bone segment may start in position A, (57a), and then rotate counterclockwise to position B, (57b), about the circle representing the joint, or pivot point, for the rotation.

(57)

a.   Position A   b.   Position B

The change from position A to position B can be captured by a rigid body transformation. The rotation in (58) captures the angular displacement of the segment.[14] In angular displacement, a body of length

---

[14] Nagahara (1988) argues for a representation for signs that uses Cartesian coordinates to represent straight movement and polar coordinates to represent movements along an arc. The approach here is similar, except that polar coordinates are applied not only to the movement of the whole hand (as will be argued in the section discussing change in orientation), but to the components of the hand as well.

r, positioned at an angle θ, rotates about a pivot point through an angle θ_k.

(58)

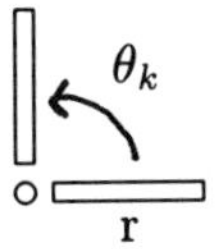

Angular Displacement: $f(r,\theta) = (r,\theta + \theta_k)$

Each segment of the finger can be modeled as a rigid body that pivots about a point. To capture the movement of the index finger from its initial to final position to articulate UNDERSTAND, each bone segment is subject to a 90° rotation about its respective joint, as illustrated by the arrows in (59a). The set of equations for the movement are listed in (59c). To capture the properties of the movement of the index finger to articulate UNDERSTAND, all three rotations must be executed simultaneously.

(59)

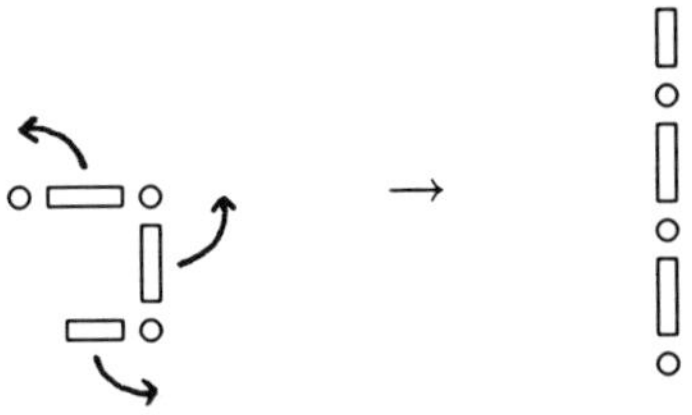

$$f(r_e,\theta) = (r_e,\theta + 90°)$$

$$f(r_m,\theta) = (r_m,\theta + 90°)$$

$$f(r_k,\theta) = (r_k,\theta + 90°)$$

a.   HS$_1$ b.   HS$_2$ c.   Rotations

4.2.3   Transition Unit

Hence the change between two postures of the hand can be specified as a set of movement functions that define the angular displacement at each of the joints involved. So the same formalism of rigid body transformations and path functions that lead to the movement function for a change in position of the whole hand can also be applied to the parts of the hand. To simplify the notation I adopt the movement function in (60).

(60)   Handshape Movement: $M(\vec{H}S_i) = HS_f,$
     where $M(\vec{H}S)$ represents a matrix of rigid body rotations
     that specifies the angular displacement of each bone segment
     involved in the movement.

Adopting $M(\vec{HS})$ as the movement function that defines the spatial unit for handshape, the transition unit and the principle of proportionality can be applied to handshape change. The transition unit for handshape change is given in (61).

(61) | Transition Unit for Handshape: $[\,HS_i, HS_f\,]_\Delta$

For example, the representation for the handshape change articulated for UNDERSTAND is given in (62).

(62) UNDERSTAND:

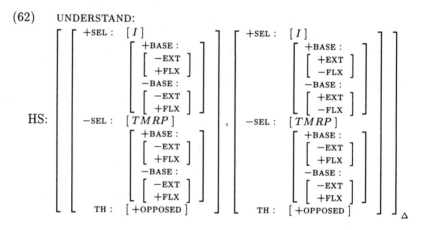

A simplified representation for the handshape change that uses the names of handshapes is given in (63).

(63) $HS : [S, G]_\Delta$

The combination of the representation in (62), the transition unit, and the principle of proportionality predicts that the gestures described in (64) are not well-formed signs.

(64) a. *(the second part of UNDERSTAND articulated twice as fast as the first part of the gesture)
b. *(the second part of UNDERSTAND articulated at only half the rate as the first part of the gesture)

Gestures like those in (64) are, in fact, ill-formed in ASL, so the analysis makes the correct predictions.

4.2.4 Doubled Transition Unit

The doubling function should also apply to handshape. As illustrated by (65), signs are articulated with repeated handshape change. At the start of (65) the fingers and thumb are curved. The hand is held in front of the signer with the palm facing to the side and the thumb-side of the hand facing up. To articulate the sign, the fingers and thumb tighten to form a fist. The gesture is articulated twice.

(65) MILK

The two small repeated gestures contrast with the ill-formed gestures described in (66).

(66) a. *(MILK articulated with one large opening and closing gesture, then with a small opening and closing gesture)

 b. *(MILK articulated with a small opening and closing of the hand, followed by a larger gesture)

The representation for (65) is given in (67).

(67) MILK

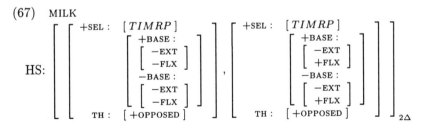

The representation in (67), in combination with the propositions for the doubled transition unit, and the principle of proportionality rule out the ill-formed gestures described in (66). So both the transition unit and doubled transition unit provide a correct account of the data.

4.2.5 Constraints on Handshape Change

Just as the transition unit for location is constrained by the properties of local signing space and the planes of articulation, so too there are constraints on handshape change. In previous accounts only a single handshape constraint has been proposed (Sandler 1989, Brentari 1990a). In this section I suggest that there is not just one, but several, constraints on handshape change.

As described in Chapter 2, a large set of handshapes occur in ASL. Based on the basic set of handshapes presented in Chapter 2, the chart in (68) depicts all logical possible sequences of those basic handshapes in ASL. The value in the left column specifies the initial handshape and the value in the top row specifies the final handshape. Where combinations occur in ASL, a sign name is given. If the combination is unattested in ASL, it is marked with an asterisk (*). An x indicates that the combination does not produce a handshape change.

(68)

Initial HS	Final HS						
	closed	curved-closed	flat-closed	curved	flat	flat-curved	open
closed	X	*	*	SHOCK	THROW	*	UNDER-STAND
curved-closed	*	X	*	*	*	*	*
flat-closed	*	*	X	*	SPRING	*	*
curved	MILK	BITE	*	X	*	*	*
flat	*	*	LIKE	*	X	*	*
flat-curved	*	*	*	*	*	X	*
open	MEMO-RIZE	*	*	*	*	WANT	X

As shown, not all handshape changes occur in ASL. Even though the chart in (68) does not take into account distributional differences based on selected fingers or repeated movements, it reveals a pattern of handshape change summarized in (69). The lines in (69) relate pairs of handshapes that participate in handshape changes with the arrowhead pointing to the final handshape.

(69)

Base Joint	Non-Base Joints		
	bent	neutral	straight
bent	*closed*	*curved-closed*	*flat-closed*
neutral	*1	*curved*	*flat*
straight	*2	*flat-curved*	*open*

Three patterns that emerge from (69) are summarized in (70). First, the handshapes with bent base joints never occur with each other in a handshape change. As indicated by (70a), a handshape change starting in a *closed* handshape and ending with a *curved-closed* handshape does not occur, nor do any other combinations of those handshapes. Second, three pairs of handshapes occur in handshape changes with each other but with no other handshapes, (70b). Third, the *closed* handshape occurs in combination with an *open*, *flat*, or *curved* handshape, and can be the final handshape if the initial handshape is *open* or *curved*, (70c).

(70) a. The following handshapes do not occur together in a handshape change: *closed, curved-closed, flat-closed*.

  b. *curved* → *curved-closed*
  flat ↔ *flat-closed*
  open → *flat-curved*

  c. *closed* → (*open, flat, curved*)
  (*open, curved*) → *closed*

The generalization in (70a) can be captured by a constraint that rules out combinations of handshape change in which both the initial and final handshape are handshapes with a bent base joint. Using joints and joint features, this is stated as (71).

(71) *([$Base$: +FLEX] → [$Base$: +FLEX])

Similar constraints can be stated on the other observed combinations, but the purpose of the section has been met. As mentioned above, the data in (68) is incomplete and opens areas for future investigation, yet it is still possible to see the need for more than one constraint on handshape change. Cross-linguistic study is crucial for testing the proposed feature set and constraints. Other factors that must be taken into account are the selected fingers that participate in the handshape changes, the relation between the fingers and thumb (discussed in more detail below), the relation between handshape and secondary movement, as well as interactions between these factors. Finally, the low occurrence of the handshapes presented here with the placeholders $*_1$ and $*_2$ requires further investigation to determine their role (if any) in other sign languages.

4.3   Change in Orientation

Arguments like those made for change in location and change in handshape can also be made for change in orientation.

4.3.1   The Data

The signs in (72) are articulated without changing the shape or location of the hand – only the orientation of the hand changes. To articulate (72a) the hand rotates from one position to another. The fingers and thumb of the moving hand are straight with the thumb at right angles to the fingers. The fingers and thumb of the static hand are wrapped loosely around the extended thumb, and the static hand is held so its palm faces down and the knuckles of the hand face away from the signer. At the start of the sign the fingertips of the moving hand point downward and the palm of the hand faces the signer. To articulate the sign the hand rotates, pivoting about the thumb until the fingertips point up and the palm faces away from the signer.

In (72b) the index finger is straight while the other fingers are curled against the palm and the thumb rests across them. The static hand is held with the palm facing down, and the forearm horizontal and parallel to the front of the body. The fingers and thumb of the static hand may be held in the same configuration as the moving hand, or may be relaxed in a neutral position. At the start of the sign the elbow of the moving arm rests on the back of the static hand, the fingertip points up, and the palm faces the side. To articulate the sign the forearm pivots about the elbow until the hand rests on the static forearm with the palm face down and the fingertip pointing to the side.

(72)   a. INCOMPETENT   b. DAY

In contrast to the well-formed signs in (72), the gestures described in (73) are physiologically possible but do not contribute to well-formed signs in ASL.

(73) a. *(INCOMPETENT articulated so fingertips point down, to the side, then up)
      b. *(second half of INCOMPETENT is twice as fast as the first part)
      c. *(second half of INCOMPETENT is half the speed of the first half)
      d. *(DAY articulated so arm moves to point fingertip away from signer, then to the side)
      e. *(second half of DAY is twice as fast as the first part)
      f. *(second half of DAY is half the speed of the first half)

In addition, recall from Chapter 2 that when the fingers are extended, there are two possible handshapes: (i) all of the joints are extended, and (ii) only the non-base joints are extended. With respect to the handshape in (72a), these related configurations are as shown in (74). In (74a) all the joints are extended and in (74b) the base joint is bent. The sign in (72a) can be pronounced with either hand configuration. As described above, if the hand configuration in (74a) is used, the whole hand rotates. But if the hand configuration in (74b) is used, at the start of the gesture the palm faces down and the fingertips point down. To articulate the sign the fingers rotate until they point upward. The physiology of the hand also forces it to rotate slightly during the last part of the gesture.

(74)   a. $\begin{bmatrix} +BASE & : & EXT \\ -BASE & : & EXT \end{bmatrix}$ b. $\begin{bmatrix} +BASE & : & FLEX \\ -BASE & : & EXT \end{bmatrix}$

The alternation of the sign between a pronunciation that uses the handshape in (74a) and one that uses the handshape in (74b) calls into question the possibility of representing the movement of the hand simply in terms of its palm orientation or handshape.

4.3.2   Rigid Body and Angular Translations

Just as for path movement, the signs in (72) are articulated with the displacement of the articulator from one place to another. But unlike path movement, which is characterized as a linear movement of the whole body from one place to another, the signs in (72) are characterized by an angular movement of a body about a pivot point. In this respect the movements in (72) resemble the movements of the bone segments about their respective joints that contribute to changes in handshape. Unlike handshape change, however, in this case only one body pivots.

Again, the part of the articulator that moves can be formalized as a rigid body and its movement can be represented as a *rigid body transformation*, specifically as a *rigid body rotation*. The angular displacement function, repeated as (75), captures the path of the rotation.

(75)

θ_k

r

Angular Displacement: $f(r, \theta) = (r, \theta + \theta_k)$

In this case only a single function need apply to the body that is moving. So the angular displacement for the movement of the fingers in INCOMPETENT is schematized in (76a), and the displacement of the forearm in DAY is schematized as (76b).

(76)

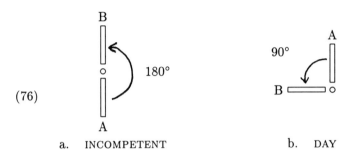

a.   INCOMPETENT   b.   DAY

4.3.3   Transition Unit

Adopting the movement function in (75), the transition unit for orientation change is specified in (77).

(77)

Transition Unit for Orientation:
$[\, OR_i(HP, LSS), OR_f(HP, LSS)\,]_\Delta$

The representations for the movements articulated in (72) are given in (78) and (79). The representation of the hand configuration used to articulate INCOMPETENT is given in (78a), and the transition unit that represents the change in orientation is in (78b).

(78)   a.   Hand Configuration for INCOMPETENT (B-handshape)

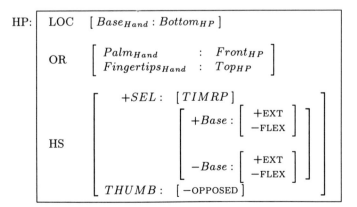

b. Transition Unit for INCOMPETENT

$$\left[\begin{array}{l} \left[\begin{array}{ll} Front_{HP}: & -Local_{LSS} \\ Top_{HP}: & +Base_{LSS} \end{array}\right], & \left[\begin{array}{ll} Front_{HP}: & +Local_{LSS} \\ Top_{HP}: & -Base_{LSS} \end{array}\right] \end{array}\right]_{\triangle}$$

The representation for the hand configuration to articulate DAY is given in (79a). The transition unit that represents the change in orientation is given in (79b). The notation *C-side* in (79b) stands for contralateral-side.

(79) a. Hand Configuration for DAY (G-handshape)

$$HP:\left[\begin{array}{l} LOC \quad [\,Elbow_{Hand}: Bottom_{HP}\,] \\[2ex] OR \quad \left[\begin{array}{lll} Palm_{Hand} & : & Front_{HP} \\ Fingertips_{Hand} & : & Top_{HP} \end{array}\right] \\[4ex] HS \quad \left[\begin{array}{l} +SEL: \;[\,I\,] \\ \qquad \left[\begin{array}{l} +Base: \left[\begin{array}{l} +\text{EXT} \\ -\text{FLEX} \end{array}\right] \\[2ex] -Base: \left[\begin{array}{l} +\text{EXT} \\ -\text{FLEX} \end{array}\right] \end{array}\right] \\[5ex] -SEL: \;[\,TMRP\,] \\ \qquad \left[\begin{array}{l} +Base: \left[\begin{array}{l} -\text{EXT} \\ +\text{FLEX} \end{array}\right] \\[2ex] -Base: \left[\begin{array}{l} -\text{EXT} \\ +\text{FLEX} \end{array}\right] \end{array}\right] \\[5ex] THUMB: \;[\,+\text{OPPOSED}\,] \end{array}\right] \end{array}\right]$$

b. Transition Unit for DAY

$$\left[\begin{array}{l} \left[\begin{array}{ll} Front_{HP}: & C\text{-}side_{LSS} \\ Top_{HP}: & -Base_{LSS} \end{array}\right], & \left[\begin{array}{ll} Front_{HP}: & +Base_{LSS} \\ Top_{HP}: & C\text{-}side_{LSS} \end{array}\right] \end{array}\right]_{\triangle}$$

In sum, by treating the hand as a single rigid body, the properties of a gesture articulated with a change in hand orientation can be captured by specifying the relation of the hand prism with respect to local signing space. Note, however, that the pivot point for articulating IN-COMPETENT is apparently the wrist, yet the pivot point for articulating DAY is the elbow. That is to say, to articulate the former, only the hand appears to rotate about the wrist, whereas to articulate the latter, the entire forearm rotates about the elbow. This information has been captured without argument by the *location* relation between the hand and hand prism in (78a) and (79a).

In the following section I present data to support this as the appropriate approach. As noted below, more work on (allophonic) variations of signs is required to fully understand the relation between articulator and hand prism.

4.3.4 Hand Prism Domain

As described above, the pronunciation for INCOMPETENT has a variant in which the fingers move about the base joint rather than the whole hand moving about the wrist. The data in (80) illustrate a sign articulated with a change in orientation which has three possible pronunciations.

To articulate (80a) the fingers and thumb are straight, the fingertips point up, the palm faces the signer, and the hand is held in front and slightly to the side of the signer. At the start of the sign the forearm is held away from the signer at a slight angle with respect to the signer. The forearm rotates about the elbow towards the signer until it can go no further. At that point the palm faces towards the signer's shoulder. The starting position for (80b) is similar to (80a). The hand is held in the same posture, but the forearm is held parallel with the front of the body. To articulate the sign the hand bends about the wrist moving towards the signer until it can go no further. The starting position for (80c) is the same as (80b). To articulate the sign the fingers bend at the knuckles towards the signer and stop when the fingertips are pointing toward the signer.

(80) a. PAST₁   b. PAST₂   c. PAST₃

To represent the properties of the gestures in (80) in terms of a transition unit, specifically a transition unit that captures a change in orientation as a rotation of the hand prism in local signing space, the hand prism might be specified as illustrated in (81). For the pronunciation in which the whole forearm rotates, the bottom of the hand prism associates with the elbow, (81a). For the pronunciation in which the hand rotates, the bottom of the hand prism associates with the wrist, (81b), and for the pronunciation in which only the fingers rotate, the bottom of the hand prism associates with the non-base joints, (81c).

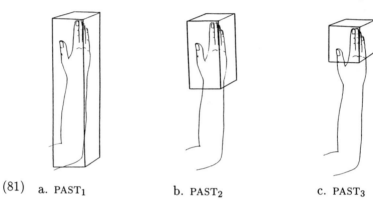

(81) a. PAST$_1$ b. PAST$_2$ c. PAST$_3$

Although signers appear to use the gestures in (81) interchangeably, it is not clear if the variants are predictable or in free variation. It is clear, however, that gestures like those described in (82) are not well-formed variations of the signs described.

(82) a. *(INCOMPETENT with fingers bending at the non-base joints)
      b. *(PAST with fingers bending at the non-base joints)

The contrast between the well-formed variants of the signs and the ill-formed but physiologically possible variants described in (82) can be captured by considering what appears to be an underlying phonetic hierarchy based on the physiological structure of the articulators, (83). The joint structure, (83a), is in this case more relevant than the bone structure in (83b). To account for the non-occurring variations in (82), the non-base joints are ruled out, as indicated by the parentheses in (83a). The variants that occur can be accounted for by specifying the highest joint in the hierarchy about which the change in orientation is articulated. For INCOMPETENT this will be the wrist, while for PAST it will be the elbow. Variations can be accounted for by allowing change in orientation to apply to joints lower in the hierarchy than specified in the underlying representation.

(83) a. Joints: *Shoulder*   b. Bones: *Upper-arm*

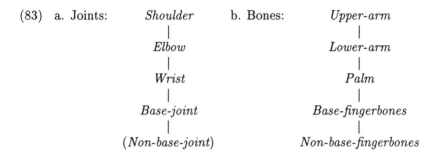

This proposal presents a possible approach for formulating the basis of a theory of visual phonetics.[15]

4.3.5   Doubled Transition Unit

Capturing the properties of change in orientation with the *transition unit* implies that the doubling function, which correctly captures the properties of changes in location and handshape, must also apply to changes in orientation. This is indeed the case, as illustrated by the sign in (84).

In (84) the fingers and thumb are bent into a fist. The palm faces away from the signer with the knuckles facing upward. To articulate the sign the hand rotates forward at the wrist through a small (about 30°) angle, returns to its original position, and then repeats the rotating movement.

(84)   YES

---

[15]Crasborn (1995) makes an initial proposal towards a visual phonetics.

This repeated movement is captured by the representation in (85). The orientation relation between the hand and hand prism is given in (85a), and the doubled transition unit is specified in (85b). Although the transition unit in (85b) captures a 90° change in the orientation of the hand, the propositions for the doubled transition unit, along with the principle of proportionality provide the reduced form of the gesture that is described for (84).

(85) a.   Hand Configuration for YES (S-handshape)

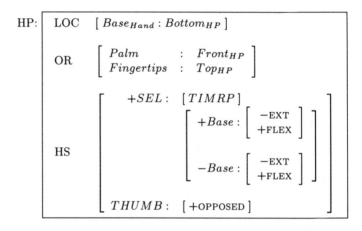

b.   Transition Unit for YES

$$\left[\left[\begin{array}{ll} Front_{HP}: & +Local_{LSS} \\ Top_{HP}: & -Base_{LSS} \end{array}\right], \left[\begin{array}{ll} Front_{HP}: & +Base_{LSS} \\ Top_{HP}: & +Local_{LSS} \end{array}\right]\right]_{2\Delta}$$

The representation in (85) rules out non-occurring but physiologically possible gestures like the ones described in (86).

(86)   a.   *(YES with a 90° rotation, followed by a 30° rotation)
       b.   *(YES with a 30° rotation, followed by a 90° rotation)
       c.   *(YES with the second rotation twice as fast as the first)

Thus the model provides the correct interpretation for repeated movements that involve a change in orientation.

4.3.6   Constraint on Orientation Change

Without giving it explicit consideration, the preceding discussion about the representation of change in orientation has captured a constraint on change in orientation. Namely, that a change in orientation for a simple sign is restricted to one rotation about a single axis. The data in (87) highlight this constraint.

Recall that the sign DAY is articulated by the forearm, with its elbow resting on the back of the static hand, rotating through a 90° angle. (87) describes gestures that are physiologically possible but that do not occur in well-formed signs. In (87a) a side-to-side rotation of the forearm is combined with its forward rotation, and in (87b) the rotation of the finger is combined with forearm rotation.

(87)   a.   *(DAY articulated with forearm rotating so that palm faces out at end of sign)
       b.   *(index finger rotates forward about knuckle as DAY is pronounced)

In fact, a transition unit of orientation applies to a single specification of the hand prism in local signing space, so it automatically rules out the gesture described in (87b). And the movement function for the transition unit of orientation specifies an angular displacement along a single dimension, so a change in the position of the hand that requires rotations about two axes, as in (87a), is also ruled out. Hence, both ill-formed gestures in (87) are ruled out by the properties of the formalism.

Moving On

In this chapter the rigid body representation of the hand from Chapter 2 has been combined with the spatial constructs from Chapter 3 to produce a formal representation of movement – the *transition unit*. Although superficially similar to previous analyses, in that the *transition unit* is a phonological unit capturing properties of movement just as the autosegment M is used in previous accounts to represent sign movement (Liddell and Johnson 1989, Perlmutter 1989, Sandler 1989, Brentari 1990b), this proposal is significant because it lays the groundwork for moving beyond simply descriptive feature-based representations for the set of properties associated with sign movements.

In this chapter I demonstrated that a cornerstone of the argument for movement as a unit, namely that path shapes are phonologically distinctive and, therefore, can be represented by path features, is untenable. Asymmetries between path movements that cannot be explained when movement is treated as an atomic phonological construct are explained by a transition-based analysis.

The key to this proposal has been to present explicit arguments for the phonological representation of each component of the sign – namely the rigid body representation of the hand and the geometric representation of signing space – and then to apply appropriate principles of physics to combine those components into a representation that captures the properties of sign movements. Unlike previous feature-based proposals which must rely on a proliferation of descriptive terms (e.g., "accelerated", "tense", "fast", "slow") to capture the properties of signs, the transition-based representation provides basic building blocks (representations of time, space, and body) to more accurately represent signs. Although a complete analysis is beyond the scope of this work, in the following chapters suggestions are made to indicate that the transition-based representation will be particularly fruitful when applied to puzzles of morphologically complex signs such as verbal and adjectival modulations which exploit the relations between body, time, and space available to the manual articulators.

But the transition unit not only accounts for the properties of movement in sign, it also unifies the three basic types of "movement" – change in location, change in handshape, and change in orientation. The rigid body representation of the manual articulators that captures the bending of a finger in the same way as the bending of the wrist is crucial to this result. In addition, the references in this chapter to the relation between bones and joints in this representation points directly towards an approach to a theory of visual phonetics to complement this representation of visual phonology.

In the next chapter I finish laying the groundwork for a formal representation of the simple sign by arguing for a phonological unit that coordinates the simultaneously articulated parts of the sign.

5

The Cell

With the *transition unit* in place to capture the properties of movement, I turn now to address the representation of the whole sign gesture. I argue for a construct, the *cell*, to account for the characteristics of the maximum and minimum sign gesture. I then show that the *cell* captures the properties of a set of complex signs, specifically agreement verbs. I present an analysis of a set of agreement verbs traditionally referred to as "backward" agreement verbs, arguing that there is really nothing backwards about them. A transition-based analysis provides a unified picture of agreement verbs.

In the process, I extend the coverage of the *cell* to complex signs, thus unifying the phonological representation of simple and complex signs. Morphologically, two levels of representation emerge – (i) a verb *root* and (ii) a verb *frame* that, strikingly unlike spoken language morphemes, are articulated simultaneously. The verb root provides information that corresponds to properties of local signing space, forming the inner verbal morphology, while the verb frame represents the location and agreement morphemes which correspond to properties of global signing space, forming the outer morphology. Hence, in a result unique to visual phonology, the work here suggests that "embedded" constructs of signing space bear a more literal correspondence to what has been treated metaphorically in spoken language as "embedded" levels of morphological structure.

5.1 Simple Signs

In the previous chapter I focused on simple signs with only one type of movement. However, simple signs can also be articulated with more than one movement. For example, the sign in (1) is articulated with both a change in location and a change in handshape.

The hand starts with the index, ring, and pinky fingers straight. The thumb and index finger are straight at the middle and end joints but bent slightly at the knuckles. All the fingers are slightly spread. The palm of the hand faces the signer and the tips of the fingers point to the side. The hand starts with both the thumb and middle finger resting lightly at the center of the chest. To articulate the sign the hand moves away from the chest for a few inches along a straight path while the thumb and middle finger move together until their tips touch. Both movements start at the same time and progress at the same rate so that the tips of the thumb and middle finger touch just as the movement away from the chest ends.

(1)   LIKE

The well-formed sign in (1) contrasts with gestures like those described in (2).

(2)   a.   *(movement away from chest ends before handshape change)
        b.   *(handshape change ends before movement away from chest)
        c.   *(hand changes shape, then moves away from chest)
        d.   *(hand moves away from chest, then changes shape)

The contrast between the data in (1) and (2) is generalized in (3).

(3)   In a well-formed sign simultaneous movements start together and end together, and progress at the same rate.

As argued in the preceding chapter, the transition unit is the appropriate phonological construct to capture each of the changes described for the well-formed sign in (1). Specifically, the fully specified transition units in (4) capture the change in handshape, (4a), and the change in location, (4b), used to articulate the movements in (1). (4a) includes the joint specifications for each of the handshapes involved in the transition. (4b) includes the location specification for each level of signing space. Local signing space is located at the center of the chest. The hand, situated in the hand prism so that the palm is associated with the front of the hand prism, moves from the base plane of local signing space which is in contact with the chest to the opposite plane which is in front of the chest.

(4) a. Change in Handshape for LIKE:

HS:

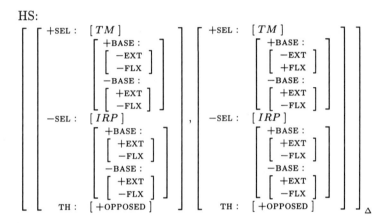

b. Change in Location for LIKE:

$$\left[LOC \quad [+Base_{LSS} : Center(Chest)_{GSS}] \quad \left[LOC \quad [Front_{HP} : +Base_{LSS}, -Base_{LSS}]_\Delta \quad \left[LOC \quad [Palm_{hand} : Front_{HP}] \right] \right] \right]$$

Simplified representations for the changes in (4) are given in (5).

(5) a. $HS : [\text{OPEN-8}, \text{CLOSED-8}]_\Delta$

b. $LOC_{LSS} : [Front_{HP} : +Base_{LSS}, -Base_{LSS}]_\Delta$

The orientation of the hand does not change during the articulation of the sign, and is captured by the static representation in (6).

(6)   Static Orientation for LIKE:

$$
\left[
\begin{array}{l}
OR \left[
\begin{array}{l}
+Base_{LSS} : Back_{GSS} \\
+Local_{LSS} : Top_{GSS}
\end{array}
\right] \\
\quad \left[
OR \left[
\begin{array}{l}
Front_{HP} : +Base_{LSS} \\
Top_{HP} : +Local_{LSS}
\end{array}
\right]
\right] \\
\quad\quad \left[
\left[
OR \left[
\begin{array}{l}
Palm_{Hand} : Front_{HP} \\
Th\text{-}Side_{Hand} : Top_{HP}
\end{array}
\right]
\right]
\right]
\end{array}
\right]
$$

To combine these representations for handshape, location, and orientation into a full representation of the sign gesture that captures the generalization in (3), I define the *cell*, a phonological construct that organizes the spatial and temporal properties of a sign.

5.1.1   The Cell

As stated in (3), the most significant observation about the sign in (1) is that the changes used to articulate it are simultaneous and proportional. To organize the information presented in (4) and (6) to represent the sign gesture, I define the *cell* as in (7). The *cell* coordinates the temporal and spatial information needed to define the sign gesture, ensuring that the initial values of the hand and its relations in space are associated with the start of the gesture and, likewise, that the final values of the hand and space are associated with the end of the gesture.

(7)

> (i)   A *cell* consists of a *time unit*, T, associated with a set of *transition units*.
>
> (ii)   The *time unit*, T, represents a duration of time that starts at time t_i and ends at t_f.
>
> (iii)   The set of *transition units* represents the spatial properties of a sign gesture, and consists of the configuration of the *manual articulator* and its spatial relations, *location* and *orientation*.
>
> (iv)   The temporal and transition units are associated so that the *manual articulator* assumes all initial spatial positions at t_i and all final spatial positions at t_f.

The notation for the *cell* is given in (8). The nested structure of the cell reflects the spatial organization of the manual articulators in signing space. When the structure includes transition units, the outer left brackets represent the initial time, t_i, and the outer right brackets represent the final time, t_f.

(8)   *Cell* Structure:

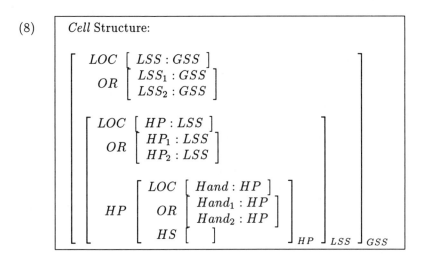

Combining the transition units for handshape and location, and the static information for orientation given above for LIKE, the cellular representation of the sign is given in (9).

(9)   LIKE:

$$
\begin{bmatrix}
\begin{bmatrix}
LOC & \begin{bmatrix} +Base_{LSS} : Center(Chest)_{GSS} \end{bmatrix} \\
OR & \begin{bmatrix} +Base_{LSS} : Back_{GSS} \\ +Local_{LSS} : Top_{GSS} \end{bmatrix}
\end{bmatrix} \\[3em]
\begin{bmatrix}
LOC & \begin{bmatrix} Front_{HP} : +Base_{LSS}, -Base_{LSS} \end{bmatrix}_{\Delta} \\
OR & \begin{bmatrix} Front_{HP} : +Base_{LSS} \\ Top_{HP} : +Local_{LSS} \end{bmatrix}
\end{bmatrix} \\[3em]
HP \begin{bmatrix}
LOC & \begin{bmatrix} Palm_{Hand} : Front_{HP} \end{bmatrix} \\
OR & \begin{bmatrix} Palm_{Hand} : Front_{HP} \\ Th\text{-}Side_{Hand} : Top_{HP} \end{bmatrix} \\
HS & \begin{bmatrix} \text{OPEN-8, CLOSED-8} \end{bmatrix}_{\Delta}
\end{bmatrix}
\end{bmatrix}
$$

The spatial and temporal properties of the transition units, marked by the subscript Δ, are coordinated by the principles in (7). Both transitions start at t_i and end at t_f, and the Principle of Proportionality applies to each of the transition units ensuring that the changes occur at the same rate. Hence, the combination of the representation for LIKE in (9) and the propositions that define the *cell* rule out the ill-formed gestures described in (2) while accounting for the well-formed properties of the sign in (1). The *cell* is crucial to this analysis, therefore it is adopted into the model.

In addition, two-handed signs of the type referred to by Sandler (1989) as *double dez*, and subject to Battison's (1978) symmetry condition can also be represented by the cell.[1] Because it is beyond the scope of the current discussion, I adopt the feature [TWO-HAND] without further argument to specify a symmetric two-handed sign.[2] When included in the cellular representation of a cell, the feature invokes a set of properties that account for the symmetric properties of the sign, where by *symmetry* I mean geometry based properties that hold on the hands and their relation in signing space. It is in the context of these symmetric two-handed signs that the rigid body transformation *reflection* is relevant.

5.1.2 Maximum Simple Sign

Logically, the cell structure for the simple sign allows up to three simultaneous transition units. In this section I argue that a cell can have at most two transition units per simple sign.

5.1.2.1 Two Transition Units

The signs in (10) are articulated with two simultaneous changes. (10a) is articulated with a simultaneous change in handshape and change in location, (10b) with simultaneous changes in handshape and orientation, and (10c) with simultaneous changes in orientation and location.

(10a) is described in the previous section. At the start of (10b) the hand is held in front of the signer with the thumb and all the fingers held straight and slightly spread. The fingertips point away from the signer and the palm faces down. To articulate the sign two movements are made simultaneously: (i) all the joints of the index finger and thumb

---

[1] "The Symmetry Condition states that (a) If both hands of a sign move independently during its articulation, then (b) both hands must be specified for the same location, the same handshape, the same movement (whether performed simultaneously or in alternation), and the specifications for orientation must be either symmetrical or identical." (Battison 1978:33).

[2] Some notes about the representation of two-handed signs in this model are made at the end of this chapter, Section 5.3.1.

bend until their tips touch to form a small circle, and (ii) the hand bends at the wrist, so that at the end of the gesture the palm of the hand faces away from the signer. Both movements start at the same time and progress at the same rate so that the finger and thumb tips touch at the same time that the hand completes its upward movement.

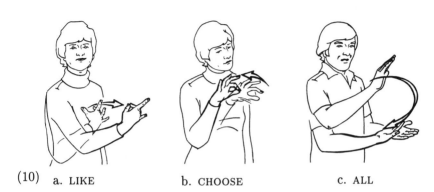

(10) a. LIKE   b. CHOOSE   c. ALL

(10c) is articulated with two hands. The fingers of the static hand are straight and together. The thumb is straight and in a relaxed position parallel to the palm of the hand. The static hand is held in front of the signer with the fingertips pointing away from the signer at about a 45° angle with respect to the front of the body and the palm facing up. The fingers and thumb of the moving hand are held in the same posture as the static hand. The moving hand starts with the fingertips pointing away from the signer and at a 90° angle with respect to the static hand. The palm faces down and the hand hovers a few inches above the static hand. To articulate the sign the hand simultaneously moves down towards the static hand while rotating so the palm ends facing upward. Both the downward movement and the rotation start at the same time, and continue at the same rate, so that the palm is facing up at the same time that its back comes to rest on the static hand.

The signs in (10) contrast with the physiologically possible gestures described in (11). In each case the gesture is similar to one of the well-formed signs but with a third movement added.

(11) a. * (articulate LIKE so the palm faces in at the start of the gesture and down at the end of the articulation)
      b. * (articulate CHOOSE while moving the hand from one location to another)
      c. * (articulate ALL so the hand changes shape between the beginning and end of the sign)

The difference between the well-formed signs in (10) and the gestures described in (11) is that the former are articulated with only two simultaneous changes, whereas the latter are articulated with three. This contrast is generalized in (12).

(12)   A well-formed simple sign is articulated with at most two simultaneous movements.

The generalization in (12) can be formalized by the proposition in (13) stated in terms of cell structure.

(13) | A well-formed cell consists of at most two transition units. |

Notationally, the constraint in (13) can be expressed as in (14).

(14) $$* \quad \begin{bmatrix} X: & [\ ]_\Delta \\ Y: & [\ ]_\Delta \\ Z: & [\ ]_\Delta \end{bmatrix}_{Cell}$$

The cellular representations for the signs in (10) are given in (15). Note in (15c) that the location relation between local signing space and global signing space includes a reference to the static hand, abbreviated as $H2$. Unfortunately, work on signs articulated with two hands is beyond the scope of the current discussion. In an elaborated representation of a two-handed sign, $H2$ would refer to a hand prism that captures the characteristics of the hand as a place of articulation.[3] The specification for $H2$ would include its handshape, and relevant location and orientation relations.

(15a) includes transition units for handshape and location, (15b) is specified for transition units for location and handshape, and (15c) is specified for transition units for location and orientation. Note that the transition units are all specified within local signing space. The relation between local signing space and global signing space is constant during the articulation of a simple sign. This contrasts significantly with the representation of morphologically complex signs (Section 5.2) like agreement verbs for which the transition units capture changes in the relation between local and global signing space.

---

[3]See Section 5.3.1 for a brief discussion about two-handed signs.

(15) a. LIKE:

$$\begin{bmatrix} LOC & \begin{bmatrix} OR & \begin{bmatrix} +Base_{LSS} : Center(Chest)_{GSS} \\ +Base_{LSS} : Back_{GSS} \\ +Local_{LSS} : Top_{GSS} \end{bmatrix} \end{bmatrix} \\[2em] \begin{bmatrix} LOC & \begin{bmatrix} OR & \begin{bmatrix} Front_{HP} : +Base_{LSS}, -Base_{LSS} \end{bmatrix}_{\Delta} \\ Front_{HP} : +Base_{LSS} \\ Top_{HP} : +Local_{LSS} \end{bmatrix} \end{bmatrix} \\[2em] \begin{bmatrix} HP & \begin{bmatrix} LOC & \begin{bmatrix} OR & \begin{bmatrix} Palm_{Hand} : Front_{HP} \\ Palm_{Hand} : Front_{HP} \\ Th\text{-}Side_{Hand} : Top_{HP} \end{bmatrix} \end{bmatrix} \\ HS & \begin{bmatrix} \text{OPEN-8, CLOSED-8} \end{bmatrix}_{\Delta} \end{bmatrix} \end{bmatrix} \end{bmatrix}$$

b. CHOOSE:

$$\begin{bmatrix} LOC & \begin{bmatrix} OR & \begin{bmatrix} +Base_{LSS} : Neutral_{GSS} \\ +Base_{LSS} : Bottom_{GSS} \\ +Local_{LSS} : Back_{GSS} \end{bmatrix} \end{bmatrix} \\[2em] \begin{bmatrix} LOC & \begin{bmatrix} OR & \begin{bmatrix} Bottom_{HP} : +Local_{LSS} \\ Front_{HP} : +Base_{LSS}, -Local_{LSS} \\ Top_{HP} : -Local_{LSS}, -Base_{LSS} \end{bmatrix}_{\Delta} \end{bmatrix} \\[2em] \begin{bmatrix} HP & \begin{bmatrix} LOC & \begin{bmatrix} OR & \begin{bmatrix} Base_{Hand} : Bottom_{HP} \\ Palm_{Hand} : Front_{HP} \\ F\text{-}tips_{Hand} : Top_{HP} \end{bmatrix} \end{bmatrix} \\ HS & \begin{bmatrix} \text{OPEN-9, CLOSED-9} \end{bmatrix}_{\Delta} \end{bmatrix} \end{bmatrix} \end{bmatrix}$$

c. ALL:

$$\begin{bmatrix} LOC & \begin{bmatrix} OR & \begin{bmatrix} +Base_{LSS} : H2_{GSS} \\ +Base_{LSS} : Bottom_{GSS} \\ +Local_{LSS} : Back_{GSS} \end{bmatrix} \end{bmatrix} \\[2em] \begin{bmatrix} LOC & \begin{bmatrix} OR & \begin{bmatrix} Back_{HP} : -Base_{LSS}, +Base_{LSS} \end{bmatrix}_{\Delta} \\ Front_{HP} : +Base_{LSS}, -Base_{LSS} \\ Top_{HP} : -Local_{LSS}, -Local_{LSS} \end{bmatrix}_{\Delta} \end{bmatrix} \\[2em] \begin{bmatrix} HP & \begin{bmatrix} LOC & \begin{bmatrix} OR & \begin{bmatrix} Base_{Hand} : Bottom_{HP} \\ Palm_{Hand} : Front_{HP} \\ F\text{-}tips_{Hand} : Top_{HP} \end{bmatrix} \end{bmatrix} \\ HS & \begin{bmatrix} \text{B} \end{bmatrix} \end{bmatrix} \end{bmatrix} \end{bmatrix}$$

By (13) the cell structures in (15) are acceptable well-formed signs because each cell includes only two transition units. In contrast, the gestures described in (11) are ruled out by (13). Thus the proposition in (13) provides a correct analysis for the data, so it is adopted into the model. A similar constraint holds on doubled unit transitions.

5.1.2.2 Doubled Transition Units

The signs in (16) are articulated with repeated changes in either hand-shape or orientation and a single change in location.

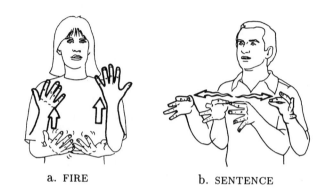

(16) a. FIRE   b. SENTENCE

In (16a) both hands are held a few inches apart in front of the upper chest. All the fingers and thumbs are straight and slightly spread. The fingertips point upward and the palms of the hands face the signer's chest. To articulate the sign the hands move upward in a straight line while the fingers wiggle. The fingerwiggling starts when the upward movement starts and ends when the upward movement stops, after the hands have moved so they are approximately in front of the signer's face. In general, the hands articulate about two cycles of the finger-waving that is characteristic of fingerwiggling.

In (16b) the thumb and index finger of both hands are curved so their tips touch while the other fingers are straight. The fingertips of both hands face away from the signer and the palms of the hands face the side (so they face each other) in the center of the space in front of the signer. To articulate the sign the hands move away from each other along a straight path for a few inches while the hands rotate back and forth so the palms alternate between facing each other and facing about a 45° angle with respect to the floor. The hands articulate about two cycles of the rotating movement. The movements start at the same time and progress at a constant rate so that the end of the second cycle of rotating coincides with the end of the movement away from the center.

The movements in both signs in (16) start together and end together. This contrasts with the physiologically possible but unacceptable gestures described in (17). Similar unacceptable combinations of the two types of movement can be described for SENTENCE.

(17)   a.   *(FIRE articulated with wiggling, followed by upward movement)

          b.   *(FIRE articulated with upward movement, followed by wiggling)

          c.   *(FIRE articulated with wiggling for half of upward movement)

          d.   *(FIRE articulated with one wiggle, upward movement, then second wiggle)

Each of the well-formed signs in (16) is articulated with repeated movement that is distributed proportionally with respect to the single change in location. In contrast, the movements in the gestures described in (17) are distributed disproportionately with respect to the overall gesture. This observation is captured by the generalization in (18).

(18)   In a well-formed sign gesture, a repeated movement is distributed proportionally with respect to a non-repeated movement.

The well-formed signs in (16) also contrast with gestures like those described in (19).

(19)   a.   *(Repeated change in location articulated simultaneously with single change in handshape)

          b.   *(Repeated change in location articulated simultaneously with single change in orientation)

          c.   *(Repeated change in handshape and single change in orientation)

          d.   *(Repeated change in orientation and single change in handshape)

          e.   *(Repeated change in two properties)

The difference between the data in (16) and (19) is that the ill-formed gestures include either repeated changes in location, (19a) and (19b), repeated changes in handshape or orientation without a single change in location, (19c) and (19d), or two repeated changes, (19e). In short, the only well-formed combination is one that includes a single change in location. This observation is generalized in (20).

(20) If a well-formed sign is articulated with a repeated gesture and a simultaneous non-repeated gesture, then the latter must be a change in location.

The proposition in (21) captures the generalizations in (20) and (18).

(21) A well-formed cell that includes a doubled transition unit may include at most a transition unit of location.

Notationally, the constraint in (21) can be expressed as in (22).

(22) Maximum Sign Structure:

$$\begin{bmatrix} LOC: & [\ ]_\Delta \\ X: & [\ ]_{2\Delta} \\ Y: & [\ ] \end{bmatrix}_{LSS} , \text{ where } X \text{ is } OR \text{ or } HP.$$

The cellular representations for the signs in (16) are given in (23).[4]

(23) a.   FIRE:

$$\begin{bmatrix} \begin{bmatrix} LOC \\ OR \end{bmatrix} \begin{bmatrix} +Base_{LSS}: Neutral_{GSS} \\ +Local_{LSS}: Back_{GSS} \\ +Base_{LSS}: Bottom_{GSS} \end{bmatrix} \\ \\ \begin{bmatrix} LOC \\ OR \end{bmatrix} \begin{bmatrix} Bottom_{HP}: +Base_{LSS}, -Base_{LSS} \\ Front_{HP}: +Local_{LSS} \\ Top_{HP}: -Base_{LSS} \end{bmatrix}_\Delta \\ \\ \begin{bmatrix} HP \end{bmatrix} \begin{bmatrix} LOC \\ OR \\ HS \end{bmatrix} \begin{bmatrix} Base_{Hand}: Bottom_{HP} \\ Palm_{Hand}: Front_{HP} \\ F\text{-}tips_{Hand}: Top_{HP} \\ 5,\ 5 \end{bmatrix}_{2\Delta} \end{bmatrix}$$

---

[4]Note that the fingerwiggling in (23a) is represented as a repeated change in handshape between the same handshapes. An argument for this approach is presented in Uyechi (1993a).

b.   SENTENCE:

$$
\left[
\begin{array}{l}
LOC \quad
\left[
\begin{array}{l}
+Base_{LSS} : Neutral_{GSS} \\
OR \quad +Base_{LSS} : Bottom_{GSS} \\
 +Local_{LSS} : Back_{GSS}
\end{array}
\right] \\[4ex]
\left[
\begin{array}{l}
LOC \quad
\left[
\begin{array}{l}
Front_{HP} : +Center_{LSS}, -Center_{LSS}
\end{array}
\right]_{\Delta} \\
OR \quad
\left[
\begin{array}{l}
Front_{HP} : C\text{-}Side_{LSS}, +Base_{LSS} \\
Top_{HP} : -Local_{LSS}, -Local_{LSS}
\end{array}
\right]_{2\Delta}
\end{array}
\right] \\[6ex]
HP \quad
\left[
\begin{array}{l}
LOC \quad
\left[
\begin{array}{l}
Base_{Hand} : Bottom_{HP}
\end{array}
\right] \\
OR \quad
\left[
\begin{array}{l}
Palm_{Hand} : Front_{HP} \\
F\text{-}tips_{Hand} : Top_{HP}
\end{array}
\right] \\
HS \;\; [\; F \;] \\
[\; 2\text{-}HAND \;]
\end{array}
\right]
\end{array}
\right]
$$

The representation in (23) complies with the proposition in (21), whereas the ill-formed gestures in (17) and (19) do not. Hence the proposition in (21) correctly accounts for the data. The proposition is crucial to the analysis, so it is adopted into the model.

In sum, the propositions in (13) and (21) define the constraints on the maximum simple sign. On the other side of the spectrum, there is also a minimum requirement on the sign gesture.

5.1.3   Minimum Sign Gesture

Recall the proposition from Chapter 2, repeated as (24).

(24)   To articulate a *sign gesture* the *manual articulator* moves.

The minimum movement of the sign gesture has been characterized as "epenthetic movement" in representations that do not specify the movement underlyingly if it is predictable as a straight movement of the hand from one place to another (e.g., Brentari 1990b). In this section I present other evidence for such "epenthetic" movement, and formalize a representation for it as the minimum cell that defines a sign.

The hand configuration in (25) is the handshape used in the manual alphabet to represent the letter W. It is articulated with the index, middle, and ring fingers extended and pointing upward while the tips of the thumb and pinky finger touch in front of the palm of the hand.

(25)   W

In isolation, (25) is articulated with a short straight movement of the hand away from the body, as if to present the hand and convey the meaning associated with the handshape.

The movement for (25) contrasts with the alternatives in (26) that could also be used to present the handshape. (26a) describes a change in handshape and (26b) describes a change in orientation. However, neither possibility is used. In fact, (26b) is the gesture used to articulate the number sign SIXTEEN. Of the possible transitions, change in location is a neutral movement.

(26)   a.   *(change handshape from closed fist to W)
        b.   *(start W-handshape with palm facing signer, then
              turn hand away from signer)

The difference between the gestures in (25) and (26) can be generalized as (27).

(27)   The default movement of a sign is a straight forward movement.

In light of the proposition in (24), the movement allows the handshapes to be pronounced.[5] The proposition in (28) captures the generalization in (27).

(28) | The minimum structure of a well-formed gesture is:

$$\begin{bmatrix} LOC : & [\ ]_\Delta \\ OR : & [\ ] \\ HP : & [\ ] \end{bmatrix}$$

---

[5]This could be viewed as analogous to saying the letters of the alphabet in English, where the pronounced name of a letter conforms to English syllable structure.

In sum, the cell is a phonological construct that organizes the transition units and provides the necessary structure to specify the minimum and maximum constraints on a sign gesture. As shown in the following section, it is also relevant to the representation of complex signs.

5.2 Agreement Verbs

In this section I extend the discussion to complex signs to demonstrate the potential power of the *cell* and *transition unit*. As mentioned before, it is at this level of morphological complexity that the relation between the local and global signing spaces is crucial.

The focus of this analysis is the set of *agreement verbs*, a class of verbs in ASL so called because they include person agreement (Padden 1988). As illustrated by (29), person information in ASL is established by assigning meaning to specific areas in signing space. First person is associated with the area around the signer, second person with the area directly in front of the signer, and third person in other areas of the signing space.[6] For example, if a signer points her index finger at herself (with all other fingers curled against the palm and the thumb resting on them), the gesture is interpreted as the first person pronoun, pointing away but directly in front of herself is second person, and pointing in any other area is interpreted as a reference to a third person. The identity of the third person referent is established by first presenting a noun or name and then pointing to the area in space to be associated with that referent.

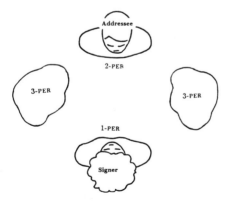

(29)   Person Agreement

---

[6]Although Meier (1990) argues for a distinction between first and non-first person, I assume the three-way person distinction.

The meaning of agreement verbs like the one in (30) are dependent on these spatial interpretations. In (30) the index finger is straight while the other fingers are curled against the palm and the thumb rests on top of them. The tip of the index finger points up. The palm of the hand faces towards a third person referent and the back of the hand faces the signer. For convenience, I adopt the terms *subject* and *object* to refer to the signer and the third person referent, respectively.[7] To articulate the sign the hand moves from the signer towards the third person referent while the middle and end joint of the index finger bend into a curved position. The movements are coordinated so they start at the same time, progress at the same rate, and end at the same time. The gesture means *I ask her/him*.

(30)   1-ASK-3

An acceptable variation of the sign in (30) is to articulate the change in the handshape without moving the hand towards the object of the verb. Unacceptable variations of the (30) are described in (31).

(31) a.   *(movement towards object ends before handshape change)
      b.   *(handshape change ends before movement towards object)
      c.   *(handshape changes, then hand moves towards object)
      d.   *(hand moves towards object, then handshape changes)

The unacceptable variations in (31) are similar to variations that were excluded for morphologically simple signs by adopting the *cell.*

---

[7]Padden (1988) presents arguments for these grammatical functions. However, as argued here for phonology, sign language grammar also needs to be analyzed in a similar non-transfer-and-test fashion before grammatical functions like *subject* and *object* can be adopted into a theoretical framework for sign language syntax.

Representing the agreement verb in (30) as a cellular structure provides the same result.

The cellular representation for 1-ASK-3 is given in (32). As noted before, the transition units for the monomorphemic signs described in the previous section impact only the characteristics of the sign within local signing space. In contrast, the transition unit for the agreement verb affects the relation between local and global signing space where the relevant locations in global signing space are represented here as 1-PER and 3-PER.

(32)   1-ASK-3:

$$
\left[
\begin{array}{l}
\left[
\begin{array}{l}
LOC \left[\ +Base_{LSS} : \text{1-PER}_{GSS}, \text{3-PER}_{GSS}\ \right]_{\Delta} \\
OR \left[
\begin{array}{l}
+Local_{LSS} : \text{1-PER}_{GSS} \\
-Local_{LSS} : \text{3-PER}_{GSS}
\end{array}
\right]
\end{array}
\right] \\
\left[
\begin{array}{l}
LOC \left[\ Bottom_{HP} : +Base_{LSS}\ \right] \\
OR \left[
\begin{array}{l}
Front_{HP} : -Local_{LSS} \\
Top_{HP} : -Base_{LSS}
\end{array}
\right]
\end{array}
\right] \\
\left[
\begin{array}{l}
HP \left[
\begin{array}{l}
LOC \left[
\begin{array}{l}
Base_{Hand} : Bottom_{HP} \\
OR \quad Palm_{Hand} : Front_{HP} \\
F\text{-}tip_{Hand} : Top_{HP}
\end{array}
\right] \\
HS \left[\ 1, \text{x}\ \right]_{\Delta}
\end{array}
\right]
\end{array}
\right]
\end{array}
\right]
$$

5.2.1   Morpho-Phonology of Agreement Verbs

An alternative pronunciation of 1-ASK-3 is articulated without the forward movement of the hand. The representation for that variation is given in (33a). It is the same as the representation in (32) but without the transition unit for location. That (32) and (33a) have the same meaning indicates that the crucial information for interpreting the sign must be available in the sparser of the two representations, namely (33a). Note that the orientation relation between local and global signing space provides redundant information, capturing a specific relation between the palm side of the hand facing the third person referent and the back of the hand facing the first person. Changing the orientation relation, as in (33b), has the effect of changing the meaning of the gesture to *he/she asks me.*

(33)   a.   1-ASK-3:

$$
\left[
\begin{array}{l}
\left[LOC \atop OR \right]
\left[
\begin{array}{l}
+Base_{LSS} : Neutral_{GSS} \\
+Local_{LSS} : \text{1-PER}_{GSS} \\
-Local_{LSS} : \text{3-PER}_{GSS}
\end{array}
\right] \\[6pt]
\left[
\begin{array}{l}
\left[LOC \atop OR \right]
\left[
\begin{array}{l}
Bottom_{HP} : +Base_{LSS} \\
Front_{HP} : -Local_{LSS} \\
Top_{HP} : -Base_{LSS}
\end{array}
\right] \\[6pt]
\left[HP \right]
\left[
\begin{array}{l}
\left[LOC \atop OR \right]
\left[
\begin{array}{l}
Base_{Hand} : Bottom_{HP} \\
Palm_{Hand} : Front_{HP} \\
F\text{-}tip_{Hand} : Top_{HP}
\end{array}
\right] \\
HS \left[1,\ \text{x} \right]_\Delta
\end{array}
\right]
\end{array}
\right]
\end{array}
\right]
$$

   b.   3-ASK-1

$$
\left[
\begin{array}{l}
\left[LOC \atop OR \right]
\left[
\begin{array}{l}
+Base_{LSS} : Neutral_{GSS} \\
+Local_{LSS} : \text{3-PER}_{GSS} \\
-Local_{LSS} : \text{1-PER}_{GSS}
\end{array}
\right] \\[6pt]
\left[
\begin{array}{l}
\left[LOC \atop OR \right]
\left[
\begin{array}{l}
Bottom_{HP} : +Base_{LSS} \\
Front_{HP} : -Local_{LSS} \\
Top_{HP} : -Base_{LSS}
\end{array}
\right] \\[6pt]
\left[HP \right]
\left[
\begin{array}{l}
\left[LOC \atop OR \right]
\left[
\begin{array}{l}
Base_{Hand} : Bottom_{HP} \\
Palm_{Hand} : Front_{HP} \\
F\text{-}tip_{Hand} : Top_{HP}
\end{array}
\right] \\
HS \left[1,\ \text{x} \right]_\Delta
\end{array}
\right]
\end{array}
\right]
\end{array}
\right]
$$

Thus, by comparing the alternations in (32) and (33), the orientation relation between local and global signing space emerges as the property of the gesture that determines person agreement. The proposition in (34) generalizes this observation.

(34)   The front of the hand faces towards the object of the verb and the back of the hand faces the subject.

The generalization in (34) is stated in formal terms as (35) where the "front" face is to be interpreted as the -LOCAL face of local signing space because it is floating in the neutral part of signing space (Section

3.4.2.2). Similarly, the "back" face is to be interpreted as the +LOCAL face of local signing space.

(35)

> The "front" face of *local signing space* faces in the direction of the subject of the verb situated in *global signing space*; the "back" face of *local signing space* faces towards the object of the verb situated in *global signing space*.

And just as all the properties of the simple sign are concentrated in local signing space, so too, the core properties the complex sign are contained in the characteristics of local signing space. Specifically, the part of the representation that is constant over the alternations of the sign in (32) and (33) is factored out in (36).

(36)   Core of ASK:

$$
\begin{bmatrix}
LOC \; [\; Bottom_{HP} : +Base_{LSS} \;] \\[2mm]
OR \begin{bmatrix} Front_{HP} : -Local_{LSS} \\ Top_{HP} : -Base_{LSS} \end{bmatrix} \\[4mm]
HP \begin{bmatrix} LOC \begin{bmatrix} Base_{Hand} : Bottom_{HP} \\ Palm_{Hand} : Front_{HP} \\ F\text{-}tip_{Hand} : Top_{HP} \end{bmatrix} \\ OR \\ HS \; [\; 1, \text{x} \;]_{\Delta} \end{bmatrix}
\end{bmatrix}
$$

The core part of the sign is, in fact, simply the representation of the hand prism in local signing space. So the root of the verb is captured by the properties of the local signing space and the agreement morphology by the relations between the local and global signing spaces.

The relation between these parts is schematized in (37). I refer to the core part of the sign gesture as the *root* and the agreement part as the *frame*. The former corresponds to the information within local signing space, and the latter corresponds to the information within global signing space. (37) also shows that, strikingly unlike spoken language phonology, the root and agreement morphology of a verb are co-temporal within a unit of phonology – the *cell*.

(37)   Morphology and Phonology of a Complex Sign

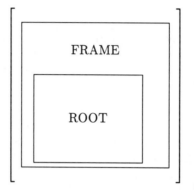

Cell

The propositions in (38) formalize the relations in (37).

(38)

Morphology and Phonology of an Agreement Verb
(i)   A *root* and *frame* combine to represent an agreement verb, where the *root* represents the morphological core of the verb, and the *frame* represents its agreement morphology.
(ii)   The phonological properties of the verb *root* are defined by the properties of *local signing space*.
(iii)   The phonological properties of the *frame* are defined by the relations between *local signing space* and *global signing space*.
(iv)   The verb *root* and *frame* are co-extensive in a *cell*.

Thus the phonological structure of the complex sign is the same as the phonological structure of the simple sign – both are represented by the cell. But whereas the simple sign is characterized by default orientation relations between local and global signing space (Section 3.4.2.2), the morphology of the complex sign demands specific meaningful relations between the two spatial constructs. The set of "backward" verbs, described in the next section, further illustrate this modality-specific relation between the morphology and phonology of agreement verbs.

5.2.2   Backward Verbs

In previous analyses, the verbs in (39) present an interesting puzzle (Padden 1988, Lillo-Martin 1991, Brentari 1988). The observation for the majority of agreement verbs is that the movement of the hands is away from the subject of the verb and towards the object of the verb, as in (39a). In contrast, verbs like (39b) are described as exhibiting the opposite behavior, or moving "backwards" because the hands move away from the object of the verb and towards the subject. As will be shown, however, these generalizations have been influenced by the word order of their English counterparts.

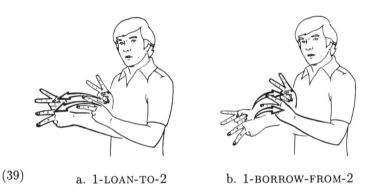

(39)   a. 1-LOAN-TO-2   b. 1-BORROW-FROM-2

For both signs the hands are held in similar positions. The index and middle fingers of both hands are straight while the other fingers are curled against the palm with the thumb resting on them. The fingertips point away from the signer and the palms face the sides. The hands are stacked one on top of the other as they are held in front of the signer with the pinky-side of one hand resting on top of the index-side of the other.

For (39a), the extended fingers are lined up between the signer (first person) and the addressee (second person). At the start of the sign the fingertips point at an upward angle. To articulate the sign the hands rotate forward so that at the end of the gesture the fingertips point toward the addressee. The sign means *I loan to you*. The sign can be articulated with only the rotating motion of the hands described here or the rotating motion can be accompanied with a slight forward movement of the hands so they move away from the signer and toward the addressee.

Similarly for (39b), the extended fingers line up between the signer and the addressee. At the start of the sign the fingers point away from the signer in the direction of the addressee. To articulate the sign the hands rotate backwards so that at the end of the gesture the fingertips point at an upward angle. The sign means *I borrow from you*. This sign, too, can be articulated with only the rotating motion of the hands, or may be accompanied with a movement of the hands in which they move away from the addressee and toward the signer.

Given that English word order is SVO, (40a), the optional movement of the hands in (39a) seems to be along a forward moving direction, (40b), because the hands move away from the first argument, subject (S), and towards the second argument, object (O). In comparison, the optional movement of the hands in (39b) seems to be along a backward trajectory, (40c), because the hands move away from the second argument, object (O), towards the first argument, subject (S).

(40)   a.   English word order: SUBJ   VERB   OBJ

        b.   Trajectory of (39a): $\longrightarrow$
                                                       "forward"

        c.   Trajectory of (39b): $\longleftarrow$
                                                        "backward"

The majority of agreement verbs are articulated with the forward seeming movement from subject towards object. Only a small number of verbs fall into the latter, "backward", category.[8]

The representations for the signs in (39) (without the optional movements) are given in (41) and (42). Combining these representations with the propositions in (35) and (38) illustrates that the assignment of subject and object is consistent for both verbs. Just as for the agreement verb ASK the back of local signing space (+LOCAL) in (41) and (42) faces the subject and the front of local signing space (-LOCAL) faces the object. The crucial difference between the signs is in the structure of their roots. They differ only by the order of the orientation relations in the transition unit. In (41) the hands start with the fingertips pointing in an upward direction and end by pointing at the addressee. In contrast, for (42) the hands start with the fingertips pointing towards the addressee and end by pointing in an upward direction.

---

[8]Other verbs in this category are: BORROW, COPY, EXTRACT, INVITE/HIRE, MOOCH, STEAL, TAKE, SUMMON, TAKE-TURN-AFTER, TAKE-ADVANTAGE-OF, REQUEST.

(41) 1-LOAN-TO-2:

$$
\begin{bmatrix}
LOC \ \begin{matrix} OR \end{matrix} \begin{bmatrix} +Base_{LSS} : Neutral_{GSS} \\ +Local_{LSS} : 1\text{-}PER_{GSS} \\ -Local_{LSS} : 2\text{-}PER_{GSS} \end{bmatrix} \\[4em]
\begin{bmatrix}
LOC \ \begin{matrix} OR \end{matrix} \begin{bmatrix} Bottom_{HP} : +Base_{LSS} \\ Front_{HP} : -Base_{LSS}, -Local_{LSS} \\ Top_{HP} : +Local_{LSS}, -Base_{LSS} \end{bmatrix}_{\Delta} \\[4em]
\begin{bmatrix}
HP \begin{bmatrix} LOC \ \begin{matrix} OR \end{matrix} \begin{bmatrix} Base_{Hand} : Bottom_{HP} \\ F\text{-}tips_{Hand} : Front_{HP} \\ Th\text{-}side_{Hand} : Top_{HP} \end{bmatrix} \\ HS \ [\ 2\ ] \\ [\ \text{TWO-HAND}\ ] \end{bmatrix}
\end{bmatrix}
\end{bmatrix}
\end{bmatrix}
$$

(42) 1-BORROW-FROM-2:

$$
\begin{bmatrix}
LOC \ \begin{matrix} OR \end{matrix} \begin{bmatrix} +Base_{LSS} : Neutral_{GSS} \\ +Local_{LSS} : 1\text{-}PER_{GSS} \\ -Local_{LSS} : 2\text{-}PER_{GSS} \end{bmatrix} \\[4em]
\begin{bmatrix}
LOC \ \begin{matrix} OR \end{matrix} \begin{bmatrix} Bottom_{HP} : +Base_{LSS} \\ Front_{HP} : -Local_{LSS}, -Base_{LSS} \\ Top_{HP} : -Base_{LSS}, +Local_{LSS} \end{bmatrix}_{\Delta} \\[4em]
\begin{bmatrix}
HP \begin{bmatrix} LOC \ \begin{matrix} OR \end{matrix} \begin{bmatrix} Base_{Hand} : Bottom_{HP} \\ F\text{-}tips_{Hand} : Front_{HP} \\ Th\text{-}side_{Hand} : Top_{HP} \end{bmatrix} \\ HS \ [\ 2\ ] \\ [\ \text{TWO-HAND}\ ] \end{bmatrix}
\end{bmatrix}
\end{bmatrix}
\end{bmatrix}
$$

Hence, the hands appear to be oriented so that the fingertips point towards the participants at the beginning and ending of the sign. Although the fingertips clearly point in the direction of the addressee, the upward turn of the fingers must be interpreted as pointing towards the signer because of the physical constraints of the articulators. With that interpretation in mind, the difference between the orientations of the hand reveal an interesting pattern with respect to the semantics of the verb. Stated in terms of thematic roles, the initial posture of the hand associates with the source of the verb, and the final posture with the goal of the verb.

The grammatical and semantic relations of the verbs are schematized in (43). In this morpho-phonological interpretation of the verbs, the orientation relation between local and global signing space in the verb frame is related to grammatical function. The order of the transition unit in the verb root is related to the thematic roles of the verb.

(43) Interpreting Agreement Verbs

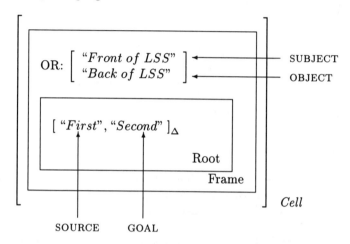

The schematic in (43) has at least two implications for the morpho-phonology of agreement verbs. First, it implies that the root of an agreement verb has at most one transition unit. This is still subject to empirical confirmation. Second, it implies that the associations of thematic roles with points in signing space are specified as relations in local signing space. Yet because specific referents are assigned at the level of global or discourse signing space, the mechanism that mediates between that information bears further investigation. In addition, there is evidence that other verb types in ASL, e.g., a spatial verb like MOVE-FROM-A-TO-B) which makes different use of space, are consistent with the morpho-phonological organization in (43) (Uyechi 1994).

To illustrate that the interpretation in (43) captures the full paradigm of the LOAN/BORROW verbs, the relation between local and global signing space is reversed in (44) and (45). According to the schematic in (43), because the verbs in 2-LOAN-TO-1 *you loan to me* and 1-LOAN-TO-2 *I loan to you* have the same meaning, the verb roots should be the same. The only difference between them are the grammatical functions associated with the first and second person. This is reflected by the modified orientation relation in (44), as compared to (41). This is the correct pronunciation of the sign. To articulate the sign the top of the hands face the addressee while the fingertips point up, then the hands rotate so the fingertips point towards the signer.

(44) 2-LOAN-TO-1:

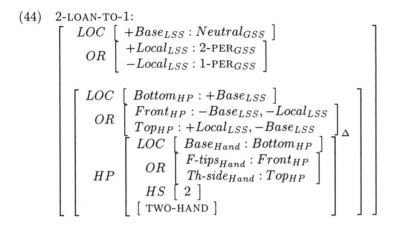

Similarly, 1-BORROW-FROM-2 *I borrow from you* and 2-BORROW-FROM-1 *you borrow from me* have the same verb and should also have the same verb root. The verbs differ only by the change in agreement morphology reflected in (45) that, when compared to the representation in (42), differs only in the orientation relation between local and global signing space. This represents the correct pronunciation of the sign. At the start of the sign the back of the hands face the addressee and the fingertips point towards the signer. To articulate the sign the hands rotate so the fingertips point up and the top of the hands face the addressee.

(45) 2-BORROW-FROM-1:

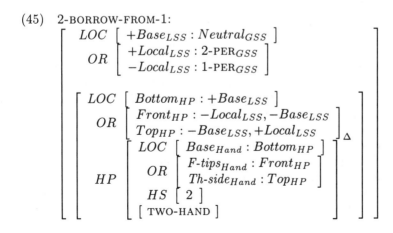

Therefore, (43) unifies the interpretation of LOAN and BORROW. From this perspective there is nothing at all backwards about any of the agreement verbs in ASL.

5.3 Transition Unit and Cell

To summarize, the *transition unit* and *cell* emerge as the organizing constructs of visual phonology. The *transition unit* represents a unit of movement of the sign gesture, capturing a change in handshape, a change in location, or a change in orientation, or, in its degenerate form, capturing a constant value of a relation over time. The *cell* represents the sign gesture, ensuring that all of the parts of the manual articulators are represented by organizing a set of co-articulated transition units. Propositions based on *cell* structure ensure that the sign gesture meets minimum and maximum properties. Both the transition unit and cell ensure that basic relations between time and space for sign gestures are coordinated appropriately.

In this chapter I have presented a brief introduction to the relation between these phonological units and the morphology of signs. The surprising result is that morphological units are co-temporal. This crucial distinction from the sequential ordering of morphological units in spoken language provides evidence that, just as for phonology, a theory of universal morphology will rely on the input from two distinct theoretical frameworks: (i) visual morphology, and (ii) spoken language morphology. Hence, the theoretical implications of the study of sign language reaches beyond the parts of the grammar that have been deemed likely to be affected by distinct language mode. So the theoretical framework for visual phonology laid out in these chapters provides a set of constructs and propositions not only for exploring the phonology of other sign languages and other parts of ASL, but also for examining the interface between phonology and the other modules of sign language grammar.

5.3.1 A Note on Two-Handed Signs

In presenting the foundation for a transition-based model of visual phonology I have focused on signs that are articulated with only one hand, yet a large number of signs are articulated with both hands. Earlier in this chapter I included without argument the feature [TWO-HAND] in the representations for LOAN-TO and BORROW-FROM. Although the feature was associated with the hand prism, it is not clear whether that accurately reflects the properties of two-handed signs. That is one of the challenges that remains for the transition-based model.

But before pursuing work on these signs, it is necessary to clarify the meaning of the term "two-handed sign". In his groundbreaking work

Battison (1978) uses the term to refer to signs articulated with both hands. Based on the Symmetry and Dominance Conditions, (46), he proposes a typology of two-handed signs.

(46) a. Symmetry Condition (Battison 1978:35)
(a) If both hands of a sign move independently during its articulation, then (b) both hands must be specified for the same location, the same handshape, the same movement (whether performed simultaneously or in alternation), and the specification for orientation must be either symmetrical or identical.

b. Dominance Condition (Battison 1978:35)
(a) If the hands of a two-handed sign do not share the same specification for handshape (i.e., they are different) then (b) one hand must be passive while the active hand articulates the movement, and (c) the specification of the passive hand is restricted to be one of a small set: A, S, B, 5, G, C, O.[a]

---

[a] A, S, B, 5, G, C, O are names for handshapes found in ASL.

The Battison typology, (47), classifies all signs articulated with two hands. Signs that meet the Symmetry Condition are Type 1 signs, signs that meet the Dominance Condition are Type 3 signs, and signs that meet neither condition are Type 2 signs.

(47) Battison's Typology of Two-Handed Signs

Type 1 Both hands active; same handshape, location, and movement.
Type 2 One hand passive; same handshape.
Type 3 One hand passive (restricted set of handshapes); different handshapes.

At the center of Battison's characterization of two-handed signs is the intuition that symmetry plays a crucial role when the manual articulators work together. Yet symmetry for Battison and others (Sandler 1993a, Brentari and Goldsmith 1993, Brentari 1995) is used only in its descriptive sense – without tapping its richer formal interpretation (Stewart and Golubitsky 1992). In fact, the geometric foundation of the transition-based model provides a potentially productive perspective from which to revisit the analysis of two-handed signs.

The representation of signing space in terms of rectangular prisms and their corresponding spatial axes provide the constructs for pursuing a formal analysis of symmetry in signs. For example, in an analysis that takes "two-handed sign" to refer to signs that are underlyingly, or phonologically, two-handed, Toole and Uyechi (1996) use the transition-based model to argue for a constraint on hand orientation in two-handed signs which clarifies ambiguities in Battison's Symmetry Condition about orientation and reduces it to an empirically verifiable proposition: *In a two-handed sign, corresponding axes must be parallel.* The *corresponding axes* are the X, Y, and Z-axes of the hand prisms that represent the hands. That the corresponding axes of the hands are aligned reflects a formal interpretation of symmetry as sameness within a system. The analysis also reveals that the set of possible hand orientations in phonological two-handed signs is a mathematically closed set derived from a single rotational transformation. Both of these results provide formal links between the abstract properties of sign language and other systems in nature.

This interpretation of and approach to the analysis of two-handed signs is, therefore, extremely promising. Hence, determining the place of the feature [TWO-HAND] in the transition-based representation of signs presents an interesting puzzle, but re-examining the symmetric properties of two-handed signs within a formally well-suited model promises to be the more exciting area for future work.

6

Segment and Syllable

In this chapter I examine three analyses of ASL that adopt the transfer-and-test model of phonology described in the first chapter (Liddell and Johnson 1989, Sandler 1989, Perlmutter 1992). Each of these analyses are developed under the assumption that the phonological framework based on spoken language phonology can be applied to sign language data, and that phonological theory can be stated in terms of a single theoretical framework. Indeed, the philosophy behind this approach is essentially correct: if it is possible to apply existing constructs and propositions to explain some new phenomenon, then the cost to the existing theory is minimal and the result may be that seemingly disparate phenomena are unified. However, a central message that emerges in this chapter is that the constructs and principles from spoken language phonology, as they are currently formulated, are not adequate to account for the properties of signs.

To highlight this problem, I present a critical examination of three proposals that are related by their focus on the phonological representation of the sign, and by the claim that the consonant and vowel have analogs in sign language phonology: (i) the moraic model (Perlmutter 1992), (ii) the movement-hold (MH) model (Liddell and Johnson 1989), and (iii) the hand tier (HT) model (Sandler 1989).

Liddell and Johnson (1989) were the first to adopt an autosegmental representation of signs and define contrasting timing segments, movement (M) and hold (H), as in (1). They were motivated by Liddell (1984) which demonstrated that signs have sequential properties that must be accounted for. The notion of "segmenting" signs based on contrasts between periods of transition and steady state followed.

(1)   a.   A *movement* is defined as a period of time during which some aspect of the articulation is in transition. (1986:447)

        b.   A *hold* is defined as a period of time during which all aspects of the articulation are in a steady state. (1986:448)

Sandler (1989) follows the Movement-Hold model by adopting an autosegmental representation of signs, but differs by arguing for a *location* (L) segment to replace the H-segment and adopting a feature geometry organization of the features in a Hand Tier model of signs. Perlmutter (1992) sidesteps the issue of the non-movement segment and takes a neutral stance at the level of the segment, proposing that feature bundles that define *positions* (P) contrast with feature bundles that define *movement* (M) in a Moraic model of signs. Although all three models are based on the assumption that sign language phonology can and should draw on the constructs and principles of spoken language phonology, Perlmutter is the first to draw substantive claims from the parallel. Whereas the Movement-Hold and Hand Tier Models focus on developing descriptive adequacy for signs, the claim of the Moraic model is that the distributional properties of signs can be accounted for by general principles of organization of the spoken language syllable.

In each case, however, finding a consistent parallel between spoken and sign language phonologies is problematic. Naturally, modality-specific properties of the theoretical framework, such as mode-specific distinctive features like *coronal* and *nasal* must be replaced with sign specific properties like *selected fingers* and *opposed thumb*, but even modality-neutral definitions of constructs such as the *segment* and *syllable* can not be transferred straightforwardly.

In spite of the problems with a claim that spoken language segments have analogs in sign language phonology, taking the proposal to its logical extremes provides a perspective of phonology that must be considered carefully before adopting the approach to visual phonology advocated here. I start by addressing Perlmutter's claims and noting its dependency on a mode-specific interpretation of sonority in sign language. Whereas the proposal has the potential to lead to a unified theoretical framework for spoken and sign language phonologies, it is heavily dependent on movement as a phonological construct – a property that, from the perspective of the framework presented here, is problematic.

I then discuss the Movement Hold and Hand Tier models. I present an analysis for the combination of two signs into one lexicalized sign (called *compounding* by the authors, but referred to as *blending* here). For both models I propose a modification to the timing unit of the segment that simplifies the representation by reducing the contrasting segments in each model to a single non-contrasting segment and resolves other problems with the analyses.

6.1 Consonants, Vowels, and Syllables

Perlmutter (1992) focuses on the properties of the prosodic structure of the sign, namely the syllable and mora, and argues that sonority plays a role in the organization of the sign syllable. The work begins with the premise that signs are represented by two types of feature complexes, movements (M) and positions (P), and that they are parallel to consonants and vowels, likening M's (movements) to V's (vowels) and P's (positions) to C's (consonants). It then draws on general principles of spoken language phonology that capture the relation of consonants and vowels in syllables to explain the distribution of properties on their sign language analogs, Ms and Ps.

In this section I focus on that interpretation of consonants and vowels in the Moraic model. A sonority hierarchy in which M is more sonorous than P is shown to be crucial to the Moraic model. Given that proposals for sonority hierarchies rely on the phonological representation of movement in signs (Corina 1990, Perlmutter 1992, Blevins 1993, Sandler 1993c, Brentari 1993), this poses serious problems for the theoretical framework set forth in this thesis in which movement is not an independent phonological construct. However, I defend the transition-based model of visual phonology by showing that the transition unit and cell present a simpler representation of the data described here.

6.1.1 The Data

Perlmutter (1992) poses two related puzzles: (i) the distribution of secondary movement, i.e., repeated movement, and (ii) the distribution of handshape change. In this section I describe the data involved and present the transition-based representation of the signs.

6.1.1.1 Secondary Movement

The data that illustrates the first puzzle is shown in (2). Detailed descriptions of the gestures follow the illustrations. The signs in (2) are both articulated with a movement of the fingers referred to as *fingerwiggling*. Fingerwiggling is regarded as an example of repeated movements referred to as secondary movement and is, along with a type of movement called circling, special because it does not appear to be analyzable as repeated changes in hand posture or palm orientation (Liddell 1990b).[1] Hence, Perlmutter bases his arguments regarding secondary movement on data articulated with fingerwiggling.

---

[1] Uyechi (1993) provides an argument that fingerwiggling is a change in handshape.

Fingerwiggling is produced by a wave-like motion of the fingers. At the start of the movement all of the fingers are straight and spread slightly apart. The wave starts with the pinky bending forward slightly at the knuckle joint. The ring finger follows, then the middle finger, and finally the index finger; each one bending slightly at the knuckle joint. As soon as the pinky finger has bent forward (even while the ring finger is starting its first movement), it moves back to its original upright position. The ring finger, then the middle finger, and finally the index finger follow suit. The total effect is a wavelike movement of the fingers that starts with the pinky. In signs like those in (2), fingerwiggling is usually articulated with two or three cycles of these "finger waves".

(2)   a. GO-UP-IN-FLAMES   b. GERMANY

In (2a) both hands are held a few inches apart in front of the signer's upper chest. The fingers and thumbs are straight and slightly spread while the fingertips point upward and the palms of the hands face the signer's chest. To articulate the sign the hands move upward in a straight line while the fingers wiggle. The fingerwiggling starts when the upward movement starts and ends when the upward movement stops. The hands move about a foot while articulating two cycles of fingerwiggling, stopping just below the signer's face.

In (2b) both hands are held a few inches in front of the signer's upper chest. The fingers of both hands are straight and spread slightly while the thumbs are extended and held parallel to the palms but at right angles to the fingers. The hands are held so the fingertips face away from the signer. The palms are turned sideways and face each other. Because it is physiologically more comfortable, the hands are held at right angles to each other so the palms assume about a 45° angle with respect to a plane of bilateral symmetry perpendicular to the signer. One hand is held on top of the other so that the pinky side of the top hand rests on the side of the index finger of the other hand and so the thumb of the lower hand rests against the palm of the upper hand. The hands are held in this position for the duration of the sign. The sign is articulated by wiggling the fingers. About two cycles of finger waves constitute a single pronunciation of the gesture.

The sign in (2a) is articulated with two simultaneously articulated movements: (i) movement of the whole hand from one position to another, and (ii) movement of the hand itself in the form of fingerwiggling. Whereas simultaneous combinations of the movements are possible, Perlmutter observes that physiologically possible combinations of those movements, such as those described in (3), do not occur in monomorphemic signs.

(3)   a.   *(Fingers wiggle while hands held in one place, then hands move from one place to another without finger-wiggling)

        b.   *(Hand moves from one place to another without finger-wiggling, then stays in one position while fingers wiggle)

In theory internal terms, Perlmutter notes that well-formed lexical signs are articulated with some movement of the hand.

A P-syllable is well formed if the P has secondary movement, if there is a handshape change on the associated handshape tier, or if there is an orientation change. (Perlmutter 1992:434)

This property of signs is captured by the proposition in (4).

(4)   To articulate a sign, the hands must move.

Both the well-formed signs in (2) and the unacceptable gestures in (3) are consistent with (4), so something more must be added to narrow the field of potential signs. The generalizations in (5) capture the properties that differentiate between the data in (2) and (3).

(5)   a.   To articulate a sign, the hands may:
            (i)   stay in one position, or
            (ii)   move from one position to another.
        b.   Fingerwiggling (secondary movement) may be articulated while the hand stays in one position.
        c.   Fingerwiggling (secondary movement) may be articulated as the hand moves from one position to another.

6.1.1.2 Handshape Change

The second puzzle presented in Perlmutter (1992) is the distribution of handshape change. For example, the signs in (6) are articulated with a change in hand posture in which the fingers and thumb of the hand change from one configuration to another. The change in hand posture in (6a) is articulated at the same time that the hand moves from one place to another. (6b) is articulated with only a change in hand posture.

(6)   a. OLD   b. UNDERSTAND

In (6a) the hand is held just in front of the chin with the fingers and thumb slightly spread in a hooked position so that only the top two joints are bent. The fingers are perpendicular to the signer's body and the palm faces to the side. To articulate the sign the hand moves downward along a straight path for a few inches while the fingers and thumb close together to form a fist. The movement of the hand along the path starts at the same time that the change in hand posture starts. The change in hand posture is articulated at the same rate as the downward movement so that at the same time that the hand completes its downward movement, the change in hand posture is complete so that the hand is closed into a fist.

In (6b) the fingers and thumb are tucked into a fist and the hand is held near the side of the forehead with the palm facing towards the signer. To articulate the sign the index finger is extended while the hand stays in the same place, and the fingers and thumb maintain their initial position.

The signs in (6) contrast with the gestures described in (7).

(7)   a.   *(Change hand posture in one place, then move the
               hands from one position to another)
        b.   *(Move move from one position to another, then change-
               hand posture while in one position)

The generalization in (8) captures the difference between the well-formed signs in (6) and the ill-formed gestures described in (7).

(8)   a.   A change in hand posture may be articulated while the hand stays in one position.

       b.   A change in hand posture may be articulated as the hand moves from one position to another.

The generalization in (8) is similar to (5b) and (5c). Both are captured by the proposition in (9).

(9)   All changes of hand posture and hand position that take place during the articulation of a sign start at the same time, t_i, and end at the same time, t_f.

6.1.2   A Transition-Based Representation

From the perspective of the transition unit and cell, the properties of the data noted in (5), (8), and (9) follow straightforwardly from the representation of the signs. The representations for the signs with repeated movement are given in (10). The properties of the transition unit and cell, along with the principle of proportionality, account for the timing of the gestures. No other propositions are needed.[2]

(10) a.   GO-UP-IN-FLAMES:

$$
\left[\begin{array}{l}
\left[LOC \begin{array}{l} OR \left[\begin{array}{l} +Base_{LSS} : Neutral_{GSS} \\ +Local_{LSS} : Back_{GSS} \\ +Base_{LSS} : Bottom_{GSS} \end{array} \right] \end{array} \right] \\[4ex]
\left[LOC \begin{array}{l} OR \left[\begin{array}{l} Bottom_{HP} : +Base_{LSS}, -Base_{LSS} \\ Front_{HP} : +Local_{LSS} \\ Top_{HP} : -Base_{LSS} \end{array} \right]_{\Delta} \end{array} \right] \\[4ex]
\left[HP \begin{array}{l} \left[LOC \begin{array}{l} OR \\ HS \end{array} \left[\begin{array}{l} Base_{Hand} : Bottom_{HP} \\ Palm_{Hand} : Front_{HP} \\ F\text{-}tips_{Hand} : Top_{HP} \\ 5, 5 \end{array} \right]_{2\Delta} \right] \end{array} \right]
\end{array} \right]
$$

---

[2]Note that for ease of representation *handshape* is represented by name. In each case, the named handshape can be decomposed into a detailed representation capturing the complete joint, finger, and thumb configuration.

b. GERMANY:

$$
\begin{bmatrix}
LOC & \begin{bmatrix} +Base_{LSS} : Neutral_{GSS} \\ OR & +Local_{LSS} : Back_{GSS} \\ +Base_{LSS} : Bottom_{GSS} \end{bmatrix} \\
& \begin{bmatrix} LOC & \begin{bmatrix} Bottom_{HP} : +Base_{LSS}, -Base_{LSS} \end{bmatrix}_\Delta \\ OR & Front_{HP} : +Local_{LSS} \\ & Top_{HP} : -Base_{LSS} \\ & HP & \begin{bmatrix} LOC & \begin{bmatrix} Base_{Hand} : Bottom_{HP} \\ OR & Palm_{Hand} : Front_{HP} \\ & F\text{-}tips_{Hand} : Top_{HP} \end{bmatrix} \\ HS & \begin{bmatrix} 5, 5 \end{bmatrix}_{2\Delta} \end{bmatrix} \end{bmatrix}
\end{bmatrix}
$$

The representations for the signs with handshape change are given in (11). Just as for the signs in (10), the properties of the transition unit and cell account for the properties of the well-formed signs and exclude the ill-formed gestures described in (7).

(11) a. OLD:

$$
\begin{bmatrix}
LOC & \begin{bmatrix} +Local_{LSS} : Bottom\text{-}of\text{-}Chin_{GSS} \\ OR & +Local_{LSS} : Top_{GSS} \\ +Base_{LSS} : Bottom_{GSS} \end{bmatrix} \\
& \begin{bmatrix} LOC & \begin{bmatrix} Top_{HP} : +Local_{LSS}, -Local_{LSS} \end{bmatrix}_\Delta \\ OR & Top_{HP} : +Local_{LSS} \\ & Front_{HP} : C\text{-}Side_{LSS} \\ & HP & \begin{bmatrix} LOC & \begin{bmatrix} P\text{-}Side_{Hand} : Bottom_{HP} \\ OR & Th\text{-}Side_{Hand} : Top_{HP} \\ & F\text{-}tips_{Hand} : Front_{HP} \end{bmatrix} \\ HS & \begin{bmatrix} C, S \end{bmatrix}_\Delta \end{bmatrix} \end{bmatrix}
\end{bmatrix}
$$

b. UNDERSTAND:

$$
\begin{bmatrix}
LOC & \begin{bmatrix} +Base_{LSS} : Side\text{-}of\text{-}forehead_{GSS} \\ OR & +Base_{LSS} : Back_{GSS} \\ +Local_{LSS} : Top_{GSS} \end{bmatrix} \\
& \begin{bmatrix} LOC & \begin{bmatrix} Bottom_{HP} : -Local_{LSS} \end{bmatrix} \\ OR & Front_{HP} : +Base_{LSS} \\ & Top_{HP} : +Local_{LSS} \\ & HP & \begin{bmatrix} LOC & \begin{bmatrix} Base_{Hand} : Bottom_{HP} \\ OR & Palm_{Hand} : Front_{HP} \\ & F\text{-}tips_{Hand} : Top_{HP} \end{bmatrix} \\ HS & \begin{bmatrix} S, 1 \end{bmatrix}_{2\Delta} \end{bmatrix} \end{bmatrix}
\end{bmatrix}
$$

So the properties of the data follow straightforwardly from the transition-based representation developed here, presenting an alternative to the approach described in the next section.

6.1.3 Consonants, Vowels, Syllables, and Sonority

To account for the distribution of secondary movement and handshape change, Perlmutter (1992) presents an analysis that imports the consonant, vowel, segment, mora, syllable, and sonority from spoken language phonology. Movement (M) and position (P) are defined as feature clusters, neutral with respect to specific representations of the segment but that parallel, respectively, the vowel and consonant. M is associated with a segment that represents a period of time that the hands move from one position to another and P is associated with a segment that represents a period of time that the hands stay in one position.

Combinations of M's and P's that are relevant to the discussion in Perlmutter (1992) are given in (12). (12b) and (12e) are representations of the signs in (2), where [*wiggle*] represents the fingerwiggling that occurs during that period of the sign. (12c) is the representation for the sign DREAM, described in Chapter 1. No specific examples of data with the properties of (12a) or (12d) are given, although PLEASANT, FINGERSPELL, LONG-AGO (1992:412) are candidates for (12a).

(12) a. $\qquad$ [*secondary*]M

     b.   GERMANY: [*wiggle*]P

     c.   DREAM: [ ]P [*bending*]M [ ]P

     d. $\qquad$ [ ]P [*secondary*]M

     e.   GO-UP-IN-FLAMES: [*wiggle*]M [ ]P

The patterns in (12) generalize to (13), where OK means that secondary movement can occur during a segment and an asterisk, *, indicates that secondary movement cannot occur during a segment. The same structures capture the distribution of handshape change, revealing that secondary movement or handshape change can always occur during an M, but can occur during a P segment only in case the P is not preceded or followed by an M segment.

(13) a. $[OK]_M$

     b. $[OK]_P$

     c. $[*]_P [OK]_M [*]_P$

     d. $[*]_P [OK]_M$

     e. $[OK]_M [*]_P$

To account for this distribution of secondary movement and hand-shape change in the data, Perlmutter adopts the general principles of organization from spoken language to apply in the sign domain. To that end, the segments from spoken language are mapped onto the proposed constructs for sign language, Ms and Ps. Then principles of organization that apply to spoken language segments are used to account for the phenomena in the new domain.

Starting with the observation that "if, instead of Ms and Ps, we had vowels and consonants, as in oral languages" (1992:417), the representations in (13) are translated into the structures in (14).

(14)   a. $[OK]_V$
        b. $[OK]_C$
        c. $[*]_C\ [OK]_V\ [*]_C$
        d. $[*]_C\ [OK]_V$
        e. $[OK]_V\ [*]_C$

The general principles (1992:417) to account for the distribution of the data are repeated in (15) and (16). (15a) and (15b) parallel (16a) and (16b). (16c) accounts for the distribution of secondary movement and handshape change, and (16d) states the sonority relation between Ms and Ps.

(15)   a.   A vowel is always a syllable nucleus.
        b.   A consonant can be the nucleus of a syllable only if it is not adjacent to a vowel.

(16)   a.   An M is always a syllable nucleus.
        b.   A P can be the nucleus of a syllable only if it is not adjacent to an M.
        c.   Secondary movement features (and handshape change) can occur only on the nucleus of a syllable. (1992:417, 423)
        d.   In sign language, M's are more sonorous than P's. (1992:418)

Given (16d), this proposal relies crucially on a dominance relation between M's and P's in order to account for the distribution of secondary movement and handshape change. In the current analysis, for lack of other major distinguishing characteristics between them, the dominance relation between the segments is linked to the contrast between movement of the hand from one place to another (M), and the hand maintaining the same placement (P).[3] Hence, in labeling M's as more sonorous than P's, movement of the whole hand is implicitly identified as the property of the sign contributing to sonority.

Yet because sonority, as applied in spoken language phonology, is mode dependent and subject to various interpretations, introducing it at this point in the analysis seems to add unnecessary complexity to the model. This raises the question as to whether one of the other possible interpretations that *consonant* and *vowel* have in spoken language phonology may be used to account for the sign language data, thereby sidestepping the need to appeal to sonority. In the next section I review those alternatives.

6.1.3.1   Alternatives to Sonority
The parallels drawn between (15a,b) and (16a,b) depend on the relations between spoken language and sign language segments given in (17).

(17)		Spoken Language		Sign Language
	a.	"vowel"	:	M-segment
	b.	"consonant"	:	P-segment

The alternatives to a sonority-based interpretation of consonants and vowels for interpreting the propositions in (16) are given in (18). (18a) are descriptive terms. The letters in (18b) represent timing segments that refer to structural positions in the syllable: C means non-syllabic and V means syllabic. The terms in (18c) are distinctive feature values from SPE (Chomsky and Halle 1968).

(18)		"consonant"	"vowel"
	a.	consonant	vowel
	b.	C	V
	c.	[+ consonantal]	[- consonantal]

Given these alternatives, the structurally-based terms in (18b) and the feature values in (18c) can be combined to yield the four logical possibilities in (19). These relate to the descriptive terms as shown: the combination in (19a) is a vowel, and the combinations in (19b-d) are consonants.

---

[3] Although as the analysis of sign languages progresses beyond the domain of ASL, other properties associated with a dominance relation may emerge.

(19)   a.   [- cons]   and   V   : vowel
         b.   [- cons]   and   C   : consonant
         c.   [+ cons]   and   V   : consonant
         d.   [+ cons]   and   C   : consonant

The example in (20) illustrates the relations in (19). The first segment is an example of the combination in (19b). It is in the onset of a syllable, so it is non-nuclear and is a C. It falls in the natural class of [-cons] and is labeled descriptively as a consonant. The second segment is an example of the combination in (19a). It is in the nucleus of the syllable, so it is a V. It falls in the natural class of [-cons] and is, in descriptive terms, a vowel. The third segment is an example of the combination in (19d). It is in the onset of a syllable, so it is non-nuclear and C. It is in the natural class of [+cons], and is referred to as a consonant. The final segment is an example of the combination in (19c). It is in the nucleus of the syllable, so it is a V. It is in the natural class of [+cons] and is descriptively classified as a consonant.

(20)   *whistle*

$$
\begin{array}{cccc}
 & \sigma & & \sigma \\
\diagup\!\!\diagup\;| & & \diagup\!\!\diagup\;| & \\
C & V & C & V \\
[-cons] & [-cons] & [+cons] & [+cons] \\
| & | & | & | \\
w & i & s & l
\end{array}
$$

Each of the interpretations of "consonant" and "vowel" in (18) can now be applied to interpret the propositions in (15). Starting with proposition (15a), *A vowel is always a syllable nucleus*, it cannot refer to the descriptive interpretation in (18a) because that results in a tautology. From (19a), a vowel is an element with the feature [-cons] in the syllable nucleus, so (15a) would read: "A [-cons] element in the syllable nucleus is always a syllable nucleus."

(15a) can also not refer to V, as in (18b), because to say that a V must always be a syllable nucleus is also a tautology. A V is, by definition, the nucleus of the syllable. Finally, (15a) cannot refer to the distinctive feature, (18c), because either [-cons] or [+cons], as in (19a) or (19c), can be a syllable nucleus. In short, (15a) has no coherent interpretation. Given the alternatives in (18), it is either false or tautological.

Now, consider proposition (15b): *A consonant can be the nucleus of a syllable only if it is not adjacent to a vowel.* Interpreted as (18a), the statement is simply false for spoken language because under some circumstances a consonant can be the nucleus of a syllable regardless of the non-nuclear components, (19c). Similarly, interpreting the statement with (18b), it is also false; a C can never be the nucleus of a syllable. It is possible to interpret the statement with (18c): "A [+cons] can be the nucleus of a syllable only if is not adjacent to a [-cons] ." But it is also not true because there are instances where [+cons] is a syllable nucleus even though it is adjacent to a [-cons]. Take, for example, the three syllable pronunciation of *rustling* [*r* ∧ *s l i n*]. [*l*] is [+cons] and a syllable nucleus, but it is immediately followed by a [-cons].

Ignoring for the moment the empirical problem with (15b), one possibility is to associate secondary movement (or handshape change) with the distinctive feature value [-cons]. Then, adopting the definition of "consonant" as [+cons] and "vowel" as [-cons], (18c), produces the interpretation of (15b) that is given in (21).

(21) A segment that does not have secondary movement (or handshape change) can be in the nucleus of the syllable only if it is not adjacent to a segment that has secondary movement (or handshape change).

The proposition in (21) rules out the non-occurring gestures in (3) and (7). Nevertheless, the propositions in (15) must necessarily hold for spoken language phonology before the parallels in (17) and the general principles in (16) can be adopted for sign language phonology. And, as shown here, neither proposition in (15) is correct for any of the interpretations for "consonant" and "vowel" in (18). In short, none of the alternatives go through, so the analysis of the data is completely dependent on the adoption of a sonority hierarchy for sign language.

6.1.4   Comparing the Proposals

Therefore, the Moraic model must import, along with consonant, vowel, and syllable, the notion of sonority. Granted, sonority is crucial to the interpretation of syllable structure in spoken language phonology. But spoken language sonority is a modality specific concept that has emerged from broad cross-linguistic comparisons to unify the properties of syllable organization across spoken languages. Thus, if the analysis of sign language is analogous to the study of spoken language, as proposed in the Moraic model, then the defense of a sign language sonority hierarchy will depend on its ability to account for cross-linguistic phenomena. As it is specified now it stands as a stipulated dominance relation between two segments whose interpretation is largely dependent on an analogy with consonants and vowels in spoken language.

In contrast, the transition-based representations of the signs presented above account for the data on the basis of only the organizational properties of the transition unit and cell. No extra stipulations are required. But the transition-based proposal is not without cost. As stated at the outset of the thesis, it requires the adoption of two mode-specific theoretical frameworks from which a single theory of universal phonology can be stated. Yet the payback in the form of the explanatory theory outlined in the previous chapters not only outweighs the cost, but also illustrates the value of distinct phonologies, if only to identify the mode-specific differences in the phonologies as discussed in Chapter 7. Furthermore, as suggested in the remainder of this chapter, the adoption of spoken language constructs may be possible, but it will only come at some cost to a spoken language-based theory of universal phonology.

6.2 Segments and Features

Liddell and Johnson (1989) present what they call a Movement Hold (MH) model for ASL, named because of the two types of autosegments they propose – movements (M) and holds (H). The purpose of their model is twofold: (i) to provide a phonetic transcription system for signs, and (ii) to provide a phonological representation that captures the sequential and simultaneous properties of signs. In this section I focus on the phonological aspect of the model.

In early work, such as Stokoe (1960) and Battison (1978), signs were analyzed as bundles of simultaneously occurring features. Liddell (1984), however, argued that signs also have sequential properties, prompting Liddell and Johnson (1989) to adopt the framework of autosegmental phonology because it organizes both sequential and simultaneous information. The timing tier provides sequential organization for the simultaneous information organized on the independent feature tiers.

By adopting autosegmental phonology, this work follows the transfer-and-test model of phonology. In this section I show that the definition of segments adopted by Liddell and Johnson leads to the overgeneration of structures. I begin by discussing the problem with the current model, and then propose a modification to their definition of segment that resolves the overgeneration problem and improves the empirical coverage of the model.

6.2.1 The Modality-Free Segment

To assess the effectiveness of a construct in a new domain, it is first necessary to provide a language-independent, or in this case, a modality-free interpretation of the construct. To that end, in this section I formulate a modality-free definition for the *segment*, the focus of the MH model.

The concept of a phonological segment in Chomsky and Halle (1968, henceforth SPE) carries the assumptions in (22). This concept of the segment is basically that of a feature bundle with inherent duration.

(22)   a.   A segment is an atomic temporal unit.

        b.   The properties of a segment are the same from its starting point to its ending point.

However the SPE assumption in (22b) does not hold for complex segments such as affricates and prenasalized stops, so in post-SPE frameworks the properties of the SPE feature bundle are factored into two parts: (i) temporal duration, represented as a time segment, X, and (ii) properties of the segment, or a melody, represented by a root node. This post-SPE concept of a segment is spelled out in (23).

(23)   a.   A *segment* consists of a *time segment* (X) associated with a melody represented by a *root node*(s).

        b.   *Time Segment*:
           (i)   A time segment has inherent duration.
           (ii)   Given any two segments, one must be temporally ordered after the other.

        c.   *Root Node*:
           (i)   A root node does not have inherent duration.
           (ii)   Given any two root nodes, one must be temporally ordered after the other.

        d.   The properties of the segmental material associated with a single root node are the same for the duration of the time segment.

The separation between time and melody provides the representation for segments as in (24). A simple segment, (24a), is represented by a one-to-one relation between a time segment, X, and a root node. A complex segment, (24b), is represented by two root nodes associated to a single timing segment, and a long vowel or geminate, (24c), is represented as two timing segments associated to a single root node.

(24)   a.   Simple   b.   Complex Segment   c.   Long Vowel/
               Segment   Geminate

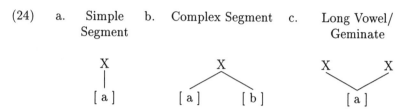

In sum, in the SPE definition of a segment, segment features are bound with the segment itself, but in post-SPE definitions, time and features are distinct. Hence, the post-SPE notion of segment explicitly differentiates between the temporal and atemporal properties of the segment; the time segment represents the former and the feature bundle the latter.

6.2.2   Movements and Holds

In the Movement Hold model, Liddell and Johnson (1986, 1989) define two distinct segment types, *movements* (M) and *holds* (H), as in (25).

(25)   a.   A *movement* is defined as a period of time during which some aspect of the articulation is in transition. (1986:447)
              For any movement... there will be an initial posture of the hand(s),a final posture of the hand(s), and a specific manner of making the transition from the first posture to the second. (1986:449)

         b.   A *hold* is defined as a period of time during which all aspects of the articulation are in a steady state. (1986:448)

As illustrated in (26), Liddell and Johnson propose that movement and hold segments are composed of two parts: (i) a segmental feature bundle and (ii) an articulatory feature bundle. The segmental features distinguish between the segment types and include information such as contour of the movement, simultaneous secondary movement, and timing information, such as duration. The articulatory features capture information relevant to the posture of the hand such as handshape and hand orientation. By definition, (25a), the movement segment must necessarily associate with two sets of articulatory features, (26a).

(26) a.   M-segment   b.   H-segment

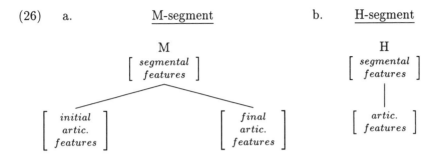

Unfortunately, the segmental representation in (26) presents an unmotivated synthesis of the SPE and post-SPE segments described above. For example, the association of segmental features with the M and H timing units is analogous to the SPE segment. At the same time the independent articulatory features are analogous to the melody proposed for post-SPE segments. Hence, in the Movement Hold model the definition of segments combines properties of both the SPE and the post-SPE segments, producing a logically incoherent notion of segment.

In the remainder of this section I present an analysis of sign language blends that highlights some empirical problems with the MH representation of signs. I propose an alternative interpretation of the M and H segments that resolves the internal inconsistencies of the segments as defined here, as well as resolving the empirical problems described below.

6.2.3   Sign Language Blends

One way to produce new signs in ASL is to combine two existing signs into a novel sign. The process is often referred to in the literature as *compounding*, but is more specifically like spoken language *blends* (Liddell 1984). In ASL when two signs combine to produce a new sign, they undergo a substantial reduction in phonological shape, bear little or no evidence of having undergone a process analogous to stress shift, and are subject to diachronic change (Frishberg 1976). These properties contrast with those of other two-sign combinations described by Klima and Bellugi (1979) as "semantic compounds" Those combinations generally retain their phonological shape, have predictable sign order, and have meanings that can be deduced from its parts. In this section I follow Liddell (1984) and refer to the former as *blends*; the latter will not be discussed here.

The signs in (27a) and (27b) combine to produce the blend in (28) that means *to make up one's own mind.* All of the signs are articulated with one hand. In (27a) the hand is held so the index finger is extended while the other fingers are bent and tucked under the thumb which is also bent. The hand starts a few inches from the side of the forehead with the index finger pointing toward the head and the palm of the hand facing down. To articulate the sign the hand moves towards the forehead in a straight line and stops when the tip of the index finger touches the forehead.

In (1b) the hand is held so all the fingers are bent into a fist. The thumb is extended and held perpendicular to the fist. The hand begins a few inches in front of the center of the signer's upper chest with the tip of the thumb pointing up and the backs of the knuckles facing away from the signer. To articulate the sign the hand moves along a straight path towards the referent of *self*. For example, if the signer is referring to herself, the direction of the movement is towards the signer's chest; if the signer is referring to someone else, the hand moves in a straight line towards the space representing that person.

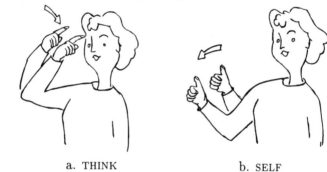

(1)   a. THINK   b. SELF

To articulate a phrasal combination of the signs, for example in the phrase I THINK SELF meaning (something like) *I think for myself* or *I think only of myself*, all movements described for (1a) and (1b) are pronounced. In contrast, the pronunciation changes noticeably when the signs are combined to form the new lexical item in (2).

To articulate (2), the hand starts in a position so that the index finger and thumb are extended and held at right angles to each other; the other fingers are bent. The tip of the index finger is held against the side of the forehead with the palm of the hand facing the opposite side of the signer's body than the hand articulating the gesture and the thumb side of the hand facing the floor. Once in this position, the hand moves along an arc-shaped path that ends in front of the signer while at the same time index finger bends at both joints to join the other fingers and the hand twists so that the tip of the thumb points upward and the knuckle-side of the hand faces towards the referent of the sign.

(28)   THINK-SELF

The blend in (28) exhibits three characteristics not found in a phrasal sequence of signs. First, the initial handshape is a blend of the handshapes in (27a) and (27b). Second, the transition between the signs merge into a single smooth movement. Finally, the simultaneous transitions are articulated proportionally; the hand posture changes at the same time the hand moves. This latter characteristic of the blend contrasts with the gestures described in (29) that are articulated with disproportionate changes and are not possible blends.

(29)   a.   *(Hand posture change complete before position change.)
        b.   *(Hand position change complete before posture change.)

In addition, Klima and Bellugi (1979) found that the mean length of a blend ('compound' in their terms) measured in visual fields on videotape is about the same as the mean length of a single sign. A summary of the differences between the phrasal combination THINK SELF and the blend THINK-SELF is given in (30). The list constitutes the set of properties that an analysis of blends must be able to account for.

(30) a.   <u>Phrasal Combination</u>   b.   <u>Blend</u>
      (i)   Two discrete   (i)   Smooth transition
            movements.   between locations.
      (ii) Distinct transitions   (ii)   Smooth transition of
            of handshape.   handshape.
      (iii) Distinct orientations.   (iii) Smooth transition of
                                             orientation.
      (iv) Duration is sum   (iv)   Duration is comparable to
            of two signs.   a lexical sign.
                                       (v)   Proportional combinations
                                             of transitions.

6.2.4 An MH Analysis

To account for the changes that signs undergo to form blends, Liddell and Johnson (1986) propose two sets of rules. The first set of rules is a combination of a Contacting Hold Rule and Movement Epenthesis which are intended to capture the synchronic formation of the blend by adjusting the segment structure of the inputs. The second set of rules is a set of "feature adjustments" which affect the diachronic changes at the feature level – what Liddell and Johnson refer to as "more finely tuned modifications in specific features" (1986:479).

Representations of the first set of rules are given in (31). The Contacting Hold Rule, (31a), is intended to capture the observation that if the hand contacts a body part, the contact is preserved in the blend. When this rule is applied only the segment and feature pair that includes the contact is preserved; all other segments and their feature complexes are deleted. Liddell and Johnson describe Movement Epenthesis as

> ...a process which inserts a movement between concatenated segments, the second of which begins with an initial articulatory bundle different from the final articulatory bundle of the preceding segment. For the most part, this process applies at the boundary between signs... (1989:237)

Although they do not state the rule formally, I present a version of it in (31b).

(31)   a.   Contacting Hold Rule
            (applies to initial sign in blend)

$$[\text{ (A)} \qquad \overset{\displaystyle\text{H}}{\underset{\displaystyle\begin{bmatrix} contact \\ body \end{bmatrix}}{\big|}} \qquad \text{(B) }]$$

$$1 \qquad\qquad 2 \qquad\qquad 3 \quad \to \quad 2$$

       b.   Movement Epenthesis

$$\emptyset \to M \ / \ \underset{[a]}{\overset{\displaystyle X}{\big|}} \ ] \_\_ [\ \underset{[b]}{\overset{\displaystyle X}{\big|}}, \quad a \neq b.$$

Given the representation of movement and hold segments in (26), the representations for the lexical signs that contribute to the blend, (27a) and (27b), are given in (32a). These form the input to the Contacting

Hold Rule. For ease of discussion, I show only the relevant feature. In this case it represents body contact. The output of the rule is shown in (32b).

(32)   a.   THINK   SELF

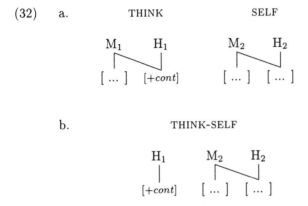

        b.   THINK-SELF

Next, applying Movement Epenthesis to the result in (32b) produces the output in (33).

(33)   THINK-SELF

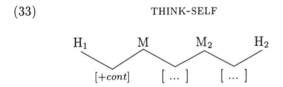

As mentioned above, the second set of rules that apply to blends are what Liddell and Johnson refer to as "feature adjustments". Of the ones that they describe, two apply to the output in (33): the Handshape Adjustment and Palm Orientation Adjustment Rules. The Handshape Adjustment Rule is formulated to capture the observation that blending creates a disfavored sequence of handshapes that is resolved by an adjustment of the initial handshape so that it better matches the characteristics of the final handshape (1986:479). In (34a), HS_k is a handshape that includes the characteristics of HS_i while at the same time anticipating the characteristics of HS_j. The Palm Orientation Adjustment Rule, (34b), is formulated to capture the observation that "the orientation features for the first articulatory bundle have changed to match those of the second" (1986:479).

(34) a. Handshape Adjustment Rule

$$HS_i \rightarrow HS_k \quad / \quad \_\_ HS_j$$

b. Palm Orientation Adjustment Rule

$$OR_i \rightarrow OR_j \quad / \quad \overset{\overset{\textstyle H}{|}}{\_\_} \quad \overset{\overset{\textstyle M}{|}}{OR_j}$$

In (35), the rules in (34) are applied to the output in (33). (35a) is the output after the application of the first set of rules, (35b) is the output of the Handshape Adjustment Rule, and (35c) is the output of the Orientation Adjustment Rule. The relevant articulatory features are included, namely handshape, body contact, and orientation. The handshapes are represented by their names: G represents the handshape with only the index finger extended, and A represents the handshape with only the thumb extended. Palm orientation is marked with the subscript p, and finger orientation is marked with the subscript f.

(35) a. Output of (31):

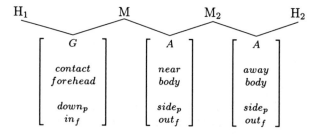

b. Handshape Adjustment Rule:

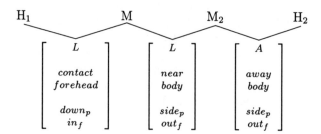

c.   Orientation Adjustment Rule:

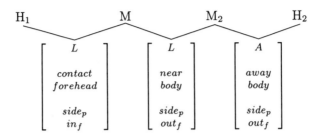

Given the list of properties of the blends in (30), the final form in (35c) is odd in at least three ways. First, there are four timing segments in the final form and only two in the input signs. This is odd, because as noted in (30b(iv)), the duration of the blend is comparable to the duration of a lexical sign. Given that the timing segments represent an interval of time, the number of timing segments in the blend should be comparable to the number in the input signs.

Second, of the four segments, two are associated with the L-handshape, one is associated with both the L- and A-handshapes, and one is associated with only the A-handshape. This asymmetric distribution appears to favor the initial L-handshape over the final A-handshape. In other words, the representation captures a gesture in which the L-handshape is held for a longer period of time than the A-handshape. But, as indicated in (30b(ii)), the transition between handshapes should be smooth.

The distribution of location features runs into similar problems. The observation in (30b(i)) is that the transition between the initial and final locations is smooth. Yet in (35c) there are three specifications for location which indicate a more triangulated movement of the hand.

So it appears that the M- and H-segments and their associated feature complexes provide some basic machinery for representing properties of the sign gesture, but fall short of accounting for the systematic changes noted in (30). In the next section I review the M- and H-segments and present an alternative representation of the segments that will (i) resolve the internal inconsistencies of these segments with the modality-free segments, and (ii) resolve the empirical problems cited here.

6.2.5   An Alternative Analysis

In this section I show that the M and H segments are problematic because they overgenerate structures. To solve that problem, resolve the incongruities with the simultaneous SPE and post-SPE properties of the

M and H segments, and provide a more satisfactory analysis of blends, I propose to reduce the M and H segments to a single segment type.

With the OCP-like stipulation in (36a) Liddell and Johnson rule out a large number of possible structures. Restated as a Principle of Shared Features, (36b), sequences like those in (36c) are ruled out for lexicalized signs.

(36)   a.   An initial posture of any segment in a string is identical to the final posture of the preceding segment...[because]... a single articulator.. can only start a gesture from the posture in which it terminated the preceding gesture (Liddell and Johnson 1989:213).

       b.   Principle of Shared Features:
            Adjacent segments in a sign share adjacent feature complexes.

       c.   (i)

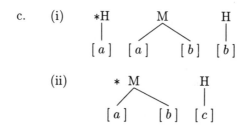

Although structures like those in (36c) are ruled out, the structures in (37) are well-formed. However, each of these well-formed structures has the same sequence of features, [a] and [b], and differ only by the sequence of timing segments. So the model predicts that signs may differ only by the minor variations in timing reflected by the combinations of M and H segments in (37). Yet there is no empirical data to support this prediction. Differences in handshape, location, and orientation as well as sequences of changes between them produce contrastive signs, but differences in timing like that reflected by the structures in (37) are not distinctive.

(37)

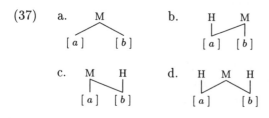

To eliminate this overgeneration of structures I propose a single segmental structure that combines the properties of both the M and H
segments. Drawing on the basic observation of the transition-based
model that movement is a transition between two points, I propose a
single timing segment, **Y**, combined into a structure that represents the
sign gesture, **SG**. The representation of the sign is defined in (38a); the
skeleton structure is given in (38b).

(38)   a.   A sign has two and only two Y segments, each associ-
              ated with a single feature bundle.

       b.

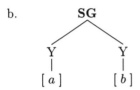

Using the structure in (38b), the representations for the signs that
contribute to the blend THINK-SELF are given in (39). The articulatory
bundles are the same as for the M-H representations.

(39)

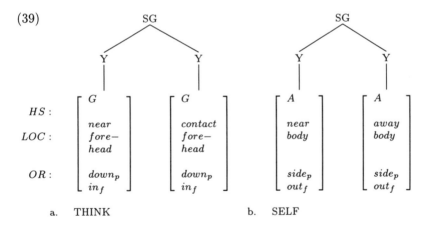

Recall that both gestures represented in (39) are articulated with a
smooth movement between two locations. For example, to articulate
(39a) the hand starts near the forehead and moves towards the forehead
until the tip of the finger touches the forehead. The gesture is smooth
because during the transition the change between the starting and ending time and between the starting and ending locations is proportional.

In order for the structures in (39) to capture those characteristics the definition of the timing segment needs to be considered.

For example, if the Y-segment is defined as having inherent duration, as for the X-segment, (23b), then the relation between time and location would follow the illustration in (40a) where location changes abruptly from LOC_1 to LOC_2 at time t_j, the juncture between the time intervals Y_1 and Y_2. As indicated by the asterisk, *, that is not the desired result. Rather, if Y is defined as a specific point in time then, as illustrated in (40b), the association between location and time more accurately reflects the properties of the gesture. At time t_i the hand starts at location LOC_1 and at time t_k it stops at location LOC_2.

(40)   a.

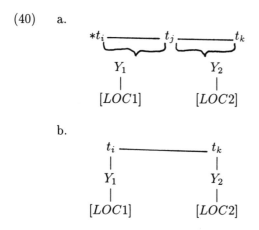

    b.

(41a) redefines the (modality-free) timing segment to represent a point in time, and (41b) is a general principle that ensures the transition from one point to another is continuous.

(41)   a.   (25b(i))' A time segment, Y, represents a discrete point in time.

    b.   Changes between parameter values are smooth.

With this proposed modification, I continue with an alternative analysis for combining signs into blends. In this analysis blending is the combination of the feature bundles from the two input signs into the basic structure for the sign gesture given in (38b) so that the initial result is a single sign structure with four feature complexes.[4] For the structure to be well-formed, however, the four feature complexes must be reduced

---

[4] As noted by Brentari (1990b) not all two-sign combinations reduce to a single sign

to two. To account for that reduction, I propose a set of general principles that apply to each category of features, namely *location, handshape, palm orientation* and *finger orientation.*
The first basic principle to apply is a form of the OCP, (42).

(42)   Adjacent segments in a sign share adjacent feature complexes.

The principles in (43) account for the reorganization of location features in blends. (43a) captures a set of dominance relations. When two feature units are in competition for a single position, the dominant one wins. Although not applicable to THINK-SELF, (43a(iii)) relates (43a(i)) and (43a(ii)). In a conflict between an edge and contact, the location with contact will be preserved. The features in (43b) are the locations contributed by the input signs. By (43a(i)), *contact forehead* is a dominant location, so it is preserved. In the absence of contact in the second input sign, the value of the right edge, *away body*, is retained. The output features for location are given in (43c).

(43)   a.   Location
      (i)   A location with contact is dominant.
      (ii)   The right edge of the sign is dominant.
      (iii)   Contact is more dominant than the right edge of the sign.

$$\text{b.} \quad \begin{bmatrix} near \\ forehead \end{bmatrix} \quad \begin{bmatrix} contact \\ forehead \end{bmatrix} \quad \begin{bmatrix} near \\ body \end{bmatrix} \quad \begin{bmatrix} away \\ body \end{bmatrix}$$

$$\text{c.} \quad \qquad\qquad \begin{bmatrix} contact \\ forehead \end{bmatrix} \qquad\qquad \begin{bmatrix} away \\ body \end{bmatrix}$$

The principle in (44a) that applies to handshape is stipulative because, for the purposes of this discussion, I treat handshape as a unit.[5] The application of the general principle in (42) to the handshape features from the input signs, (44b), produces (44c). Applying (44a) produces the final result, (44d).

---

gesture; some are articulated with two sign gestures, e.g., BLACK-NAME. I propose that the same principles formulated here will also apply in those cases. Based on general principles of maximum SG structure, it should be possible for the model to predict whether a lexicalized combination of signs will result in a single or double SG structure. Unfortunately, that analysis is beyond the scope of this discussion.

[5]It should be possible to state a more general set of principles on handshape based on joint and finger specifications. This work is left for future research.

(44)   a.   Handshape: $G \rightarrow L \: / \: \_\_ \: A$

    b. $[\,G\,]$ $[\,G\,]$ $[\,A\,]$ $[\,A\,]$

    c. $[\,G\,]$ $[\,A\,]$

    d. $[\,L\,]$ $[\,A\,]$

The principle in (45a) accounts for palm orientation. Applying the general principle in (42) to the input features in (45b) produces (45c). The palm orientation principle, (45a), then applies to (45c), with the result in (45d).

(45)   a.   Palm Orientation: Right edge is dominant.

    b. $[\,down_p\,]$ $[\,down_p\,]$ $[\,side_p\,]$ $[\,side_p\,]$

    c. $[\,down_p\,]$ $[\,side_p\,]$

    d. $[\,side_p\,]$ $[\,side_p\,]$

For finger orientation, no special principle is necessary. Only the general principle, (42), applies to the input features in (46a) to produce (46b).

(46)   a. $[\,in_f\,]$ $[\,in_f\,]$ $[\,out_f\,]$ $[\,out_f\,]$

    b. $[\,in_f\,]$ $[\,out_f\,]$

Combining the results for each feature type, the final sign gesture is shown in (47).

(47)   THINK-SELF:

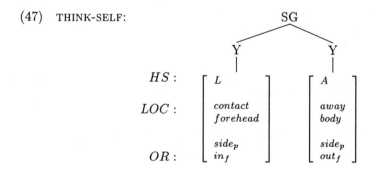

A comparison of the output of the Movement Hold model, (36c), with (47) shows that the latters provides a more satisfactory account of the data. The modified definition of the segment as a Y-segment ensures that the transitions between the feature values are smooth. The structural skeleton of the blend is also the same as the skeletons of the input signs. Hence, all the odd mismatches between the number of segments in the representation and the timing of the gesture are eliminated in this alternative analysis. In sum, the properties of the blends summarized in (30) are captured by the structure in (47).

The chart in (48) presents a comparison of the Movement Hold analysis of blends with the alternative analysis presented here. As indicated by the chart, the latter is simpler. It requires one less timing segment, presents a more restricted representation of the sign gesture, and relies on general principles of organization such as dominance, rather than specific rules to capture the systematic relation between signs.

(48)	Movement Hold Analysis	Alternative Analysis
	M-segment H-segment	Y-segment
	Contacting Hold Rule (for compounding)	LOC > LOC (CONTACT) (rt. edge)
	Handshape Adjust. Rule	Handshape rule
	Palm Orient. Adjust. Rule	Palm orientation rule
	Movement Epenthesis Rule	

(49) summarizes the problems facing the Movement Hold model. As has been shown here, an analysis that reconsiders the definition of the segment in terms specific to the properties of the sign gesture is preferable. It eliminates the overgeneration of structures, reduces the number of timing segments in blends, and eliminates the asymmetric distribution of handshape and location values in blends.

(49) a. Over-generates structures.
       b. Too many timing segments in blends.
       c. Asymmetric distribution of HS in blends.
       d. Asymmetric distribution of LOC in blends.

6.3   Feature Geometry and Segments

The final model that I consider is the *Hand Tier model* (Sandler 1989). Three observations about the MH model influence it. First, citing a lack of distinction from M-segments and a lack of explicit phonological evidence, Sandler calls into question the status of holds (H) as timing segments. Preserving the notion that there are two contrasting timing segments, she keeps the M segment, but replaces the H segment with a *location* (L) segment. Second, Sandler claims that handshape changes for monomorphemic signs are predictable, proposing that only related pairs of handshapes participate in handshape change, and that hand configuration information is a property of the morpheme and separated from the segmental organization of the sign. Finally, Sandler adopts two distinct feature geometry trees: one that organizes location features and associates with the segment, (50), and one that organizes hand configuration features, (51), and associates with the morpheme.

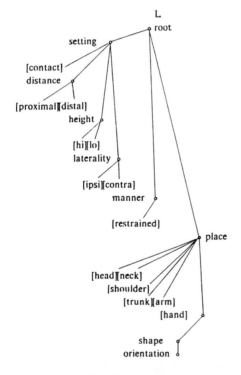

(50)   Location (Sandler 1989:134)

The internal structure of these feature geometry trees are consistent with spoken language feature trees.

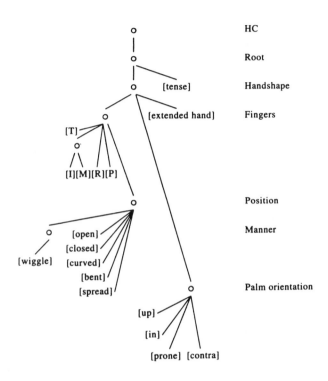

(51)   Hand Configuration (Sandler 1993:105)

Although the application of *segment* in the Hand Tier model is consistent with the modality-free segment, the notion of *feature geometry* introduces some problematic innovations. I start by presenting a modality-free definition of feature geometry.

6.3.1   Modality-free Feature Geometry

The primary motivation for *feature geometry* in spoken language is the observation that distinctive features repeatedly group themselves into natural classes that reflect regularities of distribution and alternation. To that end, a feature geometry is an organization of features into a hierarchical tree structure. The definition of feature geometry I adopt, (52), includes the assumptions from the original proposals (Mohanan 1983, Clements 1985). Subsequent developments in feature geometry exhibit a different set of assumptions that are not entirely consistent with (52), adding complexity to the structure and compromising the formalism (Sagey 1986, Archangeli and Pulleyblank 1986, McCarthy 1988).

(52)   Modality-free *Feature Geometry*:

    a. Formally, a feature geometry is the mathematical object called tree, a connected graph that does not contain any cycles. The feature geometry tree is directed and rooted, and its sister nodes are unordered.

    b. The tree is dominated by a *root node* that associates to a timing segment.

    c. A *root node* is distinct only in terms of its terminal nodes.

    d. Each non-terminal node in the tree represents a class of features. The substance of the formal statement *node A dominates node B* is that *node B is grouped under node A*.

    e. All non-terminal nodes are present for every segment.

For completeness I include the modality-free definitions of the *root node* from the previous section.

(53)   *Root Node*:
    (i) A root node does not have inherent duration.
    (ii) Given any two root nodes, one must be temporally ordered after the other.

What Sandler (1989, 1993b) refers to as the canonical timing structure of the sign is shown in (54). The timing tier is represented by a sequence of location (L) and movement (M) segments. The root node that dominates the hand configuration tree associates with each segment of the timing structure. In turn, each L-segment associates with a root node that dominates a feature geometry tree of location. The M-segment also associates with a root node that immediately branches to share the place nodes of the L-segments on either side of it. Sandler (1989) proposes three features for movement, *shape*, *setting*, and *manner*, which are independent of either tree and will not be discussed here.

(54)   Canonical Timing Structure

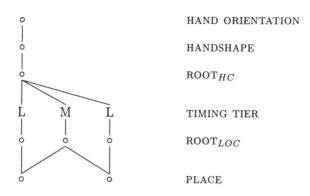

	HAND ORIENTATION
	HANDSHAPE
	$ROOT_{HC}$
	TIMING TIER
	$ROOT_{LOC}$
	PLACE

The structure in (54) is inconsistent with two parts of the definitions in (52) and (53). First, whereas (52b) specifies that a root node associates to a timing segment, in (54) the HC root node is also associated to a structure at the morphemic level. Second, (53ii) states that root nodes are temporally distinct, i.e., they cannot occur simultaneously. However, each of the three segments in (54) are associated with specifications for both $ROOT_{HC}$ and $ROOT_{LOC}$. Although the simultaneous association ensures that (52e) is met, where it could be interpreted to mean that all possible non-terminal nodes are present for every segment, the intent of the modality-free definition is that all features that represent a segment are present under a single root node.

The motivation for these innovations is centered on Sandler's claim that handshape change is predictable, subject to a single constraint, and that it is a property of the morpheme. To capture these properties, she represents handshape on a separate hand configuration (HC) tier. This is problematic on two counts. Firstly, as argued in Chapter 2, handshape change is subject to a set of constraints, not just a single constraint. Secondly, the representation of handshape change under a single root node forces the representation to allow ordered features. This is a crucial deviation from the feature geometry defined in (52a) because the sister nodes of the tree are formally unordered.[6] In this discussion I focus on the second problem.

---

[6] Although this is similar to spoken language proposals such as Sagey (1986), it still represents a modification to the tree graph that introduces extra complexity into the formal framework and requires further consideration. In other words, that the modification occurs in spoken language phonology does not automatically justify its application here.

Recall that when both the handshape and the location of a sign change during the articulation of a monomorphemic sign, they change simultaneously and the rate of change is the same. Hence one problem that immediately arises from the separation of hand configuration information and location information onto separate feature tiers is the need to coordinate their timing. To account for this, the Hand Tier model must stipulate a process of linearization (Sandler 1993b:115). As illustrated in (55), the features of the handshape contour that are associated with the position (POS) node migrate from the HC tree onto the root node for location features, mediated through the HC root node and the L timing segments. The motivation for the process is to synchronize the articulation of the handshape features with the other features of the sign.

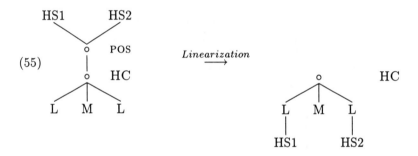

Unfortunately, a process like linearization represents a significant deviation from the idea of a modality-free interpretation of feature geometry for sign language and produces significant differences between spoken and sign language phonologies. For example, if the analogy is to hold, then the contour representation of handshape change ought to bear some resemblance to the representation of a sequence of tones in spoken language. But in that case, phonological linearization is implausible; the result would be that tones associate with two non-sequential timing segments.

In the next section I propose an alternative interpretation of the Hand Tier structures that resolves the inconsistencies of the feature geometry while preserving the major contribution of the model, namely that there is a hierarchical organization of sign features that captures the position and posture of the hand.

6.3.2   An Analysis of Blends

To illustrate the constructs and rules of the Hand Tier model, I apply it to the blend of THINK and SELF described in the previous section.

6.3.2.1   Hand Tier Analysis

The Hand Tier representations of the input signs are shown in (56). The timing segments, L and M, are at the center of the representation and associated with both the hand configuration and location trees. The hand configuration features are above the timing segments and the location features are below the timing segments. The notation for handshape (HS) includes the selected finger, I (*index finger*) and T (*thumb*), and the state of the joints. For both signs, the joints are extended (*open*). Of the three place features, the first indicates the proximity of the hand to the body, the second identifies an area of articulation, and the third identifies a specific place within that area of articulation.

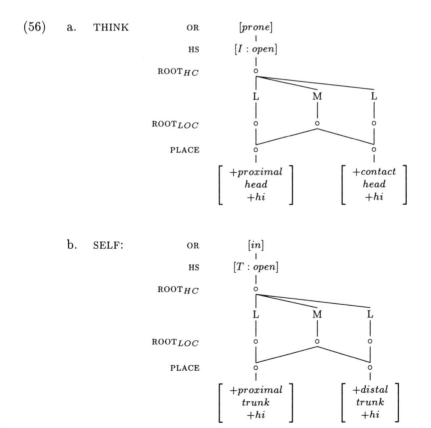

(56)   a.   THINK

b.   SELF:

Sandler (1993b:107) describes two processes that apply when signs are blended: (i) "the first location of the second sign is deleted", and (ii) "the HC that was associated to it, HC_2... does not delete, but rather spreads leftward onto the previous location". I formalize (i) as the rule in (57a); Sandler presents (ii) as the rule in (57b).

(57)   a.   Second Sign Location Deletion:

$$L \rightarrow \emptyset \; / \; [LML] \, [\text{\underline{\hspace{1em}} } ML]$$

b.   Total HC Assimilation:

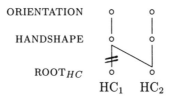

ORIENTATION	○	○
HANDSHAPE	○	○
ROOT$_{HC}$	○	○
	HC_1	HC_2

The rules in (57) alone are, however, not sufficient to account for the changes that the signs undergo during blending so, borrowing from the MH model, I include the Contacting Location Rule in (58). The rule states that if there is contact with the body in the first sign of the blend, then the segments that do not contact the body are deleted. Given the relations between the timing segments in the canonical LML structure, this means that either a sequence of LM or ML is deleted.

(58)   Contacting Location Rule:

$$\left\{ \begin{array}{c} LM \\ ML \end{array} \right\} \rightarrow \emptyset \; / \; \underset{\substack{| \\ [+contact]}}{[...L...]} \quad [LML]$$

The structures in (59) illustrate the application of the rules in (57) and (58) to the input structures in (56). To simplify the presentation I present only the parts of the signs that are affected by each rule.

(59)   a.   Input Signs:

b.   Second Sign Location Deletion:

c.   Contaction Location Rule:

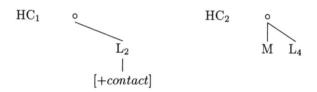

d.   Total HC Assimilation:

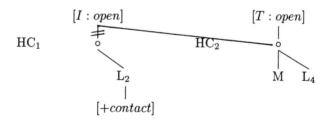

Once all the rules have applied, the parts of the input signs that remain, L_2, M, and L_4, (59d), are recombined into an LML template, as shown in (60).

(60)

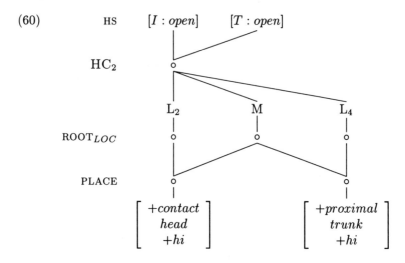

Linearization applies to (60) and results in the final form in (61). The handshape features migrate through the timing segments to the location feature tree.

(61)

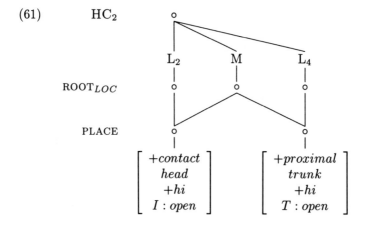

In sum, the Hand Tier model can provide a representation for blending, but the logical inconsistencies of the feature geometries persist, diminishing the inherent power of the formalism as well as its relevance to spoken language phonology and, hence, to a universal theory of phonology.

6.3.2.2 An Alternative Analysis

To resolve the inconsistencies between the modality-free feature geometry and the Hand Tier feature geometries, I present a two-pronged approach: (i) reduce the L and M timing segments to a single timing segment, and (ii) reorganize the features into a single feature geometry. This will, in addition, simplify the model.

The segments in (62) are extracted from the canonical LML sign structure in (54). From this perspective, they are structurally distinct. The location root node associated with the M-segment splits to associate with two place nodes, (62a), whereas the location root node for the L-segment, (62b), associates with a single place node.

(62)   a.   M-segment   b.   L-segment

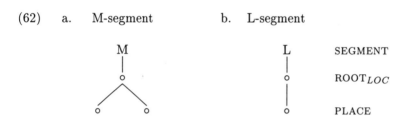

I propose that the segments in (62) be replaced with those in (63), where an M-segment is defined as a Y-segment with a branching root nodè and an L-segment is a Y-segment with a single non-branching root node. Borrowing from the discussion about the MH model, the Y-segment is the same as the spoken language segment, except that the time segment refers to a point rather than an interval of time.

(63)   a.   "M-segment"   b.   "L-segment"

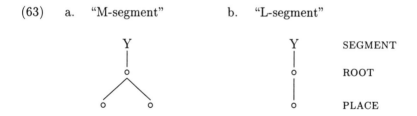

The canonical sign skeleton can be represented as (64). From this perspective, the Y-segment in the middle of the structure is redundant because it shares the place values of its neighbors. It is also associated with the same features from the HC node. The only unique information that it provides are movement features. Yet as reflected by the central position of the M segment in the canonical structure of the Hand Tier model, and its association with all available feature information, those feature values are also distributed across the sign.

(64) [HC]   Hand Config.

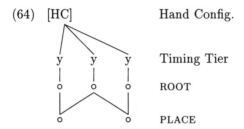

Allowing the hand configuration and movement features to migrate to the head of the sign structure, SG (sign gesture), the structure in (64) can then be simplified to (65). The introduction of the head provides a central point for representing features that apply to the whole structure.

(65)   SG   Head
       [HC, M]

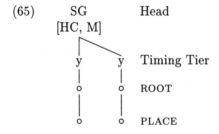

To eliminate the need for linearization the hand configuration features are re-organized with the location features into the unified feature geometry in (66).

(66)   Unified Feature Geometry

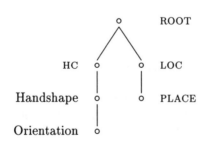

In the final representation, HC features whose domain is the sign (for example, features like *wiggle* might fall into this category) are represented in the head (SG); all other HC features are represented in the feature geometry. The autonomy between hand configuration and location is preserved by organizing them under distinct nodes joined under a single root node.

Although this structure compromises the autonomy between hand configuration and timing introduced by the Hand Tier model, it resolves the inconsistencies between the modality-free root node and the Hand Tier root node, and the modality-free feature geometry and the Hand Tier feature geometry. And, as shown below, it simplifies the analysis of blends. The modified representations for the input signs to the blend are given in (67) and (68).

(67)   THINK:

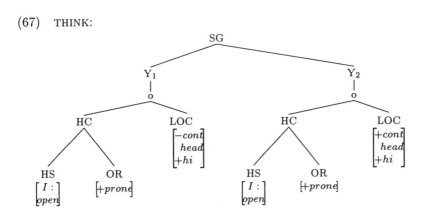

(68)   SELF:

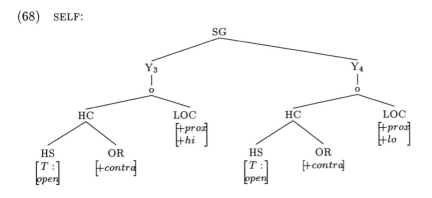

The conditions that apply in this analysis are the same as those in the alternative analysis for the MH model. They are repeated in (69).[7]

(69)   a.   If adjacent features are identical, one is deleted.

        b.   Location:

             (i)   A location with contact is dominant.

             (ii)   The right edge of the sign is dominant.

             (iii)   Contact is more dominant than the right edge of the sign.

        c.   Handshape: $[I : open] \rightarrow [TI : open] /$ ___ $[T : open]$

        d.   Palm Orientation: Right edge is dominant.

So the root nodes dominated by the segments Y_1, Y_2, Y_3, and Y_4, order the location, handshape, and orientation features on the same tiers. In (70), (71), and (72), I focus on one tier at a time and describe the result of applying the propositions in (69).

The input values for location are shown in (70a). The propositions in (69b) apply. Specifically, (69b(i)) preserves the feature cluster with contact, and (69b(ii)) preserves the right edge of the second input sign. The resulting location features for the target structure are given in (70b).

$$(70) \quad a. \quad \begin{bmatrix} -contact \\ head \\ +hi \end{bmatrix} \begin{bmatrix} +contact \\ head \\ +hi \end{bmatrix} \begin{bmatrix} +prox \\ +hi \end{bmatrix} \begin{bmatrix} +prox \\ +lo \end{bmatrix}$$

$$b. \quad \begin{bmatrix} +contact \\ head \\ +hi \end{bmatrix} \qquad\qquad \begin{bmatrix} +prox \\ +lo \end{bmatrix}$$

The input values for handshape are given in (71a). First the OCP-like rule in (69a) applies, (71b), then the handshape specific proposition in (69c) applies with the final result in (71c).

(71)   a. $[\,I : open\,]$ $[\,I : open\,]$ $[\,T : open\,]$ $[\,T : open\,]$

        b. $[\,I : open\,]$ $[\,T : open\,]$

        c. $[\,TI : open\,]$ $[\,T : open\,]$

---

[7]For some signs, the blend might require two SG structures. General principles of dominance apply; i.e., given a conflict between two values, the more dominant one wins.

The input values for palm orientation are given in (72a). (69a) applies with the result in (72b), then (69d) applies with the final values in (72c).[8]

(72) a.   [+prone] [+prone]   [+contra] [+contra]

    b.   [+prone]   [+contra]

    c.   [+contra]   [+contra]

Recombining the parts into the sign template produces the structure in (73).

(73) THINK-SELF:

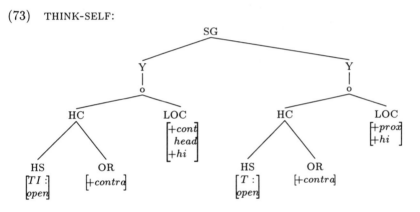

In sum, by proposing two modifications to Sandler's model, namely (i) reduce the M and L segments to a Y segment, and (ii) combine the feature geometries under a single root node, the model is simplified. Inconsistencies between spoken language feature geometry representations and the Hand Tier model are resolved, and the linearization process is no longer necessary.

The result is similar to the alternative proposal presented in the previous section for the MH model, albeit with the addition of the organization of the features into a feature geometry. Crucially, the difference between the spoken language segment and the Y segment is the specification of time — for the former it is a time interval, for the latter it is a point in time. This difference reflects the asymmetry between visual images and auditory "images" noted in the first chapter. Recall that

---

[8]Although finger orientation is significant (see the alternative analysis in the MH model), Sandler only represents palm orientation.

a visual image requires only a moment in time to capture, whereas an auditory image requires a time interval.

Moving On

In this chapter I have reviewed three models of sign structure that adopt a transfer-and-test model for sign analysis. The Moraic model is dependent on the notion of a sign specific sonority hierarchy that requires further cross-linguistic consideration. The Movement Hold and Hand Tier models can be simplified with an adjustment to a modality-independent definition of the segment. In all three cases, the transfer of the spoken language phonology to account for sign language data is not unproblematic.

In the final chapter I compare the structural properties of the spoken language segment and syllable with the properties of the transition unit and syllable. The differences between them provide more clues towards understanding the types of differences between language modes that plague a transfer-and-test model of signs.

7

A Different Mode

At the outset of the thesis I proposed that language mode, visual or spoken, matters to a theory of phonology and that a modality independent universal theory of phonology will depend on being able to generalize from two mode specific theories of phonology. In this final chapter I summarize the findings of the geometry based approach to visual phonology developed in this thesis. In particular I compare the phonological constructs from visual phonology, the *transition unit* and *cell*, with what appears organizationally to be their spoken language counterparts, the *segment* and *syllable*. I show that they are distinct in ways that reflect the language modes they represent.

I conclude that, with respect to a theory of universal phonology, neither the current organization of phonological structure, the segment and syllable, nor the set of constructs argued for in this thesis are sufficiently abstract to account for both modes of data. Whether a single, sufficiently abstract, theoretical framework can resolve the differences and apply to both modes of language, or whether distinct language modes will always require distinct theoretical frameworks remains a question to be answered in a program that undertakes research of both sign and spoken languages. Whatever the final result, either outcome should lead to a single universal theory of phonology. In spite of their differences, the constructs of the visual and spoken language phonologies crucially share formal organizational properties that are best explained in terms of a universal theory of phonology.

7.1 The Geometry of Visual Phonology

The work in this thesis demonstrates that, of the formal languages available, geometry is the appropriate one for representing the properties of the sign gesture. Recognizing that the form of the hand and its constituents remain constant under change, the parts of the manual articulator are modeled as *rigid bodies*. Their movements can then be characterized as *rigid body transformations*, functions that characterize how a rigid body moves. Of specific interest are rigid body *translation*, movement of a body from one point to another, and rigid body *rotation*, movement of a body about a point. Because a rigid body transformation applies without regard to the path between the initial and final positions of the body, other geometric functions are adopted, specifically formulae for linear path, circular path, and angular displacement.

What this subset of geometry means for the representation of signs is that the movements of the hand can be formalized mathematically. In this model, manual movements to articulate signs are classified into three categories: change in location, change in orientation, and change in handshape. As summarized in (1), each of these categories of movements are based on characteristics captured by the formalisms mentioned above: the scope of the rigid body, the transformation that applies to the body, and the formula for the path of the transformation.

(1)	Rigid Body	Transformation	Path Function
Change in Location	Whole Hand	Translation	Line Circle
Change in Orientation	Forearm, Hand, or Fingers	Rotation	Angular displacement
Change in Handshape	Individual Joints of Fingers	Rotation	(Matrix of) Angular displacement

Signing space is also formalized in terms of geometry. The space that the hand moves in is represented as a set of four embedded rectangular prisms: *hand prism, local signing space, global signing space,* and *discourse signing space.* The prisms are related at each level by *location* and *orientation,* dyadic relations that specify the position of one prism relative to the prism it is nested in.

Taken together, namely the rigid body characterization of the hand, rigid body transformations, path functions, spatial constructs, and location and orientation, geometry provides the formal language for representing the complete sign gesture capturing both static and dynamic properties of the hands.

7.2   The Phonology of Visual Geometry

In this phonology the sign gesture is characterized as a rigid body moving through space. One set of phonological constructs refers to properties of the hand, and another refers to properties and relations of space. The two are combined in the organizational constructs, the *transition unit* and *cell*.

7.2.1   Hand

The distributional asymmetries and alternations of signs lead to the hierarchical organization of the hand in (2).

(2)

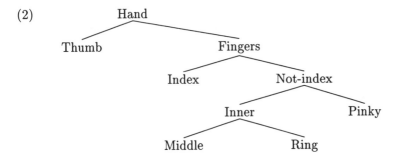

Each finger and the thumb are further subdivided into joints, as in (3). Although there are three joints per finger or thumb, only two sets, *base* and *non-base*, are phonologically significant.

(3)

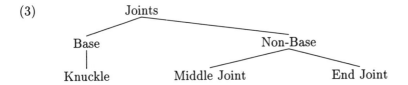

A handshape is specified by three pieces of information: (i) *selected* and *unselected* fingers (and thumb), (ii) *opposed* or *unopposed* thumb, and (iii) binary joint features, [EXT] and [FLEX]. In terms of the hierarchical structure in (2), fingers and thumb are *selected* at the level of the hand node, only the thumb node is specified for *opposition*, and each of the terminal nodes is specified for the binary features [EXT] and [FLEX]. Although the organization presented in (2) and (3) resemble the trees of spoken language feature geometry, the properties of handshape require further investigation before being characterized as a feature geometry of visual phonology.

7.2.2 Space

Each of the spatial constructs, *hand prism, local signing space, global signing space*, and *discourse signing space*, provides a frame of reference for the space nested immediately inside it, so the location and orientation for each prism is stated in terms of its reference frame.

With respect to location, the base of the hand (or forearm, or wrist for some signs) associates with the bottom of the hand prism in a fixed position. In turn, the hand prism is situated in local signing space with respect to phonologically relevant reference planes: the *base plane*, the *non-base plane*, the *center*, and the *ipsilateral* and *contralateral sides*. The location of local signing space in global signing space is specified as one of several places on or near the body included in a currently stipulative inventory of places.

With respect to orientation, each side of the hand is associated with one of the six faces of the hand prism. In turn, the orientation of the hand prism is specified relative to the planes of local signing space. The orientation of local signing space in global signing space is morphologically significant, in particular for the interpretation of agreement verbs. Hence, the orientation relation at different levels of signing space is one property that links visual phonology to other parts of the grammar.

Another interesting property of the relations between the spatial constructs is the relaxation of constraints on spatial relations as the space under consideration gets bigger. In other words, the bigger the space, the greater the number of options. For example, the location of the hand in the hand prism is fixed, but the hand prism may be located at any of the six faces of local signing space. At the next level of the spatial hierarchy, the location of local signing space in global signing space is less constrained. Location is no longer bound to just the planes of global signing space. Rather, local signing space can be situated in a number of different places on the body as well as in the space in front of the body. Similar levels of relaxation on the constraints on orientation can also be identified. These properties of the spatial hierarchy bear further consideration.

In particular, findings about the characteristics of signs at specific levels of signing space may prove relevant to issues about the phonological primacy of movements (Sandler 1989, 1993). As noted in the thesis, the paths of the hand within local signing space are restricted to the line and circle. However, data like that in (4) illustrate a verbal modulation which exhibits a combination of a linear and arc-shaped path. This deviation from the constraints imposed on signs at the lexical level can be explained by considering the relation between visual morphology and the properties of the spatial hierarchy described above.

(4) a. LOOK-AT$_{regularly}$ b. LOOK-AT$_{over-and-over-again}$

The range of variation and the representation of these paths are left as tasks for future work.

7.2.3 Transition Unit

The *transition unit* relates timing information to the spatial constructs for hand and space to capture the dynamic properties of the sign gesture. In the unmarked case the relation between space and time in the transition unit is dictated by the Principle of Proportionality. In the marked cases the model provides the means to specify more complex relations between space and time.

For example, a verb may be articulated quickly or slowly to reflect the speed with which the action transpires. With the information captured by the transition unit this property of signs can be captured as a specific relation between time and space. (5a) represents the unmarked case in which the change in time and space are proportional. In contrast, (5b) represents a situation in which the sign takes twice as long to articulate, and (5c) represents a situation in which the sign is articulated in half the time, or at twice the speed of the unmarked case.

(5) a. $$\frac{P_f - P_i}{t_f - t_i} = \frac{\Delta P}{\Delta t} = speed$$

 b. $$\frac{P_f - P_i}{2(t_f - t_i)} = \frac{\Delta P}{2\Delta t} = \frac{speed}{2}$$

 c. $$\frac{2(P_f - P_i)}{t_f - t_i} = \frac{2\Delta P}{\Delta t} = 2(speed)$$

Similarly, signs may be articulated with a characteristic that has been described as "tenseness". For example, the sign for GOOD can be articulated with a tensed movement that results in a gesture meaning *really good*. The sensation of tenseness, however, corresponds to the acceleration of the hand. In terms of physics, acceleration is expressed as a change in speed over a change in time, and can be specified in terms of the information provided in the transition unit. The formula for this is given in (6).

(6) Acceleration ("tenseness")

$$\frac{speed_f - speed_i}{t_f - t_i} \quad = \quad \frac{\frac{\Delta P_f}{\Delta t} - \frac{\Delta P_i}{\Delta t}}{\Delta t} \quad = \quad \frac{\Delta P_f - \Delta P_i}{\Delta t^2}$$

Independent of the mathematical details, the point here is to suggest that the properties of the sign captured by the transition unit can be used to provide formal representations for other properties of signs, in particular adverbial and verbal modulations of signs that hitherto have eluded or complicated formal phonological representations of signs.

7.2.4 Cell

Finally, the *cell* organizes transition units to specify a sign gesture. The usefulness of the cell has been demonstrated through the specification of minimum and maximum constraints on the sign gesture, as well as accounting for the properties of agreement verbs.

7.3 Segment, Syllable, Transition Unit, and Cell

In this section I compare the spoken language constructs *segment* and *syllable* with the constructs from the visual phonology, *transition unit* and *cell*. The similarities and differences that emerge are instructive in two ways. First, they shed light on why attempts to apply the segment and syllable directly to sign language phenomena are problematic, and second, they provide information for formulating strategies to work towards a theory of universal phonology.

7.3.1 Segment and Transition Unit

Independent of theoretical frameworks, in spoken language phonology the notion *segment* captures two properties of speech: (i) the state of the speech articulators (ii) over a period of time. In visual phonology the *transition unit* captures the state of part of the speech articulators at and between two points in time. In spoken language phonology the segment is a component of the syllable, and in visual phonology the transition unit is a component of the cell. Thus, these are good candidates for comparison.

The properties of the segment and transition unit are summarized in (7).

(7)

		Segment	Transition Unit
	a.	A segment associates a time unit with a feature geometry.	A transition unit associates a time unit with a spatial unit.
	b.	A segment represents a duration of time.	A transition unit represents a duration of time, specified by distinct endpoints
	c.	A distinctive feature is relevant only at the level of phonology.	A parameter in a spatial unit may relate to morphological, syntactic or semantic structure.
	d.	Given any two segments, one must follow the other.	Transition units may co-occur.
	e.	Feature values are the same for the duration of a simple segment; values change for a complex segment.	Spatial values may remain the same or change during a transition unit.
	f.	A segment represents all the properties of an articulatory gesture.	A transition unit represents part of the properties of an articulatory gesture.

The segment and transition unit are similar because they relate gestural information to time, and because they mediate between that combination of information and the next level of organization – for spoken language phonology, the syllable, and for visual phonology, the cell. But after that initial set of similarities, the properties of the constructs diverge. Specifically, they differ in their interpretation of time and their organization of information.

Whereas the entire time interval for the segment is an atomic unit, the endpoints of a time interval are crucial to the transition unit. The organization of the information associated with each construct reflects these distinct interpretations of time. Segments are classified by the values of their distinctive features – features that are generally relevant only

at the level of phonology. In contrast, the nature of the spatial information organized by the transition unit varies according to the morphological, syntactic, and semantic setting of the sign. This is an interesting
distinction that I return to later.

In addition, whereas the segment represents the state of all parts
of the speech articulators over an interval of time, the transition unit
presents only a partial picture of the manual articulators. That is, a
transition unit only captures information about handshape, location, or
orientation, but never a combination of them. This latter contrast is
related to the other temporal discrepancy between the units, namely
that segments may not co-exist in time, whereas transition units can.
In other words, given two spoken language segments, one is temporally
ordered with respect to the other. Crucially, transition units may co-
occur.

Clearly, the transition unit and segment differ in a number of ways,
but the differences can be split into two categories: (i) the specification
of time, and (ii) the properties of the information they organize.

In spoken language phonology, the root node and the information
associated with it is associated with an interval of time. The content of
a simple segment is the same throughout the interval of time, but for a
complex segment the information dominated by a root node may change.
In a similar fashion, the spatial properties associated with a transition
unit may remain the same over a time interval, as for a simple segment,
or they may change, as for a complex segment. Unlike the complex
segment, however, the distinct gestural information in a transition unit
bears a specific relation to time. The initial properties of a gesture
associate with the start of the time interval, and the final properties
associate with the end of the interval. In contrast, the specific relation
between temporal and gestural information in a complex segment is not
as clear.

This contrast raises an interesting question about the feature geometry representation of complex segments. In its original form, feature
geometry is not a geometry at all, but a representation from a branch of
mathematics known as graph theory. The tree-based organization of features in phonology is formally a rooted, directed, and connected graph
without cycles. In its original formulation (Mohanan 1983, Clements
1985) the sister nodes are unordered; the graph captures only dominance relations (constituency). In subsequent proposals, branching and,
consequently, ordering under the root node is allowed to account for
the properties of change associated with complex segments. This addition of sequential information complicates the original formalism without
specifically addressing the distribution of the feature values over time.

One possibility raised by this comparison between the transition unit and segment is that a more elaborate timing structure might also be relevant to a representation of spoken language. If that is the case, then in terms of timing characteristics, the segment and transition unit might not differ so greatly.

The other difference between the complex segment and transition unit is more difficult to reconcile. The segment organizes distinctive features, constructs that in spoken language figure almost exclusively at the level of phonology. For example, place features like *coronal* and *labial* reflect properties of the articulators that rarely, if at all, are related to verb morphology. In contrast, as discussed in Chapter 5, the location and orientation of local signing space in global signing space, both inherently phonological properties, are crucial to the interpretation of verb agreement.

That the transition unit routinely organizes information that extends beyond the domain of phonology, whereas such phenomenon are rare in spoken language phonology, presents an intriguing asymmetry between the phonologies. In this model of visual phonology the difference is reflected by an organization of phonological constructs unlike that of spoken language constructs. Whereas the constructs in spoken language phonology are distinctive features that classify segments, the constructs in visual phonology such as *location* and *orientation* are dyadic relations that specify relations between constructs. From this perspective the differences are unlikely to be resolved by adjusting the organization of the spoken language phonology to accommodate the properties of the visual phonology, or tweaking the constructs of visual phonology to more closely resemble spoken language constructs. If these differences can be resolved at all, the resolution will likely depend on understanding more about the relations between visual phonology and other modules of the grammar.

7.3.2 Syllable and Cell

The properties of the syllable and cell are summarized in (8). They are remarkably similar, reflecting more general organizational properties of phonology. As noted already, the syllable organizes a group of segments and a cell organizes transition units. In addition, both units impose minimal requirements on the units they organize; in the case of the syllable it is a specific segment, and in the case of the cell it is a transition unit that specifies a change. Both units also occupy distinct periods of time. If there are two syllables, one must follow the other; likewise, if there are two cells, one must follow the other.

(8)

Syllable	Cell
a. A syllable organizes a group of segments.	A cell organizes a set of transition units.
b. A syllable has an obligatory head.	The minimal cell includes a non-static transition unit.
c. Given any two syllables, one must follow the other.	Given any two cells, one must follow the other.
d. In a syllable segments are ordered sequentially.	In a cell transition units occur simultaneously.
e. In a syllable the number of segments may vary.	In a cell all properties of the manual articulators must be represented.

Just as for the transition unit and segment, the differences between the syllable and cell reflect different relations between temporal and informational organization. Whereas the syllable imposes sequential order on its components, the cell imposes simultaneous order on its components. And whereas the number of components in a syllable may vary, the cell requires all properties of the articulators to be represented. In this way the cell is more like the spoken language segment because it is at the highest level of the feature geometry that all properties of the speech articulators are included in the representation.

Unlike the segment, however, the cell (for a simple sign) can be composed of two simultaneously articulated transition units. In terms of the spoken language phonology, this is like a "super-complex" segment composed of two simultaneously changing distinctive features, an unattested phenomenon in spoken language. Again, this indicates that for either framework of phonology to account for the phenomena in the domain of the other would require extensive adjustments. The nature of those changes are left for future consideration.

A more intriguing situation is posed by the similar minimum requirements on the syllable and cell juxtaposed with their distinct temporal structure. With respect to (8b), it is not just that any segment may serve as the head of the syllable. Rather, a segment is eligible to serve as the syllable head only if it meets some minimal sonority criteria. Given that a single transition (of location) is the minimal requirement for a transition unit to serve as a minimal cell, this comparison seems to imply that some notion of sonority hierarchy is relevant to the visual phonology. However, the parallel is short-lived because the role of sonority is not only for the syllable to identify a head, but also to impose order on a string of segments. Given the temporal organization of the cell, namely the simultaneous nature of its components, this latter property of the sonority hierarchy is irrelevant in visual phonology. Unless it can be demonstrated that sonority plays an analogous role in the spatial organization of the cell, it seems unreasonable to count it among the relevant phonological properties of signs.

In sum, the property of simultaneity in the visual mode is likely to remain a major factor for differentiating two types of phonologies.

7.4 Universal Phonology

The theme that emerges from comparing the segment and transition unit, and the syllable and cell, is the difference between their temporal and spatial properties. In the visual mode information is presented simultaneously; in the spoken mode it is presented sequentially.

In the visual mode the phonological organization of spatial constructs is more directly linked to the morphological and syntactic properties of the language. For example, for some verbs the orientation of LSS in GSS is crucial to the meaning of the sign. Given that the rate at which the spoken articulators produce linguistic information outstrips the rate of the manual articulators, a similar link between grammatical modules in the spoken mode would be less critical. Thus it would appear that a general principle of conservation on the rate of information presentation across modes might hold on the language faculty, and that it will be reflected in the underlying representation of language.

Recall now the difference in vision and hearing presented in Chapter 1 and repeated in (9). A visual image can be captured in a moment at a discrete point in time, but a parallel does not exist for sound. In contrast, both visual and audio images can be captured over an interval of time.

(9)

	Vision	Hearing
Discrete point in time	Discrete image (snapshot)	*
Interval of time	Continuous image (videotape)	Continuous sound (audio-tape)

It is now possible to understand how this asymmetry contributes to differences between the constructs of the visual and spoken language phonologies. In this work on sign language the organization of the phonology is such that the atomic unit of the representation is a single piece of information, either handshape, location, or orientation, that defines the posture of the articulator at a discrete point in time – in effect, producing a snapshot of a part of the articulator. The phonology needs to have only a snapshot of the articulator at the start of the gesture and another at the end of the gesture to represent a sign gesture. General principles of the system apply to produce a continuous gesture. In contrast, the spoken language phonology must be organized to capture an image of the speech gesture – a task that requires the representation of all parts of the articulator over an interval of time. An image of the articulators at a specific point in time simply does not have the same status in the spoken language phonology as in the visual phonology. Determining how these distinct representational and organizational properties of the phonologies can be resolved to produce a uniform theory of universal phonology is now the challenge for future work.

Bibliography

Anderson, Stephen R. 1993. Linguistic Expression and Its Relation to Modality. In *Phonetics and Phonology, Volume 3: Current Issues in ASL Phonology*, ed. Geoffrey R. Coulter. 273–290. Academic Press.

Ann, Jean. 1993. *A Linguistic Investigation of the Relationship Between Physiology and Handshape*. Doctoral dissertation, University of Arizona.

Archangeli, Diana, and Douglas Pulleyblank. 1986. The content and structure of phonological representation. Tucson, Arizona: University of Arizona.

Baker, Charlotte. 1976. What's not on the other hand in American Sign Language. *CLS* 12:195–278.

Baker-Shenk, Charlotte, and Dennis Cokely. 1980. *American Sign Language: A Teacher's Resource Text on Grammar and Culture*. Washington, DC: Clerc Books, Gallaudet University Press.

Battison, Robbin. 1978. *Lexical Borrowing in American Sign Language*. Silver Spring, Maryland: Linstok Press.

Blevins, Juliette. 1993. The Nature of Constraints on the Nondominant Hand in ASL. In *Phonetics and Phonology: Volume 3, Current Issues in ASL Phonology*, ed. Geoffrey R. Coulter. 43–62. Academic Press.

Boyes-Braem, Penny Kaye. 1981. *Features of the Handshape in American Sign Language*. Doctoral dissertation, University of California, Berkeley.

Brentari, Diane. 1988. Backwards Verbs in ASL: Agreement Re-Opened. *CLS* 24:16–27.

Brentari, Diane. 1990a. Licensing in ASL Handshape Change. In *Sign Language Research: Theoretical Issues*, ed. Ceil Lucas. 57–68. Washington, D.C.: Gallaudet University Press.

Brentari, Diane. 1990b. *Theoretical Foundations of American Sign Language Phonology*. Doctoral dissertation, University of Chicago.

Brentari, Diane. 1992. Phonological representation in American Sign Language. *Language* 68:359–374. Review of Sandler (1989).

Brentari, Diane. 1993. Establishing a Sonority Hierarchy in American Sign Language: The Use of Simultaneous Structure in Phonology. *Phonology* 10:281–306.

Brentari, Diane. 1995. A prosodic account of two-handed signs. Paper presented at University of Groningen, Holland.

Brentari, Diane, and John A. Goldsmith. 1993. Secondary Licensing and the Nondominant Hand in ASL. In *Phonetics and Phonology: Volume 3, Current Issues in ASL Phonology*, ed. Geoffrey R. Coulter. 19–41. Academic Press.

Chomsky, Noam, and Morris Halle. 1968. *The Sound Pattern of English*. New York: Harper and Row.

Clements, G.N. 1985. The Geometry of Phonological Features. *Phonology Yearbook* 2:225–252.

Corina, David. 1990a. Handshape Assimilations in Hierarchical Phonological Representation. In *Sign Language Research: Theoretical Issues*, ed. Ceil Lucas. 27–49. Washington, D.C.: Gallaudet University Press.

Corina, David. 1990b. Reassessing the role of sonority in syllable structure: Evidence from a visual gestural language. *CLS* 25:33–43.

Corina, David. 1993. To Branch or Not to Branch: Underspecification in ASL Handshape Contours. In *Phonetics and Phonology: Volume 3, Current Issues in ASL Phonology*, ed. Geoffrey R. Coulter. 63–95. Academic Press.

Corina, David, and E. Sagey. 1989. Are Phonological Hierarchies Universal?: Evidence from American Sign Language. *ESCOL* 6:73–83.

Corina, David, and Wendy Sandler. 1993. On the nature of phonological structure in sign language. *Phonology* 10:165–207.

Crasborn, Onno. 1995. Articulatory Symmetry in Two-Handed Signs. Master's thesis, University of Nijmegen, Holland.

Friedman, Lynn A. 1976. *Phonology of a Soundless Language: Phonological Structure of American Sign Language*. Doctoral dissertation, University of California, Berkeley.

Frishberg, Nancy. 1976. *Some Aspects of the Historical Development of American Sign Language*. Doctoral dissertation, University of California, San Diego.

Gannon, Jack R. 1989. *The Week the World Heard Gallaudet*. Washington, D.C.: Gallaudet University Press.

Gerilee Gustason, Donna Pfetzing, Esther Zawolkow. 1980. *Signing Exact English*. Silver Spring, Maryland: Modern Signs Press. Illustrated by Carolyn B. Norris.

Goldsmith, John. 1976. *Autosegmental Phonology*. Doctoral dissertation, MIT. Distributed by the Indiana University Linguistics Club.

Hayes, Bruce. 1993. Against Movement: Comments on Liddell's Paper. In *Phonetics and Phonology: Volume 3, Current Issues in ASL Phonology*, ed. Geoffrey R. Coulter. 213–226. Academic Press.

Humphries, Tom, and Carol Padden. 1988. *Deaf in America: Voices from a Culture*. Cambridge, Massachusetts: Harvard University Press.

Humphries, Tom, and Carol Padden. 1992. *Learning American Sign Language*. Englewood Cliffs, New Jersey: Prentice Hall.

Humphries, Tom, Carol Padden, and Terrence J. O'Rourke. 1980. *A Basic Course in American Sign Language*. Silver Spring, Maryland: T.J. Publishers. Illustrated by Frank A. Paul.

Johnson, Robert. 1986. Metathesis in American Sign Language. Paper presented at the Theoretical Issues in Sign Language Research I Conference, Rochester, New York.

Klima, Edward S., and Ursala Bellugi. 1979. *The Signs of Language*. Cambridge, Massachusetts: Harvard University Press.

Liddell, Scott. 1984. Think and Believe: Sequentiality in American Sign Language. *Language* 60(2):372–399.

Liddell, Scott, and Robert Johnson. 1986. American Sign Language compound formation processes: lexicalization and phonological remnants. *Natural Language and Linguistic Theory* 4:445–513.

Liddell, Scott, and Robert Johnson. 1989. American Sign Language: The Phonological Base. *Sign Language Studies* 64:195–278.

Liddell, Scott K. 1980. *American Sign Language Syntax*. The Hague: Mouton Publishers.

Liddell, Scott K. 1990a. Four Functions of a Locus: Reexamining the Structure of Space in ASL. In *Sign Language Research: Theoretical Issues*, ed. Ceil Lucas. 176–198. Washington, D.C.: Gallaudet University Press.

Liddell, Scott K. 1990b. Structures for Representing Handshape and Local Movement at the Phonemic Level. In *Theoretical Issues in Sign Language Research, Volume 1: Linguistics*, ed. Susan D. Fischer and Patricia Siple. 37–65. Chicago, Illinois: The University of Chicago Press.

Lillo-Martin, Diane C. 1991. *Universal Grammar and American Sign Language*. The Netherlands: Kluwer Academic Publishers.

Lucas, Ceil. 1993. Internal Constraints on ASL Signs: The Case of DEAF. Paper presented at NWAVE 22, University of Ottawa.

Mandel, Mark Alan. 1981. *Phonotactics and Morphophonology in American Sign Language Phonology*. Doctoral dissertation, University of California, Berkeley.

McCarthy, John. 1988. Feature geometry and dependency: A review. *Phonetica* 43:84–108.

Meier, Richard P. 1990. Person Deixis in American Sign Language. In *Theoretical Issues in Sign Language Research, Volume 1: Linguistics*, ed. Susan D. Fischer and Patricia Siple. 175–190. Chicago, Illinois: The University of Chicago Press.

Mohanan, K.P. 1983. The Structure of the Melody. MIT.

Nagahara, Hiroyuki. 1988. Toward an Explicit Phonological Representation for American Sign Language. Master's thesis, University of California, Los Angeles.

Padden, Carol. 1988. *The Interaction of Morphology and Syntax in American Sign Language*. New York, New York: Garland Press. Outstanding Dissertation Series.

Padden, Carol A., and David M. Perlmutter. 1987. American Sign Language and the Architecture of Phonological Theory. *Natural Language and Linguistic Theory* 5:335–375.

Perlmutter, David. 1989. A moraic Theory of American Sign Language Syllable Structure. University of California, San Diego.

Perlmutter, David M. 1992. Sonority and Syllable Structure in American Sign Language. *Linguistic Inquiry* 23(3):407–442.

Sagey, E. 1986. *The representation of feature and relations in non-linear phonology.* Doctoral dissertation, MIT.

Sandler, Wendy. 1989. *Phonological Representation of the Sign: Linearity and Nonlinearity in American Sign Language.* Dordrecht: Foris.

Sandler, Wendy. 1993a. Hand in hand: The roles of the nondominant hand in sign language phonology. *The Linguistic Review* 10:337–390.

Sandler, Wendy. 1993b. Linearization of Phonological Tiers in ASL. In *Phonetics and Phonology: Volume 3, Current Issues in ASL Phonology,* ed. Geoffrey R. Coulter. 103–129. Academic Press.

Sandler, Wendy. 1993c. A Sonority Cycle in American Sign Language. *Phonology* 10:243–279.

Schick, Brenda S. 1990. Classifier Predicates in American Sign Language. *International Journal of Sign Linguistics* 1(1):15–40.

Stack, Kelly M. 1988. Tiers and Syllable Structure in American Sign Language: Evidence from Phonotactics. Master's thesis, University of California, Los Angeles.

Stewart, Ian, and Martin Golubitsky. 1992. *Fearful Symmetry: Is God a Geometer?* England: Blackwell Publishers.

Stokoe, William. 1960. Sign Language Structure: An outline of the visual communication systems of the American Deaf. *Studies in Linguistics, Occasional Papers 8.* Available from Silver Spring, Maryland: Linstok Press.

Stokoe, William C., Dorothy C. Casterline, and Carl G. Croneberg. 1965. *A Dictionary of American Sign Language on Linguistic Principles.* Silver Spring, Maryland: Linstok Press. New Edition, 1976, Linstok Press.

Supalla, Ted. 1978. Morphology of verbs of motion and location in American Sign Language. In *Proceedings of the Second National Symposium on Sign Language Research and Teaching,* ed. F. Caccamise. Silver Spring, Md.: National Association of the Deaf.

Supalla, Ted. 1982. *Structure and Acquisition of Verbs of Motion and Location in American Sign Language Phonology.* Doctoral dissertation, University of California, San Diego.

Supalla, Ted. 1986. The Classifier System in American Sign Language. In *Noun Classes and Categorizations,* ed. Colette Craig. 181–214. John Benjamin.

Supalla, Ted, and Elissa L. Newport. 1978. How Many Seats in a Chair? The Derivation of Nouns and Verbs in American Sign Language. In *Under-*

standing Language Through Sign Language Research, ed. Patricia Siple. 91–132. New York, New York: Academic Press.

Toole, Janine, and Linda Uyechi. 1996. Another perspective on hand orientation in American Sign Language. *WECOL*.

Uyechi, Linda. 1992. Secondary Signing Location in American Sign Language. *BLS* 18:248–259.

Uyechi, Linda. 1993a. Against *wiggling* and *circling* as movement in American Sign Language. Paper presented at the 67th meeting of the LSA, Los Angeles, California.

Uyechi, Linda. 1993b. Another look at two-handed signs in American Sign Language. *MIT Working Papers in Linguistics: Papers from the 5th Student Conference in Linguistics*. 225–270.

Uyechi, Linda. 1994. Local and Global Signing Space in American Sign Language. *NELS* 24:589–603.

Valli, Clayton, and Ceil Lucas. 1992. *Linguistics of American Sign Language: A Resource Text for ASL Users*. Washington, DC: Clerc Books, Gallaudet University Press.

van der Hulst, Harry. 1993. Units in the analysis of signs. *Phonology* 10:209–241.

Weyl, Hermann. 1969. *Symmetry*. Princeton, New Jersey: Princeton University Press.

Wilbur, Ronnie B. 1990. Why Syllables? What the Notion Means for ASL Research. In *Theoretical Issues in Sign Language Research, Volume 1: Linguistics*, ed. Susan D. Fischer and Patricia Siple. 81–108. Chicago, Illinois: The University of Chicago Press.

Wilbur, Ronnie B. 1993. Syllables and Segments: Hold the Movement and Move the Holds! In *Phonetics and Phonology, Volume 3: Current Issues in ASL Phonology*, ed. Geoffrey R. Coulter. 135–168. Academic Press.

Index

Other titles in the
Dissertations in Linguistics Series

Possessive Descriptions
Chris Barker

Although possessives are one of the most commonly used construction types cross-linguistically, they have seldom received detailed or sustained study from a semantic point of view. Taking the work of Abney, May, and Heim as a starting point, this book develops a comprehensive analysis of the contribution of possessive NPs to the truth conditions of the sentences in which they occur. The behavior of possessives gives strong evidence that certain large classes of underived nouns (including kinship terms and body part terms) are "transitive" (i.e., have more than one argument position) both syntactically and semantically. Building on this basic idea, examination of quantificational possessives suggests that possessor phrases do not behave like determiners or specifiers semantically, but rather more like definite or indefinite descriptions. Yet possessives have properties distinct both from simple definite descriptions and from simple indefinite descriptions—in other words, they are their own type of description: possessive descriptions.
202 p. ISBN: 1-881526-73-9 (cloth); ISBN: 1-881526-72-0 (paper)

Theoretical Aspects of Kashaya Phonology and Morphology
Eugene Buckley

This study discusses a wide range of phonological and morphological phenomena in Kashaya, a Pomoan language of northern California, and considers their implications for current theories of generative grammar. The volume raises issues in feature theory, presents prosodic analysis, and discusses numerous morphological patterns.
420 p. ISBN: 1-881526-03-8 (cloth); ISBN: 1-881526-02-X (paper)

The Structure of Complex Predicates in Urdu
Miriam Butt

This volume takes a detailed look at two differing complex predicates in the South Asian language Urdu. The Urdu permissive in particular brings into focus the problem of syntax-semantics mismatch. Urdu shows that argument structure must be considered independent of syntactic structures, but be related to grammatical relations via a theory of linking. This work counters that the recent move towards increasingly abstract argument structure representations do not allow an adequate characterization of the case marking patterns, and that semantic factors such as volitionality must play a role in linking.
257 p. ISBN: 1-881526-59-3 (cloth); ISBN: 0-937073-58-5 (paper)

On the Placement and Morphology of Clitics
Aaron Halpern

Using data from a variety of languages, this book investigates the place clitics in the theory of language structure, and their implications for the relationships between syntax, morphology, and phonology. It is argued that the least powerful theory of language requires us to recognize at least two classes of clitics, one with the syntax of independent phrases and the other with the syntax of inflectional affixes. These classes may be diagnosed on the basis of both distributional and morphological differences although there is considerable overlap.
260 p. ISBN: 1-881526-48-8 (cloth); ISBN: 1-881526-47-X (paper)

Context and Binding in Japanese
Masayo Iida

Iida investigates the proper treatment of zibun-binding, reviewing the status of the syntactic subjecthood condition. She proposes a conjunctive theory of zibun-binding in which both a syntactic condition and a nonsyntactic condition apply to every instance of zibun-binding. This approach is contrasted with a disjunctive approach adopted in many theories of zibun-binding, which views the subjecthood condition as a fundamental licensing condition, supplemented by semantic or discourse binding condition to account for nonsubject binding, when the syntactic condition would be violated.
392 p. ISBN: 1-881526-75-5 (cloth); ISBN: 1-881526-74-7 (paper)

Configuring Topic and Focus in Russian
Tracy Holloway King

This work examines word order and the encoding of topic and focus in Russian. As has long been observed, word order in Russian encodes specific discourse information: with neutral intonation, topics precede discourse-neutral constituents which precede foci. The author extends this idea to show that word order encodes different types of topic and focus in a principled manner. The interaction of topic and focus with the syntax and the nature of phrase structure in general has been vigorously debated in recent linguistic literature. This work's in-depth analysis of Russian elucidates this debate since Russian contains both configurational and non-configurational characteristics.
272 p. ISBN: 1-881526-63-1 (cloth); ISBN: 1-881526-62-3 (paper)

Phrase Structure and Grammatical Relations in Tagalog
Paul Kroeger

This volume examines the history of the subjecthood debate in the syntax of Philippine languages. Using data from Tagalog, the assertion is made that grammati-

cal relations such as subject and object are syntactic notions, and must be identified on the basis of syntactic properties, rather than by semantic roles or discourse functions. The conclusions drawn entail consequences for many approaches to syntax including the Government-Binding theory.
240 p. ISBN: 0-937073-87-3 (cloth); ISBN: 0-937073-86-5 (paper)

Ergativity: Argument Structure and Grammatical Relations
Christopher D. Manning

This book considers the proper treatment of syntactic ergativity within modern syntactic frameworks, arguing for the decoupling of grammatical relations and argument structure. The result is two notions of subject, grammatical subject and argument structure subject, and a uniform analysis of syntactically ergative and Philippine languages as languages that allow an inverse mapping between these two levels. Argument structure is shown to be particularly well motivated by the examination of ergative languages, and a treatment of binding and control based on argument structure is presented. These phenomena are always accusative or neutral, but if one examines constraints on surface syntactic properties, which are universally sensitive to grammatical relations, then many languages are indeed syntactically ergative. As well as developing a general approach to syntactic ergativity and contrasting this approach with other recent proposals, the book includes in-depth discussion of the ergative language Inuit, as a testbed for the proposals made.
240 p. ISBN: 1-57586-037-6 (cloth); ISBN: 1-57586-036-8 (paper)

Argument Structure in Hindi
Tara Mohanan

Arguing for a conception of linguistic organization, this book involves the factor-ization of syntactically relevant information into at least four parallel dimensions of structure: semantic structure, argument structure, grammatical function struc-ture, and gram-matical category structure. The author argues that these dimen-sions are co-present, being simultaneously accessible for the statement of regularities.
285 p. ISBN: 1-881526-44-5 (cloth); ISBN: 1-881526-43-7 (paper)

Stricture in Feature Geometry
Jaye Padgett

This work represents an in-depth investigation into the pervasive interaction of place of articulation features and constriction degree features (stricture features) in pho-nological processes. The central claim, a development of Feature Geome-try theory, is that place features and oral stricture features like [continuant] and [consonantal] form a phonological unit called the articulator group. This proposal finds motivation in a wide range of empirical areas, including place assimilation processes, complex segment contrasts, dissimilatory effects, spirantization and phonetic considerations. Theoretical topics of particular concern include the organization of phonological features, feature underspecification, feature cooccurrence conditions and structure preservation, the application of the Obligatory Contour Principle, and the phonetics-phonology interface.

232 p. ISBN: 1-881526-67-4 (cloth); ISBN: 1-881526-66-6 (paper)

The Semantic Basis of Argument Structure
Stephen Wechsler

A central problem on the syntax-semantics interface is the mapping between semantic roles and syntactic arguments, usually termed 'linking.' This book presents a clear and concise treatment of linking which departs significantly from models employing a problem-atical intermediate level where roles are classified into thematic role types such as 'agent' and 'goal'. Instead, the connection between a verb's meaning and its argument structure is assumed to be quite direct. This direct connection appeals to fundamental aspects of verb meaning, while more specific semantic relations such as 'goal' are relevant to linking only when such relations are associated with the meanings of prepositions and similar forms. As a result, the theory is firmly grounded in the semantic content of verbs and prepositions.

Among the topics treated are the dative alternation and preposition selection. The final chapter implements this analysis within a hierarchical lexicon in the framework of Head-Driven Phrase Structure Grammar.

168 p. ISBN: 1-881526-69-0 (cloth); ISBN: 1-881526-68-2 (paper)

For a complete list of our titles, please visit our World-Wide Web site at:
http://csli-www.stanford.edu/publications/

CSLI Publications are distributed by

CAMBRIDGE
UNIVERSITY PRESS